I0119339

Studies in Logic

Logic and Argumentation

Volume 100

The Fallacy of Composition

Critical Reviews, Conceptual Analyses, and Case Studies

Studies in Logic Series Editor
Dov Gabbay   dov.gabbay@kcl.ac.uk

The Fallacy of Composition

Critical Reviews, Conceptual Analyses, and Case Studies

Maurice A. Finocchiaro

© Individual authors and College Publications, 2023
All rights reserved.

ISBN 978-1-84890-435-4

College Publications
Scientific Director: Dov Gabbay
Managing Director: Jane Spurr

http://www.collegepublications.co.uk

All rights reserved. No part of this publication may be reproduced,
stored in a retrieval system or transmitted in any form, or by any
means, electronic, mechanical, photocopying, recording or
otherwise without prior permission, in writing, from the publisher.

Contents

Preface and Acknowledgments

This book is a collection of essays of mine which have been published in scholarly journals, anthologies, and conference proceedings during the past decade (2013-2023). Thus, here I want to express my acknowledgments to the original publishers for their permissions to republish these essays; to the many scholars from whom my work has benefitted; and to the institutions that have supported my research. The details are as follows.

Chapter 1 was originally published as "Debts, Oligarchies, and Holisms: Deconstructing the Fallacy of Composition," in *Informal Logic*, 33(2013): 143-74. The journal editor has informed me that the copyright belongs to me as the author.

Chapter 2 was originally published as "The Fallacy of Composition and Meta-argumentation," in *Virtues of Argumentation: Proceedings of the 10th International Conference of the Ontario Society for the Study of Argumentation (OSSA), 22-26 May 2013*, ed. Dima Mohammed and Marcin Lewiński (Windsor, ON: Ontario Society for the Study of Argumentation, 2013). This is available on Open Access.

Chapter 3 was originally published as "Ubiquity, Ambiguity, and Metarationality: Searching for the Fallacy of Composition," in *Reflections on Theoretical Issues in Argumentation Theory*, ed. Frans H. van Eemeren and Bart Garssen, 131-41 (Dordrecht: Springer Nature, 2015). It was based on a paper originally presented at the 8th Conference of the International Society for the Study of Argumentation (ISSA), Amsterdam, 2014. It is republished here with permission from Springer Nature, through the RightsLink of the Copyright Clearance Center.

Chapter 4 was originally published as "The Fallacy of Composition: Guiding Concepts, Historical Cases, and Research Problems," in *Journal of Applied Logic*, vol. 13, issue 2, part B, June 2015, pp. 24–43. This journal was published by Elsevier, and this essay is republished here with permission from Elsevier, through the RightsLink of the Copyright Clearance Center.

Chapter 5 was originally published as "Economic Reasoning and Fallacy of Composition, Part I: The Problem," in *Eris: Rivista internazionale di argomentazione e dibattito* (ISSN 2421-6747), vol. 1, no. 2, 2016, pp. 17-38. It was based on a paper originally presented at the 11th International Conference of the Ontario Society for the Study of Argumentation (OSSA), University of Windsor (ON, Canada), May 18-21, 2016. The journal editor has informed me that I have the right to republish this essay as I deem appropriate.

The Appendix to Chapter 5 is authored by John Woods. It was originally published as "Economic Reasoning and Fallacy of Composition, Part II:

Comments on Maurice Finocchiaro's Paper," in *Eris: Rivista internazionale di argomentazione e dibattito* (ISSN 2421-6747), vol. 1, no. 2, 2016, pp. 39-45. It was based on a commentary by Woods originally presented at the 11th International Conference of the Ontario Society for the Study of Argumentation (OSSA), University of Windsor (ON, Canada), May 18-21, 2016. The journal editor has informed me that we have the right to republish this essay as we deem appropriate.

Chapter 6 was originally published as "Economic Reasoning and Fallacy of Composition, Part III: Response to John Woods's Comments," in *Eris: Rivista internazionale di argomentazione e dibattito* (ISSN 2421-6747), vol. 1, no. 2, 2016, pp. 46-56. The journal editor has informed me that I have the right to republish this essay as I deem appropriate.

The Appendix to Chapter 6 is authored by John Woods. It was originally published as "Economic Reasoning and Fallacy of Composition, Part IV: Some Parting Words," in *Eris*: *Rivista internazionale di argomentazione e dibattito* (ISSN 2421-6747), vol. 1, no. 2, 2016, pp. 57-61. The journal editor has informed me that we have the right to republish this essay as we deem appropriate.

Chapter 7 was originally published as "Samuelson on the Fallacy of Composition in Economics: A Woodsian Critique," in *Natural Arguments: A Tribute to John Woods*, ed. Dov Gabbay, Lorenzo Magnani, Woosuk Park, and Ahti Veikko Pietarinen, 125-72 (London: College Publications, 2019). It is republished here by this same organization.

Chapter 8 was originally published as "Argumentation Schemes for Composition and Division Arguments: A Critique of Walton's Account," in *Journal of Applied Logics: IfCoLog Journal of Logics and their Applications*, 8(2021): 53-73. This journal is published by College Publications of London, and so this essay is republished here by the same organization.

Chapter 9 was originally published as "Do Arguments for Global Warming Commit a Fallacy of Composition?", in *Argumentation*, 37(2023): 201-215. This journal is published by Springer Nature, and this essay is republished here with permission from Springer Nature, through the RightsLink of the Copyright Clearance Center.

With regard to individual scholars, I should begin by expressing my gratitude to John Woods: he has been an inimitable source of inspiration, encouragement, and support for all these essays and for the whole book; many of his works have served explicitly as the subjects of critical appreciations on my part, especially in Chapters 5, 6, and 7; and, last but not least, his commentary on my 2016 OSSA presentation was so valuable as to generate the four-part dialogue here recorded in Chapters 5 and 6, each of which has an appendix authored by John himself.

Also noteworthy is my indebtedness to Hans Hansen, for his organizational and editorial efforts regarding: the 10th OSSA conference in

2013, which was the original venue for Chapter 2; the 11th OSSA conference in 2016, which was the original venue for Chapters 5 and 6; and the special issue of *Argumentation*, dealing with fallacies, and containing the original publication of Chapter 9. I also owe a similar debt of gratitude to Frans van Eemeren and Bart Garssen for their organizational and editorial efforts regarding: the 8th ISSA Conference in 2014, and the volume of selected contributions, which were instrumental to the creation of Chapter 3; and, again, the special issue of *Argumentation* on fallacies, which provided the motivation for Chapter 9.

Next, I want to thank Tony Blair and Ralph Johnson for having edited the special issue of *Informal Logic* in honor of Trudy Govier, where my Chapter 1 was originally published. Here, I must also confess my enormous debt to Trudy herself, however indirect. That is, Chapter 1 was originally conceived as, and still remains, a critical appreciation of her work on the fallacy of composition. This critical appreciation was my first scholarly involvement and publication on this topic, and it happened to embody many fruitful research questions. It was the pursuit of these questions, obviously with the addition of other inputs, that generated the rest of the chapters in this book.

Acknowledgments are also due to a number of other scholars who happened to provide useful comments on various versions of the original manuscripts of these chapters: Derek Allen, Ian Dove, Michel Dufour, Jean Goodwin, Melvin Jameson, and Bernard Malamud.

Finally, in a class by itself is the special debt of gratitude which I owe to the University of Nevada, Las Vegas, in particular the College of Liberal Arts, the Philosophy Department, the Chair of the Philosophy Department (David Forman), the Administrative Assistant of the Philosophy Department (Nicole Moore), my departmental colleagues, and the staff in the Office of Information Technology (Hector Ibarra and Nick Panissidi). They have continued to provide institutional, material, and moral support, even after (in 2003) I decided to retire from formal teaching in order to work full time on research, scholarship, and writing.

Introduction: Arguments from
Parts to Whole, Micro to Macro, and Some to All

The focus of this book is the fallacy of composition, and this topic is approached through a series of critical reviews, conceptual analyses, and case studies.

The critical reviews elaborate interpretations and evaluations of relevant works by such distinguished scholars as these: philosophers John Woods, Trudy Govier, Douglas Walton, and Chaim Perelman; economists Paul Samuelson, William Nordhaus, and Paul Krugman; and political sociologists Robert Michels, Robert Dahl, and Seymour Martin Lipset. To a smaller extent, I also discuss arguments from such classics as Aristotle, Galileo, and Hume.

The conceptual analyses attempt to bring some clarity and order to notions such as the following: argument of composition, fallacy of composition, arguments and fallacies of division, arguments confusing the distributive and collective meaning of terms, arguments from a property of some group members to the same property for the entire group, hasty generalizations, flawed arguments from analogy, argument schemes, principles of evaluation, fallaciousness vs. incorrectness, and meta-argumentation.

The case studies advance textually-based and historically-sensitive accounts of argumentation involving the following: Aristotle's geocentric-geostatic argument from natural motion, the design argument for the existence of God, Michels's iron law of oligarchy, the paradox of thrift, the argument from private to public debt, bank creation of money, the paradox of the bumper harvest, the general demand for labor, beggar-thy-neighbor policies, current arguments for global warming, and jury decisions of guilt in jurisprudence. A sketch of these case studies is perhaps the best way to introduce the topic and the approach. That is, this book deals with arguments such as the following.

For thousands of years, before the Copernican Revolution, most scientists and philosophers, as well as common people, believed that the earth stood still at the center of the universe. This belief was based on direct observation and indirectly on many arguments of various types and strength. One of these claimed that the earth must be standing still at the center of the universe, because all parts of the earth (such as rocks and water droplets) can be seen to move naturally toward the center, and thus if free to move the whole earth would move the same way; but once the whole earth had reached the center it could not move in any other way, and so the only thing it could do would be to stand still therein.

1

Such an argument can be found, for example, in Aristotle's *On the Heavens*. It was criticized by Galileo, along with most other geocentric and geostatic arguments, in his *Dialogue on the Two Chief World Systems, Ptolemaic and Copernican* (1632). Galileo began by pointing out that there is a crucial ambiguity in the key premise that all parts of the earth can be seen to have a natural motion toward the center. If this is an observation report, then the "center" in question must be the center of the earth; in this case, the conclusion to be drawn (in accordance with the principle that whatever is true of the parts is also true of the whole) would be that the natural motion of the whole earth is to move toward its own center. However, it is an intrinsic logical impossibility for a whole object to move toward its own center. On the other hand, if the "center" mentioned in the key premise is the center of the universe, it would be possible for the whole earth to move towards it, but then that key premise would no longer be an observation report; indeed, it would be groundless, and the argument would be begging the question.

Besides arguments for and against the motion and location of the earth, another comparably rich collection in the whole history of thought has been the arguments for and against the existence of God. One of the arguments in favor is the argument from design. It starts with the analogical claim that the universe is like a machine; then it adds the generalization that machines are made by (human) intelligent designers; and it concludes that the universe was created by an intelligent designer (called God).

This argument was criticized by David Hume in his *Dialogues Concerning Natural Religion* (1779). He objected that the first premise is a hasty generalization, because although many parts of the universe are machines produced by intelligent design, many other parts (even when orderly arranged) are produced by natural causes such as attraction and heat. His second objection was that, even if all parts of the universe were machine-like, we could not be sure that the same would apply to the universe as a whole; here, Hume is charging that this step commits a fallacy of composition.

Another instructive and important case study, concerns the so-called iron law of oligarchy. It was first elaborated by Robert Michels in a book originally published in German in 1911, and then translated into English as *Political Parties: A Sociological Study of the Oligarchical Tendencies of Modern Democracy* (1915). Michels discovered that political parties, even those advocating democracy (such as the German Social Democratic Party), had insurmountable oligarchical (anti-democratic) tendencies; then, assuming that what was true of political parties was also true of governmental institutions or societies as a whole, he concluded that that every bureaucratic organization has oligarchical tendencies which are impossible to overcome, and that this applies even to democratic governments, which are thus doomed to become undemocratic.

Michels's critics agreed that his argument has some plausibility because they admitted that there are some important similarities between political parties or labor unions and societies or national governments, e.g., the tendency for previously elected leaders to be re-elected. However, in *Democracy and Its Critics* (1989), Robert Dahl objected that there is a crucial dissimilarity, i.e., that in political systems that allow competition among political parties, the oligarchic tendencies that exist within parties are counteracted at the macro societal level. Another critic was Seymour Martin Lipset, who wrote the introduction to the 1962 edition of Michels's book. He pointed out that there is another crucial difference, definable in terms of a condition present in democratic societies but absent in undemocratic ones and in particular institutions of democratic ones: a constitutional provision that prevents any one entity from exercising despotic power over opposing entities.

The most explicit, frequent, and consequential discussions of the fallacy of composition are by professional economists. One theme of their discussions is that common people who have not studied the science of economics often commit this fallacy when thinking about economic matters; and that by learning this science they can avoid such fallacious reasoning and think correctly about wages, prices, savings, debts, banking, commerce, etc. In fact, economists often connect the ability to think correctly about such matters and avoid this fallacy to a proper understanding of the relationship between microeconomics and macroeconomics; and they usually attribute the elaboration of this relationship to the epoch-making scientific contributions of John M. Keynes (1883-1946). The topic also frequently comes up in controversial public discussions when professional economists, writing as editorialists and columnists, accuse each other of committing this fallacy.

Thus, in several chapters of this book, I discuss as a pervasive case study the concept and examples of fallacy of composition in Paul Samuelson's *Economics*, since this is one of the most influential textbooks ever written, by one of the most distinguished economists who ever lived. His most common example is the popular argument from private to public deficits and debts, that is: it is obviously wrong and irresponsible for a family or a firm to constantly operate with an unbalanced budget, to constantly borrow money, and to accumulate a continuously growing debt; therefore, unbalanced budgets and a growing debt are wrong and irresponsible for the national government. That is, this argument is attributing to the whole society the same financial limitation which its parts are known to have.

Samuelson criticizes this argument by elaborating some objections which he himself quotes from the nineteenth-century English historian Lord Thomas B. Macaulay. That is, there are some crucially relevant differences that make private debts harmful in ways which do not apply to public debts, and make the latter beneficial in ways in which the former are not: private

3

debts are normally external (namely, owed to entities outside the private organization), whereas the public debt is mostly internal (namely, owed by a society to its own citizens); and private debts lack the benefits which the public debt enjoys, deriving from its effect on private wealth and consumption and on monetary policy and debt management. However, note that these same differences, especially the first one, are such that even a public debt can become problematic if and insofar as it is owed to foreign countries or citizens (thus becoming external).

One of the most frequent problems in practical politics is that of unemployment: how to help people who do not have a job find one; how to make sure that people who are employed do not lose their jobs; what benefits to provide to them as long as they remain unemployed; etc. A common argument from the right wing of the ideological spectrum is along the following lines, and it can be stated with various degrees of harshness: unemployment benefits should be reduced or eliminated, because doing so would provide a crucial incentive to look for and accept a job, even at a low wage, and (if need be) at a lower wage than other workers; such an incentive would create more competition among workers; this competition would lead to lower wages; lower wages would encourage more hiring by employers; and this in turn would increase employment and benefit the whole economy.

In December 2013, such an issue was being discussed in the American Congress, although this was neither the first nor the last time. However, it did provide the occasion for a memorable criticism by Paul Krugman, in a column published in the *New York Times*, on December 9, 2013, entitled "The Punishment Cure." According to Krugman "that argument involves a fallacy of composition. Cut the wages of some workers relative to those of other workers, and those accepting the wage cuts may gain a competitive edge. Cut everyone's wages, however, and nobody gains an edge. All that happens is a general fall in income."

Next, it will be instructive to mention another case study concerning an issue originating from the other (the left) side of the ideological spectrum. It involves a proposal made by the President of the United States, Barack Obama, in January 2015. He proposed to allow qualified students to attend community colleges free of tuition charges for two years, the qualifications being sufficiently good grades and sufficient progress toward graduation. The proposal was applauded by left leaning politicians; for example, it was later advocated by Bernie Sanders, during his campaign to be the Democratic-Party candidate in the 2016 presidential election.

However, the proposal was also criticized by right leaning politicians, thinkers, and news media, for example, in an opinion column by William A. Kelly Jr. and Elizabeth Sawyer Kelly, in *The Wall Street Journal* of February 4, 2015. They labeled the proposal explicitly a fallacy of composition: "President Obama ... has fallen victim to the fallacy of composition. He has made the mistake of believing that if one person benefits from an action, then everyone else who takes the same action will also benefit. Economics teaches us otherwise. Although getting an associate degree or some college education at a community college may benefit any one person, in the aggregate a policy that increases the supply of people with associate degrees can backfire unless it has been designed to fill an existing excess demand. Otherwise such a policy will merely exacerbate an existing excess supply of labor with that level of educational attainment. That looks likely to happen here."

Finally, there is one case study which was impossible to miss or ignore in the present context, since it involves the possibility, or at least the allegation, that the claim of global warming is based on a fallacy of composition. This allegation has been made by some philosophers, on the grounds that the conclusion that the planet earth is warming is inferred from the evidence that the parts of the earth are experiencing warming. Now, it is indeed true that the structure of this reasoning is that of an argument of composition. However, then the issue becomes whether or not this particular argument of composition is fallacious.

I hope that this sketch of these case studies conveys a sense of what this book is about. The focus is on a special class of arguments: that is, arguments that reason from what is true of parts to the same being true of the whole; arguments from what is true in microeconomics to the same being true in macroeconomics; and arguments from what is true of some members of a group to the same being true of all in the group. And the focus is twofold: that is, concerned about the structures of such arguments, and about whether or not they are invalid, incorrect, or fallacious. Moreover, I hope that this sketch also succeeds in showing that in this book this key topic is being approached through a series of critical reviews of what other scholars have written on the topic; and through a series of definitions, clarifications, and analyses of the concepts involved; and through a series of studies of actual arguments in real controversies, past and present.

On the other hand, the nine essays that make up the nine chapters of this book all had a somewhat autonomous origin; each discusses a relatively distinct issue; and they can all be read independently of one another. In the book they are arranged in chronological order, and thus a reader can also notice and detect the overlap and the progress as time goes on. To provide the reader with some options along these lines, I feel it is also a good idea to provide an overview, by summarizing the various chapters here.

Chapter 1 is a critical appreciation of Trudy Govier's keynote address at the 2006 conference of the International Society for the Study of Argumentation, dealing with the fallacy of composition in general and with economists' writings on this fallacy in economics. I argue that the "fallacy of composition" is a problematical concept, because it does not denote a distinctive kind of argument but rather a plurality, and it does not constitute a distinctive kind of error but rather reduces to oversimplification in arguing from micro to macro. Finally, I propose further testing of this claim based on examples involving public vs. private debt in economics, oligarchic tendencies in politics, and the emergence of societal wholes in sociology.

Chapter 2 discusses three ideas: that, although the fallacy of composition is little studied and trivially illustrated, some view it as ubiquitous and paramount; that, although definitions regard the concept as unproblematic, it contains three distinct elements, often confused; and that, although some scholars apparently claim that fallacies are figments of a critic's imagination, they are really proposing to study fallacies in the context of meta-argumentation. Guided by these ideas, I discuss the important historical example of Michels's iron law of oligarchy.

In Chapter 3, "ubiquity" refers to the hypothesis that fallacies of composition are ubiquitous; "ambiguity" refers to the hypothesis that "fallacy of composition" has at least three distinct meanings, often confused; and "metarationality" refers to the hypothesis that the best places to search for fallacies of composition are meta-arguments whose conclusions attribute this fallacy to ground-level arguments. While testing these working hypotheses, I have found some historically important cases, for example, a step in the design argument for the existence of God, as critiqued by Hume.

Chapter 4 continues, refines, elaborates, and extends the previous topics. Again, although the fallacy of composition is little studied by theorists and trivially illustrated in textbooks, some view it as ubiquitous and highly significant. Furthermore, although definitions regard the concept as unproblematic, it contains three distinct elements that are often confused, and it is often carelessly conflated with the fallacy of division. And although some apparently claim that fallacies are figments of a critic's imagination, they are really proposing to study fallacies in the context of meta-argumentation. Guided by these ideas, I find three important historical examples: Aristotle's geocentric argument from natural motion, as critiqued by Galileo; a step in the theological argument from design, as critiqued by Hume; and Michels's iron law of oligarchy, as critiqued by political sociologists Robert Dahl and Seymour Martin Lipset. Finally, I formulate some problems for future research on compositional arguments: distinguishing incorrectness from fallaciousness; elaborating general principles of evaluation; clarifying the three distinct subtypes; shifting from the arbitrary pluralism of argument-identification to the normal meta-argumentation of argument-analysis; and further historical-empirical search for such fallacies in various controversies, over holism, over global warming, and over national debts.

Chapter 5 argues that John Woods and Douglas Walton deserve credit for including (in all three editions of their textbook *Argument*) a discussion of "economic reasoning" and its susceptibility to the "fallacy of composition." Unfortunately, they did not sufficiently pursue the topic, and argumentation scholars have apparently ignored their pioneering effort. Yet, obviously, economic argumentation is extremely important, and economists constantly harp on this fallacy. This essay calls attention to this problem, elaborating my own approach, which is empirical, historical, and meta-argumentational. Accordingly, by way of illustration, I examine relevant claims found in three types of economic writings: textbooks, including Paul Samuelson's classic *Economics*; technical articles in professional journals discussing such issues as the problem of increases versus decreases in commodity prices and the problem of the dynamics of international trade; and columnists' opinions about current issues such as government spending and deficits, including writings by Paul Krugman and his critics.

Chapter 5 has an appendix authored by John Woods, containing a commentary on the previous part of the chapter. Woods discusses the empirical turn in logic, the elusiveness of the concept of compositionality, the problem of reasoning about economics and by economists, and the conceptual relevance of jury decisions in criminal trials.

Chapter 6 is an analysis of the points of agreement and disagreement between myself and John Woods. They involve methodological issues, such as the nature of the empirical approach to logic; theoretical issues, such as the correctness and incorrectness of arguments of composition; the acceptability of economists' own evaluations of economic arguments; and the relevance and significance of jury decisions in criminal trials.

Chapter 6 also has an appendix authored by John Woods, containing his final commentary. Woods discusses the problems of over-abstraction, complex systems, and thermodynamic costs.

Chapter 7 is a critical examination of the conception and examples of the fallacy of composition in Paul Samuelson's textbook *Economics*; his examples involve the paradox of thrift, the argument from private to public debt, bank creation of money, the paradox of the bumper harvest, the general demand for labor, and beggar-thy-neighbor policies. More generally, this chapter aims to illustrate my version of the naturalized approach to the study of reasoning, which stresses historical texts and meta-arguments. More specifically, it covers all nineteen editions of Samuelson's textbook (1948-2010); tries not only to understand, but also to evaluate, its claims; and tries to determine whether his definition is conceptually adequate, and whether his economic examples are really fallacies of composition. Finally, it is an explicit follow-up to my previous discussion with John Woods (here in Chapters 5 and 6). My conclusion is that Samuelson's definition is problematic, and his examples are either non-fallacious or non-compositional or non-arguments.

Chapter 8 begins with a description of my acquaintance with Douglas Walton's scholarly work: this acquaintance goes back some five decades, but it is relatively meager given his enormous output, and yet I recently renewed and deepened it for the purpose of the present contribution. For this purpose, I decided to focus on a topic at the borderland of two things: the notion of argumentation schemes which seems to have earned Walton the greatest notoriety lately, and the fallacy of composition on which I have focused in the last several years. Thus, next I summarize Walton's account of argumentation schemes for the fallacy (and argument) of composition (and of division); unfortunately, it seems to be highly unsatisfactory. I also examine Chaim Perelman's account of the same topic since Walton refers to his work; Perelman's account is terminologically anomalous but seems to make some conceptual sense, and yet it magnifies further the inadequacy of Walton's account. Finally, I undertake a more constructive effort and sketch what I feel is a promising and more adequate account, elaborating several argumentation schemes and several evaluative principles, based on realistic examples.

Chapter 9 begins with a brief description of my approach to the study of argumentation and fallacies which is empirical, historical-textual, dialectical, and meta-argumentational. It then focuses on the fallacy of composition and elaborates a number of conceptual definitions and distinctions: argument of composition; fallacy of composition; arguments and fallacies of division; arguments that confuse the distributive and collective meaning of terms; arguments from a property belonging to members of a group to its belonging to the entire group; several nuanced schemes for arguments of composition; and several principles for the evaluation of such arguments. I then call attention to the fact that some scholars have claimed that the basic argument for global warming commits the fallacy of composition, and I undertake a critical analysis of this claim. I show that the global-warming argument is not a fallacy of composition, but is rather a deductively valid argument of composition from the temperature of the parts to the temperature of the whole earth; moreover, I criticize the meta-argumentation of these scholars by showing that the global-warming argument is not similar to the one for global pollution, which is indeed fallacious; finally, I argue that these scholars confuse the global-warming argument with the argument claiming that all effects of global warming are harmful, which is indeed incorrect as a hasty generalization.

Chapter 1
Debts, Oligarchies, and Holisms:
Deconstructing the Fallacy of Composition

1. Govier on the Fallacy of Composition

In 2006, Trudy Govier delivered a keynote address to the sixth conference of the International Society for the Study of Argumentation (Govier 2007; 2009). Its revealing title was "Duets, Cartoons, and Tragedies: Struggles with the Fallacy of Composition." In it, she insightfully discusses a number of problems stemming from the following fundamental fact: that "we apply to *groups* the intentional language of emotions, attitudes, and beliefs. Such language is paradigmatically individual in application and yet we apply it to groups of all sizes—small, medium, large and very large—and of varying degrees and kinds of organization" (Govier 2009, 91).[1]

In elaborating her account, Govier follows and exhibits an approach or orientation which is fruitful and deserves greater diffusion, and which I would characterize as judicious. I define judiciousness, or balanced judgment, as the avoidance of one-sidedness and of extremes, and I certainly endorse such an approach.[2]

In fact, to begin with, Govier rejects "the supposition that, with respect to intentional language, group attributions are problematical whereas individual attributions are not" (92); this would amount to an undesirable "dichotomous contrast between individual and group" (92). Furthermore, she rejects both of two extreme positions: that "all intentional language, as applied to groups, is based on error … [and] should be banned" (94); and that "intentional language as applied to groups must be legitimate … it passes the only realistic and sensible test of legitimacy—namely actual use" (94).

Govier's formulation of the problem and description of the project provide another good example of judiciousness. To see this, let us begin with Govier's stipulation of the nominal definition to "call the application of

---

[1] Subsequent references to Govier 2009 will be given by mentioning just the page number(s).

[2] I have argued before that judiciousness is an important element of Galileo's scientific approach, and of the scientific method in general (Finocchiaro 1980, 145-66; 2005, 361-430; 2010, 121-34); that it is the plausible kernel of Hegelian dialectic, and a valuable and viable approach in the social sciences and humanistic disciplines (Finocchiaro 1988, 228-30; 2005, 207-30); and that a judicious-minded approach is a fruitful orientation to follow in logic and argumentation theory (Finocchiaro 2005, 21-108; 2013, 4-17).

intentional language to groups the *compositional phenomenon*" (92), and the attribution of an intentional predicate to a group a *compositional attribution*. Then the problem is this: "compositional attributions pose questions, especially when claims about group actions and attitudes are based on evidence about individuals. Real issues arise. The challenge is to acknowledge the gap and the problem, and find ways in which the gap can be bridged" (95).

In a large and important class of cases, "the gap ... can be bridged insofar as group structures and relationships provide contexts for people to think together and act on the basis of their joint deliberations. We can understand how the deliberations and actions of an interactive group provide grounds for attributing to it attitudes and beliefs: the individuals are not considered purely individualistically when they think and act together; thus they stand in relationships and constitute a group" (103). This happens when groups have some kind of elected executive that represents the members, and the members can explicitly or tacitly express their consent or disapproval.

Besides following such a sound judicious approach to the compositional phenomenon and compositional attribution, Govier's account deserves credit for practicing a realistic approach, in the sense that she discusses real or realistic examples and materials. That is, her analysis is meant to shed light on actual practical problems in all their complexity, as contrasted to artificial, abstract, or invented examples in an oversimplified context. And such realism is not an accidental feature of Govier's 2006 ISSA address, for she has regularly practiced it in other works and reflectively advocated it on various occasions (Govier 1987; 1999; 2000, 289-90). I also advocate such a methodological approach, as do other scholars, although it goes under various labels, such as empirical, historical, pragmatic, and naturalized.[3]

For example, Govier analyzes the case of the newspaper cartoons about the prophet Mohammed, which were published in Denmark in 2006 and elicited widespread protest by Muslims, especially in Islamic countries. Here, she valiantly tries to sort out who is attributing what violent attitudes to such groups and wholes as Denmark, the West, and Islam, on the basis of facts about the behavior and attitudes of individual Danish journalists and cartoonists and individual Islamic terrorists and protesters. The importance and relevance of such analytical efforts were underscored just recently, in the autumn of 2012, with the eruption in Muslim countries of similar protests elicited by the private production in the United States of an amateurish video about the prophet Mohammed.

---

[3] Cf. Barth, Vandormael, and Vandamme 1992; Finocchiaro (2005, 21-91, 128-47; 2013, 4-17); Fisher 2004; Johnson 2000; Woods 2013. The last mentioned work strikes me as being a novel departure from some of Woods's earlier work (such as Woods and Walton 1977a; 1977b), although undoubtedly there is some continuity of evolution and development between the two.

Govier also discusses certain aspects of the activities of the South African Truth and Reconciliation Commission (99-100). She examines ways of bridging the gap between the reconciliation of individuals with each other, however numerous, and national reconciliation between races in the society at large. Govier also mentions briefly the much-discussed "tragedy of the commons," in which individuals can benefit, and do benefit, by exploiting a common good, but only as long as the whole group does *not* undertake such an exploitation; for example, one farmer may be able to make a living by grazing his cattle on public land, but if all farmers graze their cattle on the same public land there may not be enough pasture for all. And she also mentions briefly the problem of world hunger, and whether it can be effectively solved or alleviated by means of actions and attitudes analogous to those whereby a family deals with the hunger of some of its members. On all such examples, Govier has insightful things to say and to convey on several levels: substantive social commentary, methodological illustration of the judicious and realistic approaches, and theoretical analysis of the compositional phenomenon and compositional attributes.

Let us now ask what any of this has got to do with logic and argumentation theory in general, and the "fallacy of composition" in particular. For, after all, Govier's key aim in her 2006 address is "to relate this problem more specifically to issues about argument and argumentation" (95).

We may begin by focusing on the common nominal definition which Govier adopts: "what I have in mind here is the Fallacy of Composition, in which we mistakenly infer conclusions about wholes or groups from premises about parts or individuals" (92). Let me note, however, that in this passage as well as in the rest of her essay, she always spells the term 'fallacy of composition' with initial capital letters. This orthographical minutia turns out to be very revealing, for, as we shall see later, Govier's account embodies a questionable hypostatization of the "fallacy of composition."

On the other hand, here Govier wisely ignores "the fallacy of arguing from premises in which a term is used distributively to a conclusion in which it is used collectively" (*Webster's Third New International Dictionary* 1976, p. 818), which many authors mention as a special case of the fallacy of composition. For example, Copi (1968, 81) illustrates this notion with the example: "because a bus uses more gasoline than an automobile, therefore all buses use more gasoline than all automobiles." And this notion has the historical pedigree of being traceable to the *Port Royal Logic* (Arnauld and Nicole 1996, 199-200). However, the amalgamation of this notion with the compositional phenomenon of which Govier speaks would only introduce confusion into the discussion, perhaps even committing a fallacy of equivocation. Thus, Govier is right to say nothing about it. But this is not to deny that it would be useful to have a historical account of the various definitions of the fallacy of composition, or of its various elements. In this regard, Woods's (2012) general account of the history of fallacies is useful, but only a start.

We may also agree that the compositional phenomenon, the problem of compositional attribution, and Govier's real examples have *something* to do with the fallacy of composition so defined; this seems obvious at an intuitive level and from the point of view of over-all judgment. To have seen such a connection and to have attempted to articulate it is a very valuable aspect of Govier's essay. This value may be better appreciated if one reads other works dealing with the same topic (i.e., the relationship between claims about individuals and claims about groups), which are full of useful information and subtle and insightful analyses, but do not as much as mention the fallacy of composition.[4] But the challenge is to articulate clearly what precisely the connection is between such realistic material and cognitive phenomena on the one hand, and logic, argumentation theory, and the fallacy of composition on the other.

For example, is it the case that "the Fallacy of Composition is genuinely a fallacy, and an important one" (92)? And that "the existence and understanding of this gap [in compositional attributions] underpin the tradition of the Fallacy of Composition … this fallacy is genuine and important" (102)? I am not sure that this is the case, or that Govier succeeds in showing that it is. On the contrary, what she herself says and argues shows almost the opposite.

In fact, let us be clear about what her project of "gap-bridging" is and what it accomplishes. She is correctly claiming that there is indeed a gap between the intentional predicates attributed to individuals and to groups, but that the gap can sometimes be bridged; the real challenge is to determine when the gap can, and when it cannot be bridged, and what are the factors and conditions that allow the gap to be bridged. What this means is that compositional attributions are sometimes correctly made on the basis of the behavior and characteristics of individuals. Thus, in such cases, no fallacy of composition is being committed.

Now, it would be a misconception to describe this situation by saying that the fallacy of composition is not always fallacious, for this claim would be tantamount to a self-contradiction: that it is not always mistaken, erroneous, or incorrect to "mistakenly infer conclusions about wholes or groups from premises about parts or individuals" (92). However, such a self-contradiction is easily avoided, with resources that are contained in Govier's own essay.

---

[4] The most outstanding example of such non-logical and non-argument-theoretical approach is Jones (2003; 2010). However, the materials and analyses in these works could be exploited and adapted from the point of view of the fallacy of composition (as well as the reverse fallacy of division).

That is, before defining the fallacy of composition we should define what might be called the *argument* from composition.[5] In the present context we need not decide whether this term should be preferred to several others that easily come to mind: *compositional* argument, argument *of* composition, and argument *by* composition. Govier herself comes close to formulating such a definition in the concluding section, where she speaks of arguments "when premises are about individuals and conclusions are about groups" (102). Similarly, after presenting the compositional phenomenon and the problem of compositional attribution in general, she starts to elaborate a connection with logic or argumentation by focusing on "reasoning from premises about parts to a conclusion about a whole" (95). But the notion can also be defined by appropriately modifying the definition of this fallacy which she adapts from traditional accounts. Thus, in the definition I quoted (six paragraphs) above, we can drop the word "mistakenly," and then we get that a compositional argument is one "in which we … infer conclusions about wholes or groups from premises about parts or individuals" (92). Such a notion of compositional argument is essentially the logical or argument-theoretical translation or analogue of the compositional phenomenon and of compositional attribution.

Once we have such a notion of compositional argument, then we could utilize Govier's account of gap bridging or filling to claim the following. If and insofar as the gap between premises and conclusion in a compositional argument has been bridged, such a compositional argument is cogent or correct. If and to the extent that the gap has not been bridged, such a compositional argument is erroneous or mistaken. We could then try to define a fallacy of composition as a compositional argument that is erroneous. At least this would avoid the misconception or self-contradiction mentioned earlier, that *fallacies* of composition are sometimes *cogent* arguments.

So far, such a modified definition of fallacy of composition would be satisfying only two of the necessary conditions for something (a cognitive practice or sequence of thoughts) to be a fallacy: that it be argumentation or reasoning, and that it be erroneous or mistaken. However, the traditional concept of fallacy includes other necessary conditions: the fallacy must be a *kind* of argument or *manner* of reasoning; it must be *commonly* or *frequently* committed; and it must have the *appearance* to be correct, i.e., must be *deceptive* (although not in the sense of being accompanied by an intention to mislead, but rather in the sense of being perceived as correct by oneself and others). In short, the traditional concept of fallacy amounts to this: a fallacy is a (1) common (2) kind of (3) argument that (4) seems correct but (5) is

---

[5] Walton, Reed, and Maccagno (2008, 113) also take such a step; but then they seem to stop there, in the sense that what they go on to say regarding the critical evaluation of such arguments is unhelpful.

not.[6]

The historical pedigree of this concept could be documented from sources such as the following,[7] where I have inserted numbers labeling various clauses to make them correspond to my formulation just given. In *Elements of Logic*, Richard Whately (1826, 131) states that "by a Fallacy is commonly understood 'any [5] unsound [2] mode of [3] reasoning, which [4] appears to demand our conviction, and to be decisive of the question at hand, when in fairness [5] it is not'." Furthermore, in "A History of the Fallacies in Western Logic," John Woods (2012, 514) states that "roughly speaking, the traditional concept of fallacy is that of a [5] mistake of [3] reasoning which people [2] in general tend to commit with a [1] notable frequency and which, even after successful diagnosis, are [4] subject to this same inclination to commit." And Govier herself agrees that "by definition, a fallacy is a [5] mistake in [3] reasoning, a mistake which occurs with some [1] frequency in real arguments and which is characteristically [4] deceptive" (1995, 172).[8]

Without worrying here about conditions (1) and (4), and having already discussed (3) and (5), let us focus on condition (2). When Whately speaks of a "mode" of reasoning, we may take this to refer to a manner or style of reasoning, as distinct from merely an instance or particular occurrence of reasoning. When Woods requires that a fallacy be such that thinkers "in general tend to commit" it, he may be construed as referring to a general habit or universal tendency, not to occasional occurrences or individual episodes of mistaken reasoning. When in my own formulation above I spoke of "kind," I meant it to be a natural kind, definable in terms of some concrete or tangible or deep-structural property, as distinct from some epiphenomenal or superficial or artificial characteristic.

In Govier's formulation quoted above, she does not explicitly include this condition. Thus, it is not absolutely clear whether or not she would accept it. But it is likely that she would, because this is suggested by her saying that

---

[6] This claim, together with my critique below, has been inspired by Woods (2013), who argues in detail that the traditional concept of fallacy has these features, and that at least fourteen of the traditional list of eighteen fallacies do not really instantiate the traditional concept. Needless to say, I am not attributing to Woods the critical argument I develop here, but the inspirational connection and subjective debt on my part are present. Readers acquainted with Woods (2013) should not be surprised at this, given that they can easily see this attitude of mine to be a kind of mirror image of the one displayed therein by Woods towards Finocchiaro (1981; 1987). Concerning the latter, see also Govier (1982; 1987, chapter 9; 1995).

[7] However, see the criticism of such a historical thesis advanced by Hansen (2002). Still, I do not think his criticism undermines my main point here, partly because the target of his criticism is a much more oversimplified concept of fallacy than the one I am advocating.

[8] For the last two references, see also, respectively, Woods 2013, chapter 4.6; Govier 2010, 66, 85.

fallacies are "characteristically" deceptive. This seems to mean that they are *typically* deceptive, and they *tend* to be deceptive. And such a characteristic, typical, or tendential deceptiveness could hardly subsist or happen without the argument in question being a member of a real class or natural kind.

This condition of generality is relevant and important in the present context because the fallacy of composition as defined so far, even according to the modified definition given above, is not a real type or natural kind of argument. In fact, in an analysis which is both cogent and interesting, Govier herself shows that the fallacy of composition is not an argument type. Recall that, in accordance with the modified definition, a fallacy of composition must be, and can only be, a fallacious argument from composition; and that an argument from composition is one containing reasoning from premises about the properties of parts or individuals to a conclusion about the properties of wholes or groups.

The passage containing this analysis is worth quoting in its entirety, but to be fully and immediately transparent, it is useful to recall and elaborate some aspects of the content and structure of Govier's examples. So far, I have not even mentioned the "duet" example which she briefly discusses: "John is a terrific tenor and Susan is a brilliant soprano. So a duet by John and Susan will be superb" (95). Wisely and mercifully, Govier wastes no time and space on this example. Here, she is presumably echoing the example of Copi (1968, 80): "since every part of a certain machine is light in weight, the machine 'as a whole' is light in weight." Nevertheless, it may be worth pointing out that such arguments are deductively invalid, and so if they are regarded as deductive arguments, they are incorrect.

Let us now consider the example of the Danish newspaper cartoons about the prophet Mohammed and the violent Muslim demonstrations against them in Islamic countries. Govier elaborates how some key aspects of some people's thinking about this were inductive generalizations, but hasty ones; for example, some Danes have offended some Muslims, therefore Denmark (or the West) has offended Islam; or, some Muslims have committed violence against some Westerners, therefore Islam has committed violence against the West. The tragedy of the commons also has an element of hasty generalization.

The world-hunger example appears, instead, to involve analogical reasoning. The argument would be that the world community should take some action to alleviate world hunger, because in a family no one would prepare dinner but exclude a family member from the table. Here, the whole world is being regarded as analogous to a part of it—the family.

Finally, in her analysis, to be quoted presently, Govier says that some instances of the fallacy of composition may be interpreted as inferences to the best explanation. However, she gives no explicit example of this connection, and as far as I can tell none of the examples she gives can be

15

viewed in this manner.

With these points in mind, we are now ready to appreciate the full cogency of Govier's meta-argument:

> In terms of the theory of argument, it is interesting to note that the Fallacy of Composition can appear in arguments of different types. If an argument is taken to be *deductive*, and the premises are about individuals while the conclusion is about a group, clearly that argument will be deductively invalid in the straightforward sense that it will be possible for the premises to be true while the conclusion is false. We may locate the Fallacy of Composition within this gap. If an argument is taken to be an *analogical* argument in which the primary subject is a macro phenomenon, while the analogue is described at the micro level, the analogy will be inadequate because there are relevant differences between the analogue and the primary subject. We consider the Fallacy of Composition in considering the nature and relevance of these differences. If an argument from individual to group is taken as *inductive generalization*, it can be criticized as hasty; the individual cases do not give sufficient evidence about the group as a whole. If it is regarded as an *inference-to-the-best-explanation*, there will be doubts about whether a compositional attribution to a group does, indeed, provide the best explanation of the possession of characteristics by an individual or individuals, given that individuals within the group may differ from each other and can exert a certain degree of autonomy. [96]

The upshot of these last considerations is that compositional arguments do not constitute a "kind" of argument, at least not in the sense in which this notion applies to deductions, arguments from analogy, inductive generalizations, and inferences to the best explanation. One implication of this regards the slightly revised, self-consistent notion of the fallacy of composition. That is, even if we define the "fallacy of composition" as a mistaken argument of composition, it does not seem to be a fallacy in the traditional sense, since it fails to satisfy the generality condition, number (2). In short, so defined, fallacies of composition are not really fallacies.[9]

---

[9] It could be objected that the main strand of my argument in this paragraph assumes that a "kind" of argument must be distinct from other "kinds," and this assumption is unwarranted because all argumentation schemes overlap. However, although it is true that some schemes overlap, not all do, and so the compositional scheme could very well be one of those that do not. Moreover, it seems to me that it would be pointless to define a kind that was not distinct from other kinds, and so a kind must be sufficiently well defined to be distinctive.

Another objection might be that what I call the generality condition (no. 2) can be satisfied in another way than the direct manner of the reasoning instantiating the properties that make up the definiens of the kind. This alternative might be an indirect method, along the lines of what Walton (2010) calls "paraschemes"; that is, a given instance of reasoning would be classified as belonging to the scheme of compositional argument because it is psychologically perceived as belonging to

The consequences for Govier's notion of the Fallacy of Composition are perhaps even worse. Earlier we saw that the Fallacy of Composition (as defined by Govier) was not always a fallacy, since some compositional arguments were not mistaken, according to her own gap-bridging analysis. Thus, one might say that Govier's "Fallacy of Composition" is not an evaluative category, in the sense that it is not a principle or rule that would enable, or assist, us in determining whether or not a given argument or piece of reasoning is correct or erroneous. Additionally, from the last considerations, it seems that Govier's Fallacy of Composition is not an interpretive concept either, for it is not a concept whose application to a real case tells us much, if anything, about the type, kind, or manner of reasoning involved. It follows that it is unclear what role, if any, such a Fallacy of Composition plays in logic and argumentation theory.

In short, Govier's Fallacy of Composition is not really a fallacy, in the traditional sense. There are at least two reasons for this: the Fallacy of Composition is not always a mistake, but rather sometimes correct; and the Fallacy of Composition is not a kind of argument or manner of reasoning, but rather a mere instance of argument or reasoning.

2. The Fallacy of Composition in Economics

The preceding critical appreciation of Govier's account should not be regarded as the end of the story, but rather as something of a beginning—an introduction to the study of the fallacy of composition. For it would be a violation of balanced judgment to interpret the main conclusion of my critique as claiming prematurely that the fallacy of composition is a chimera of no importance or relevance to logic and argumentation theory. Moreover, the realistic approach suggests or requires that we examine more empirical material or actual examples involving compositional phenomena, attributions, and arguments. Thirdly, although, as we have seen, Govier's account suggests that the fallacy of composition be self-consistently defined as an erroneous argument of composition, and although the notion of compositional argument can be criticized as not constituting a natural kind or normal type of argument, it is proper to attempt to clarify this notion further; for example, one could try to determine whether compositional arguments, besides their nominal definitional property, have other theoretically or methodologically significant characteristics that might enable us to interpret

---

some simplified "parascheme" heuristically associated with that scheme. Here my short answer to this objection is that I find Walton's concept and application of parascheme so obscure that the project strikes me as an attempt to explain a relatively puzzling phenomenon (that fallacies appear to be better arguments than they are) in terms of things that are even more difficult to understand.

them more deeply and evaluate them more effectively. Finally, Govier herself makes an apparently incidental remark that turns out to be very revealing and fruitful, and so I have no hesitation in crediting her for suggesting or inspiring a novel line of investigation.[10] Let us then reconstruct such a novel research project.

About halfway into her essay, Govier casually mentions that "the Fallacy of Composition ... has been strikingly memorialized in a sculpture by that name at the University of Groningen. This sculpture, a lighted structure, by Trudi van Berg and Jos Steenmeijer, occupies most of a wall on the building for the Faculty of Economics" (95). She cites a website, which is relatively user-friendly, and where one can view an image of the sculpture. The site also contains some comments, the most relevant of which is the following: "this work ... was inspired by an economic concept. The work of John M. Keynes led to valuable insights, including the fact that macro-economy—the behaviour of aggregated variables—is very different to micro-economy, or the behaviour of individuals. The whole behaves very differently to the sum of its parts. This is known as 'the fallacy of composition'. In 1998 the Faculty of Economics celebrated its 50th anniversary."[11]

That is, this Groningen website seems to be claiming that a key achievement of Keynesian economics was to expose the fallacy of composition presumably committed in the economic thinking of common people and of previous economists. Such a judgment is very widely shared. For example, if one consults the entry "Keynes" in the *Cambridge Dictionary of Philosophy* (Nelson 1999), one finds an interpretation that implicitly reinforces it. Although the entry does not mention the fallacy of composition, it does attribute to Keynes a focus on the distinction between micro and macro economics, and on ways to interrelate them.

Such hints revived my memory of having taken, during my undergraduate studies, an introductory economics course taught by the famous economist Paul Samuelson, and I seemed to recollect some discussions of the fallacy of composition. This led me to consult his textbook *Economics* (Samuelson 1955), which is still in my possession. I was amazed, but not surprised, to discover that it is full of critical discussions of economic examples of the fallacy of composition. Here then is a goldmine of material that deserves serious attention and careful study by logicians and argumentation theorists, and I will presently undertake a preliminary examination of it. But before doing that, it is worth mentioning a number of economic-related points that attest to the general cultural relevance and

---

[10] It should also be mentioned that the title of my essay is modeled on hers, although I also adopted (*mutatis mutandis*) the title of Woods (1988), which may have served as her own model in the first place.

[11] http://www.rug.nl/science-and-society/sculpture-project/sculpture1998?lang=en; consulted on July 24, 2012.

awareness of the fallacy of composition in economics: after exposure to Samuelson's textbook, such points can be easily retrieved from many sources; and conversely, noticing such points can serve as a clue for the general cultural importance of the problem of economic composition.

In *Elements of Logic*, Whately has a four-page discussion of the fallacies of composition and division, which would need to be examined carefully in a full treatment of this topic. Here I only wish to call attention to the fact that among his many more or less realistic examples, there are two that relate to economics: "the imprudent spendthrift, finding that he is able to afford this, *or* that, *or* the other expense, forgets that *all of them together* will ruin him" (Whately 1826, 176). The second example is one in which people sometimes skirt their responsibility by telling themselves that they are "not bound to contribute to this charity in particular; nor to that; nor to the other: the *practical* conclusion which they draw, is, that *all* charity may be dispensed with" (Whately 1826, 176).

The spendthrift example was later quoted by John S. Mill in his two-page discussion of the fallacy of composition in *A System of Logic* (1961, 536-37). A similar example is given in what seems to be the only study of this fallacy published in the journal *Informal Logic*. The author (Pole 1981) regards the fallacy of composition as one of several kinds of fallacies involving the part-whole distinction, and he also discusses a special case of composition, which he labels the "salesman's fallacy." This presumably occurs when a salesman tries to sell us a product (e.g., an automobile or a house) which is really beyond our means, by focusing on each part or accessory and stressing the point that we can afford that particular accessory. The fallacy is presumably the argument that the whole automobile is affordable because each part is affordable.

It is also interesting that the 1976 unabridged edition of *Webster's Third New International Dictionary* saw it fit to give an example in its entry on the fallacy of composition, and it is an economic example: "if my money bought more goods I should be better off; therefore, we should all benefit if prices were lower" (p. 818).

Let us now look at the considered reflective judgment of some economists, before we examine their examples. In the third edition of his famous textbook *Economics*, Samuelson (1955) has an introductory chapter in which one of several sections is entitled "the whole and the part: the 'fallacy of composition' " (p. 9). In it, he starts by giving seven examples of paradoxical-sounding statements that are nevertheless true, such as: "1. If all farmers work hard and nature cooperates in producing a bumper crop, total farm income *may fall*. ... 6. Attempts of individuals to save more in depression *may lessen the total* of the community's savings" (Samuelson 1955, 9). He claims that these statements can be easily and clearly shown to be true, as he actually does at various points in the book, when the various particular topics come up for discussion. And then comes the connection with the present topic: "many of the above paradoxes hinge upon one single confusion or fallacy, called by logicians the 'fallacy of composition'. In books on logic, this is defined as follows: '*A fallacy in which what is true of a part is, on that account alone, alleged to be also true of the whole*'. Very definitely, in the field of economics, it turns out that what seems to be true for each individual is not always true for society as a whole" (Samuelson 1955, 10).

By way of general introduction, it should also be noted that the term "fallacy of composition" is duly listed in the book's index, and that it is the only fallacy listed there. That index gives several references, including three to important examples not mentioned in the introduction: private debt vs. public debt, individual banks vs. the banking system, and the connection between commodity prices and land rents.

Such quotations from a distinguished economist are meant here primarily to help document the cultural ubiquity of the economic fallacy of composition. I believe they provide some degree of support, even though there are two potentially damaging issues that cannot be ignored at this point.

First, let us call attention to the clause "on that account alone," in the definition which Samuelson adopts from logic books; it may be labeled the "exclusionary clause." He seems to be referring to arguments concluding that the whole has a certain property *just because* the parts have that property; this may be contrasted to saying *partly because* or *primarily because*. In other words, he is talking about compositional arguments whose only premises are claims that attribute a certain property to the parts, thus excluding other premises that might assert something about the relationship among the parts. And he is talking about arguments claiming more than that the truth of the premises makes the truth of the conclusion likely, and much more than that they provide some support to the conclusion. Samuelson's exclusionary clause does indeed increase the likelihood that the inference is erroneous, for as we saw in our discussion of Govier's account, it would exclude adding any gap-bridging premises. At the same time, we should note that such exclusionary compositional arguments are not automatically or necessarily deductively invalid. In fact there are instances that are valid, such as the following variant of Copi's hackneyed example: since every part of this machine has weight (mass), the machine as a whole has weight (mass).

The second qualification involves the distinction between appearance and reality. Note that Samuelson says that in economics what *seems* to be true for each individual *is not* always true for the whole society. However, it is also the case that what seems to be true for each individual is not always really true of that individual. And when this happens, the main reason why the inference to the whole society does not hold may be that the individuals do not actually have the property in question in the first place, and so the compositional argument in question is not simply an instance of reasoning from parts to the whole, but has two steps: from apparent properties of parts to actual properties of parts, and from the latter to actual properties of the whole; now, the weak point may be the first step of this chain inference rather than the second.

Let us now go on to a much later edition of Samuelson's textbook, the 13th of 1989, co-authored with his former student Nordhaus. By and large, there is slightly less emphasis on the fallacy of composition, and fewer and less frequent examples are discussed. Nevertheless, this fallacy is still referenced in the index; included in a new "Glossary" of terms; illustrated concretely in three different chapters; and discussed generally in a two-page section of the introductory chapter. In that general introduction, the fallacy is now presented as only one of several "pitfalls in economic reasoning," the others being the fallacy of *post hoc, ergo propter hoc*, and the failure to appreciate the qualification "other things being equal," to appreciate that observation and perception are theory-laden, and to appreciate that economic laws are statistical and not exact.

That introductory discussion begins with the following words: "Have you ever seen people jump up at a football game to gain a better view? They usually find that, once everybody is standing up, the view has not improved at all. Such behavior, where what is true for an individual is not necessarily true for everyone, illustrates the 'fallacy of composition', which is defined as follows: *the fallacy of composition occurs when what is true of a part is therefore believed to be true for the whole*" (Samuelson and Nordhaus 1989, 7-8). Then four brief examples are given, corresponding to some of those in the list of the 1955 edition. As we can see, the earlier exclusionary clause is gone from the general definition; gone is also the earlier tendency to confuse this issue with the issue of appearance vs. reality; and an incisive non-economic example is given, involving people viewing an athletic game in a stadium.

Another piece of evidence for the cultural ubiquity of the economic fallacy of composition is an internet essay entitled "Teaching the Fallacy of Composition: The Federal Budget Deficit," by L. Randall Wray, a professor of economics at the University of Missouri-Kansas City. This article appeared as the second item, at the top of a list of 1,130,000 items, found by a Google search of the "fallacy of composition" (consulted on October 19, 2012). Wray states that "one of the most important concepts taught in economics is the notion of the fallacy of composition: what might be true for individuals is probably not true for society as a whole." Then he gives three brief examples overlapping with Samuelson's list: the paradox of thrift; the causes (individual vs. social) of unemployment; and the effects (micro vs. macro) of a minimum-wage law. And then he elaborates a great length the all-important example of public vs. private debt.

The only thing to note at the moment is that Wray's definition explicitly injects the notion of probability into the inference from parts to whole. This is an improvement, for the probability clause makes it clear that compositional arguments are normally meant to be inductive and defeasible, not deductive.

To conclude this section, although the story does not end here either, it would seem rash or injudicious to dismiss such economists' talk of the fallacy of composition. In the domain of economic affairs and thinking, the fallacy of composition seems to have some reality and robustness, above and beyond the trivial and hackneyed examples of logic textbooks.

3. The Fallacy of Composition as an Error of Oversimplification

One of the internet comments on Wray's essay is also culturally important. Moreover, it raises a relatively novel issue, potentially significant from the point of view of logic and argumentation theory. It is one of 29 comments and was posted on August 23, 2009 by an anonymous respondent, using the label "Razorback". The most relevant claim is: "read a classic from Hazlitt, *Economics in One Lesson*. It deals (extensively) with the pervasive logical 'fallacy of composition', which basically is a tendency of most thinkers to oversimplify the 'micro' effects and then perform a simple sigma summation to derive the 'macro' and then apply further reasoning from there."[12]

This respondent is referring to a book which was first published in 1946; became a best seller; and had a second edition in 1979. The author is Henry Hazlitt, a libertarian economist (and philosopher) belonging to the "Austrian school" of economics. In this book, his main thesis is that "the whole of economics can be reduced to a single lesson, and that lesson can be reduced to a single sentence. *The art of economics consists in looking not merely at the immediate but at the longer effects of any act or policy; it consists in tracing the consequences of that policy not merely for one group but for all groups*" (Hazlitt 1979, 17). He also has a negative way of expressing this key point: "economics is haunted by more fallacies than any other study known to man" (Hazlitt 1979, 15); and "nine-tenths of the economic fallacies that are working such dreadful harm in the world today are the result of ignoring this lesson. Those fallacies all stem from one of the two central fallacies, or both: that of looking only at the immediate consequences of an act or proposal, and that of looking at the consequences only from a particular group to the neglect of other groups" (Hazlitt 1979, 17).

The most immediate thing to note here is that, insofar as Hazlitt is dealing

---

[12] http://neweconomicperspectives.org/2009/08/teaching-fallacy-of-composition-federal.html; consulted on October 19, 2012.

with the fallacy of composition, his work adds another dimension to its cultural ubiquity. This stems from the fact that he may be regarded as an important representative of conservative or right-wing thinking, just as Samuelson may be regarded as a leading exponent of liberal or left-wing thinking. To that extent, the exposure of the fallacy of composition seems to be a concern common to both sides of the political and ideological spectrum, and so it is not merely an ideological tool of one side against the other.

However, let us ask whether Hazlitt is really talking about this fallacy. In fact, he does not explicitly use the term "fallacy of composition." Thus, if we want to attribute the concept to him, as the anonymous respondent to Wray does, then we need to interpret the fallacy or fallacies described but not named by Hazlitt as either a generalization or a special case of composition. And this may be what the anonymous respondent is suggesting.

To address this issue, let us begin by noting that the anonymous respondent is not just reiterating the usual definition of the fallacy of composition, but is rather giving an interesting interpretation of it, which I would in turn interpret as follows. He is focusing on arguments that try to derive macro effects from micro ones, which correspond to what I have called compositional arguments. And he is claiming that such arguments are often erroneous, insofar as they embody an oversimplification that does not properly take into account various complications, but instead simply generalizes the properties of the micro phenomena to the macro level. Such erroneous compositional arguments are fallacies of composition.

Next, let us note that Hazlitt is concerned, first and foremost, to contrast short-term with long-term consequences, and the effects on a single particular group with the effects on the aggregate of all groups, i.e., on the whole society. Now, both of these contrasts may be seen as special cases of the distinction between the micro and the macro level, which almost everyone writing on this topic makes. With the first contrast, Hazlitt is extending the micro vs. macro distinction to the temporal domain, by viewing the short term as a micro period of time, and the long term as a macro period. With the second contrast, Hazlitt is extending the parts vs. whole distinction by focusing on parts of a whole society that are themselves aggregates of individuals, rather than just on individuals. Both extensions seem plausible. Thus, Hazlitt is really dealing with the compositional phenomenon, compositional attributes, and compositional arguments, after all.

In his negative, critical thesis, Hazlitt is concerned with exposing the error of over-emphasizing the parts or micro phenomena in understating the whole or macro phenomena. One such typical error would be to start with what is known about the micro or parts, and then argue that the exact same thing is true about the macro level of the whole. Such argumentation runs the risks of which the anonymous respondent speaks: an oversimplification of the description of the micro phenomena, and/or an oversimplification of the way in which they are added up or combined to yield the macro phenomena. Thus, what is usually called the fallacy of composition becomes a special case of the error of oversimplification. (Whether we should speak of the fallacy of oversimplification, I leave it as an open question at the moment.) In short, the anonymous respondent seems to have a point in claiming that the key concern of Hazlitt's book is to expose the fallacy of composition in economic thinking, even though Hazlitt does not use the usual label and is generalizing the usual distinction of micro vs. macro.

On the other hand, it may not be an accident that Hazlitt does not speak of the fallacy of composition. Perhaps he is really concerned with exposing the error of oversimplification in economic affairs, committed through the neglect of considerations of the long run (as contrasted to the short run) and/or of the whole society (as contrasted to a part), and through the neglect of complexities in combining the micro to yield the macro. Here the key issue would seem to be the avoidance of one-sidedness and of extremes; that is, judiciousness or balanced judgment, in my terminology introduced above. It is not at all obvious that there is any advantage in speaking of the fallacy of composition rather than speaking of oversimplification and injudiciousness. If there is no such advantage, then Hazlitt's work cannot be used to strengthen the case for the cultural ubiquity of the economic fallacy of composition.

More importantly, from the point of view of logic and argumentation theory, perhaps fallacies of composition are basically errors of oversimplification. If so, this would provide another reason why the concept of fallacy of composition is problematical: for this would amount to saying that (at best) fallacies of composition are not a distinctive kind of error, since they would be special cases of the error of oversimplification, and the concept of oversimplification is neither simple nor unified but rather subsumes a multiplicity of oversights. This reason may be added to the one which earlier I extracted from Govier's account, namely that fallacies of composition are not a distinct kind of argument, because compositional arguments do not constitute a natural or distinctive kind. Putting the two together, we get that fallacies of composition are neither a distinctive kind of argument nor a distinctive kind of error. What are they, then? They are instances of compositional arguments that oversimplify the relationship between the micro and macro levels, the parts and the whole, the individual and society.

4. Further Testing and Extended Examples

These deconstructionist[13] claims about the fallacy of composition need

---

[13] Needless to say, my talk of deconstruction is not meant to have the technical meaning stemming from the philosophy of Jacques Derrida and related systems of

further testing. Although this testing cannot be undertaken in this essay, here it will be useful to sketch and summarize the material and the extended examples I have in mind for this purpose.

One next step would be to undertake a detailed, concrete, and substantive examination of what I regard as the best examples of economic fallacies of composition that can be gleaned from Samuelson's and Wray's works mentioned above. One of these examples involves the topic of private or personal vs. public or national debt, and the question whether it is fallacious to argue that a constant or excessive national debt is irresponsible or ruinous just because (or primarily because, or partly because) a constant or excessive personal debt is irresponsible or ruinous.[14] Another paradigm example concerns the phenomenon that the whole banking system can expand the money supply even though a single bank cannot, and the fallaciousness of arguing that since no single bank by itself can create money, neither can the banking system as a whole do so (Samuelson 1955, 273-78). The third important example deals with the relationship between commodity prices and land rents: at the level of an individual entrepreneur or firm, land rents contribute to determining commodity prices, whereas, at the macro level of the whole economy, the reverse happens (commodity prices contribute to determining land rents); here the fallacy of composition would be to argue that since at the micro level the direction of causation is from rents to prices, therefore at the macro level the direction is also from rents to prices (Samuelson 1955, 504-505; Samuelson and Nordhaus 1989, 667-668).

A second project would search for compositional arguments and fallacies of composition in political science. In particular, there happens to be some material which is highly relevant, and involves one of the most famous and widely-discussed principles in that field—the so-called "iron law of oligarchy": that every bureaucratic organization has oligarchical tendencies which are impossible to overcome, and that this applies even to democratic institutions, which are thus doomed to become undemocratic. This law was advanced in a book by Robert Michels, first published in German in 1911, and later in English in 1962, revealigly entitled *Political Parties: A Sociological Study of the Oligarchical Tendencies of Modern Parties*.

Now, some of the most distinguished social scientists of the twentieth century have criticized Michels's argument in support of the law by charging him with errors that are clearly reminiscent of the fallacy of composition,

---

thought. Rather it is meant to have the ordinary meaning of this term, which is "the analytic examination of something (as a theory) often in order to reveal its inadequacy" (Merriam-Webster Dictionary online, available at http://www.merriam-webster.com/dictionary/deconstruction, consulted on February 15, 2013).

[14] Samuelson 1955, 350-52; Samuelson and Nordhaus 1989, 399-404; Wray 2006, 2-5.

even though these critics do not use this label. One of these critics is Robert Dahl, the founder of a field known as democratic theory (Dahl 1956; 1989). Dahl charges that Michels begins by studying the workings of political parties, in particular the German Social Democratic Party; he discovers that even parties advocating democracy have insurmountable oligarchical (anti-democratic) tendencies; he concludes that what is true of political parties is also true of governmental institutions or societies as a whole; and thus he commits an error of reasoning, consisting of illegitimately generalizing from parts to the whole (Dahl 1989, 275-77). Another important criticism is advanced by Seymour Martin Lipset, a political sociologist who wrote the introduction to the English translation of Michels's book. Lipset's key charge is that Michels failed to appreciate that a whole society can be democratic (anti-oligarchical) even though it is composed of parts that are oligarchical (anti-democratic); this happens when there exist institutions that prevent any one group from exercising despotic power over opposing groups (Lipset 1962, 36-37).

A third project would be to attempt to relate the controversy of holism vs. individualism in sociology to the fallacy of composition, that is, to interpret that controversy in argumentation-theoretical terms in general, and compositional arguments in particular. In fact, at the descriptive or semantic level, individualism affirms, and holism denies, that all properties of the whole can be defined in terms of properties of the parts; whereas at the explanatory or epistemic level, individualism affirms, and holism denies, that all properties or laws at the macro or social level are in principle derivable from, explicable by, or reducible to the properties or laws at the micro or individual level (cf. Addis 1999; Jones 2003). Thus, individualism would seem to correspond to the claim that compositional arguments can in principle be correct; whereas holism would correspond to the thesis that some compositional argument must be fallacious.

5. Epilogue

I began with a critical appreciation of Govier's account of the fallacy of composition. I endorsed her approach insofar as it typically displays balanced judgment (by avoiding one-sidedness and extremes), and insofar as it embodies a sound realism (by focusing on important actual or realistic examples). And I found acceptable some of her substantive claims: that compositional attributions are problematic; and that compositional arguments exemplify a variety of argument kinds, such as deductive, analogical, and generalization. However, I questioned her notion of the fallacy of composition, by arguing that she has a tendency to hypostatize the concept; that is, she wavers between the notion of a compositional argument (that can be correct or incorrect) and the notion of the fallacy of composition (as a mistaken argument of composition), thus depriving her account of genuine evaluative value; and she fails to see that the multiplicity of argument kinds subsumed under the notion of fallacy of composition deprive it of interpretive significance.

Then I undertook a critical appreciation of the topic of the fallacy of composition in economic thinking and in the writings of some economists. The first positive point was that there is considerable prima facie evidence that the economic fallacy of composition is ubiquitous in our culture; although this is apparently unknown or little discussed among philosophers, the exposure of such a fallacy is a constant refrain among economists on both the right and left wings of the political spectrum. A second positive point was the claim that the essential flaw of economic fallacies of composition is an error of oversimplification in dealing with inferences from the micro to the macro level; I extracted this thesis from some of these writings. On a critical note, from the point of view of logic and argumentation theory, insofar as fallacies of composition are essentially errors of oversimplification, they do not constitute a distinctive kind of error.

Finally, I proposed some further testing of my "deconstructionist" claim that the so-called fallacy of composition is neither a distinctive kind of argument nor a distinctive type of error. The tests involve concrete and important examples of alleged fallacies of composition from the social sciences. In economics, there is the all-important issue of public vs. private debt, as well as the question of effects on the money supply of a particular bank and of the whole banking system, and the problem of the micro-level vs. macro-level direction of causation between commodity prices and land rents. In political science, we have the issue of whether, and if so how, a whole society can be democratic even when it consists of particular institutions that tend to be oligarchic or anti-democratic. And in sociology the issue of holism vs. individualism provides examples of compositional arguments that may or may not be fallacies of composition.

References

Addis, Laird. 1999. Holism. In *Cambridge Dictionary of Philosophy*, 2nd edn., ed. Robert Audi, 390-91. New York: Cambridge University Press.

Arnauld, Antoine, and P. Nicole. 1996. *Logic or the Art of Thinking*. Trans. J.V. Buroker. Cambridge: Cambridge University Press.

Barth, Else M., J. Vandormael, and F. Vandamme, eds. 1992. *From an Empirical Point of View: The Empirical Turn in Logic*. Ghent: Communication and Cognition.

Copi, Irving M. 1968. *Introduction to Logic*, 3rd edn. New York: MacMillan.

Dahl, Robert A. 1956. *A Preface to Democratic Theory*. Chicago: University of Chicago Press.

Dahl, Robert A. 1989. *Democracy and Its Critics*. New Haven: Yale University Press.

Finocchiaro, Maurice A. 1980. *Galileo and the Art of Reasoning: Rhetorical Foundations of Logic and Scientific Method*. (Boston Studies in the Philosophy of Science, vol. 61.) Dordrecht: Reidel [now Springer].

Finocchiaro, Maurice A. 1981. Fallacies and the evaluation of reasoning. *American Philosophical Quarterly* 18: 13-22. Reprinted in Finocchiaro 2005, 109-27.

Finocchiaro, Maurice A. 1987. Six types of fallaciousness: Toward a realistic theory of logical criticism. *Argumentation* 1: 263-82. Reprinted in Finocchiaro 2005, 128-47.

Finocchiaro, Maurice A. 1988. *Gramsci and the History of Dialectical Thought*. Cambridge: Cambridge University Press.

Finocchiaro, Maurice A. 2005. *Arguments about Arguments: Systematic, Critical, and Historical essays in Logical Theory*. New York: Cambridge University Press.

Finocchiaro, Maurice A. 2010. *Defending Copernicus and Galileo: Critical Reasoning in the Two Affairs*. (Boston Studies in the Philosophy of Science, vol. 280.) Dordrecht: Springer.

Finocchiaro, Maurice A. 2013. *Meta-argumentation: An Approach to Logic and Argumentation Theory*. (Studies in Logic, vol. 42.) London: College Publications.

Fisher, Alec. 2004. *The Logic of Real Arguments*, 2nd. edn. Cambridge: Cambridge University Press.

Govier, Trudy. 1982. Who says there are no fallacies? *Informal Logic Newsletter*, vol. v, no. i, pp. 2-10.

Govier, Trudy. 1987. *Problems in Argument Analysis and Evaluation*. Dordrecht: Foris.

Govier, Trudy. 1995. Reply to Massey. In *Fallacies: Classical and Contemporary Readings*, ed. H.V. Hansen and R.C. Pinto, 172-80. University Park: The Pennsylvania State University Press.

Govier, Trudy. 1999. *The Philosophy of Argument*. Newport News: Vale Press.

Govier, Trudy. 2000. Critical review: Johnson's *Manifest Rationality*. *Informal Logic* 20: 281-91.

Govier, Trudy. 2007. Duets, cartoons, and tragedies: Struggles with the fallacy of composition. In *Proceedings of the Sixth Conference of the International Society for the Study of Argumentation*, ed. F.H. van Eemeren, J.A. Blair, C.A. Willard, and B. Garssen, 505-11. Amsterdam: Sic Sat.

Govier, Trudy. 2009. Duets, cartoons, and tragedies: Struggles with the fallacy of composition. In *Pondering on Problems of Argumentation*, ed. F.H. van Eemeren and B. Garssen, 91-104. Dordrecht: Springer.

Govier, Trudy. 2010. *A Practical Study of Argument*, 7th edn. Belmont: Wadsworth.

Hansen, Hans H. 2002. The straw thing of fallacy theory: The standard definition of 'fallacy'. *Argumentation* 16: 133-55.

Hazlitt, Henry. 1979. *Economics in One Lesson*. New Rochelle: Arlington House Publishers. 1st edn., 1946.

Johnson, Ralph H. 2000. *Manifest Rationality: A Pragmatic Theory of Argument*. Mahwah: Lawrence Erlbaum Associates.

Jones, Todd. 2003. The failure of the best arguments against social reduction (and what that failure doesn't mean). *Southern Journal of Philosophy* 41: 547-81.

Jones, Todd. 2010. *What People Believe when They Say That People Believe: Folk Sociology and the Nature of Group Intentions*. Lanham: Lexington Books.

Lipset, Seymour M. 1962. Introduction to Michels 1962, 15-39.

Michels, Robert. 1962. *Political Parties: A Sociological Study of the Oligarchical Tendencies of Modern Parties*. Trans. E. Paul and C. Paul. New York: Collier.

Mill, John Stuart. 1961. *A System of Logic: Ratiocinative and Inductive*. London: Spottiswoode. 1st edn., London: Longmans, 1843.

Nelson, Alan. 1999. Keynes. In *Cambridge Dictionary of Philosophy*, 2nd edn., ed. R. Audi, 467-68. New York: Cambridge University Press.

Pole, Nelson. 1981. Part/whole fallacies. *Informal Logic Newsletter*, vol. 3, no. 3, June, pp. 11-13.

Samuelson, Paul A. 1955. *Economics: An Introductory Analysis*, 3rd edn. New York: McGraw-Hill.

Samuelson, Paul A., and William D. Nordhaus. 1989. *Economics*, 13th edn. New York: McGraw-Hill.

Walton, Douglas. 2010. Why fallacies appear to be better arguments than they are. *Informal Logic* 30: 159-84.

Walton, Douglas, C. Reed, and F. Maccagno. 2008. *Argumentation Schemes*. Cambridge: Cambridge University Press.

Whately, Richard. 1826. *Elements of Logic*. London: J. Mawman. Rpt., Bologna, Italy: Editrice CLUEB, 1988.

Woods, John. 1988. Buttercups, GNP's, and quarks: Are fallacies theoretical entities? *Informal Logic* 10: 67-76. Reprinted in Woods 2004, 161-70.

Woods, John. 2004. *The Death of Argument: Fallacies in Agent-Based Reasoning*. Dordrecht: Kluwer.

Woods, John. 2012. A history of the fallacies in Western logic. In *Logic: A History of Its Central Concepts*, ed. D.M. Gabbay, F.J. Pelletier, and J. Woods, 513-610. Amsterdam: North-Holland.

Woods, John. 2013. *Errors of Reasoning: Naturalizing the Logic of Inference*. (Studies in Logic, vol. 45.) London: College Publications.

Woods, John, and D.N. Walton. 1977a. Composition and division. *Studia Logica* 36: 381-406. Reprinted in Woods and Walton 1989, 93-119.

Woods, John, and D.N. Walton. 1977b. Post hoc, ergo propter hoc. *Review of Metaphysics* 30: 569-93. Reprinted in Woods and Walton 1989, 121-41.

Woods, John, and D.N. Walton. 1989. *Fallacies: Selected Papers 1972-1982*. Dordrecht: Foris Publications.

Wray, L. Randall. 2006. Teaching the fallacy of composition: The federal budget deficit. At https://edi.bard.edu/research/cfeps-archive/; first consulted on October 19, 2012; later on May 25, 2023.

Chapter 2
The Fallacy of Composition and Meta-Argumentation

1. The Problem: Significance vs. Triviality

Vices may be regarded as the opposite of virtues; and fallacies are, arguably, vices of argumentation.[1] Thus, one may study the virtues of argumentation indirectly by studying fallacies. In any case, of course, the study of fallacies is a well-established area of logic and argumentation theory (cf. Hamblin 1970; Woods 2013), and so no elaborate justification and motivation are needed.

Now, among the fallacies, there is one—the fallacy of composition—whose importance has been widely claimed. For example, in 1826, in the *Elements of Logic*, Richard Whately explicitly named and discussed this fallacy, saying among other things: "there is no fallacy more common, or more likely to deceive, than the one now before us" (Whately 1826, 174-75). Moreover, at least since the epoch-making contributions of John Maynard Keynes (who died in 1946), economists tend to regard the fallacy of composition as the single worst pitfall in economic reasoning; they also consider the exposure of it to be the greatest accomplishment of the modern science of economics; they deem the avoidance of it the most important lesson one can learn from this science; and such claims are easily found in the writings of economists of both the left and right wings of the ideological spectrum.[2] Additionally, in 1981, an article was published in the journal *Informal Logic*, dealing with "part/whole fallacies," of which composition may be regarded as a special case; the author argued that there is "a virtual epidemic of part/whole fallacies perpetrated on an unsuspecting public" (Pole 1981, 11). Finally, in 2006, Trudy Govier saw it fit to devote to the fallacy of composition her keynote address to the International Society for the Study of Argumentation; in it she followed her usual realistic and judicious approach, and thus examined some important recent examples of this fallacy, involving issues such as individual vs. national reconciliation in South Africa, and individual vs. collective actions and blame in the post-nine-eleven relations between Islam and the West.[3]

However, despite such attention and such claims, scholars in logic and argumentation theory do not seem to have done much work on the fallacy of

---

[1] Cf. Finocchiaro 1980, 338; 1981, 17; 2005, 116.
[2] Cf. Hazlitt 1979; Nelson 1999; Samuelson 1955; Samuelson and Nordhaus 1989; Wray 2006; and Finocchiaro 2013a.
[3] Govier 2007; 2009. Cf. Finocchiaro 2013a.

31

composition, although textbooks tend to pay lip service to it. For example, the journal *Informal Logic* has not published any more articles on this fallacy in the intervening thirty-one years (i.e., through 2012). Furthermore, there is no sustained discussion of it in the volume on *Fallacies and Argument Appraisal* of the Cambridge University Press series on critical reasoning and argumentation; instead, the author only mentions it briefly in some introductory remarks on problems with language (Tindale 2007, 57-58). And in his latest book on *Errors of Reasoning*, even the inimitable John Woods (2013) does not get around to elaborating a critique of this particular fallacy, as he does for at least fourteen others of the so-called gang of eighteen traditional fallacies; however, here it must be added that this book is full of insights and should serve as a model to emulate, both with regard to the substantive theory of fallacies and to the methodological approach of naturalism which it develops (cf. Finocchiaro 2013a; 2013b); moreover, he does give it due coverage in his history of fallacies (Woods 2012).

Sometimes this scholarly neglect of the fallacy of composition is explained and partly justified in terms of its rarity or infrequency. For example, in the 1973 edition of his textbook *Logic and Philosophy*, Howard Kahane has a brief discussion of this fallacy together with its reverse twin, the fallacy of division. Here are his revealing words: "since non-trivial real life examples of these two fallacies … are unusual, textbook examples tend to be contrived or trivial" (Kahane 1973, 244).

Obviously, this explanation of the scholarly neglect conflicts with the ubiquity thesis reported earlier. Thus, the question arises whether the fallacy of composition is common and important, or uncommon and unimportant; although such a question arises for fallacies in general,[4] in this case the problem is more serious because the conflict seems deeper. The issue is largely an empirical question, to be resolved by following an empirical approach. However, the investigation cannot be conducted with a *tabula rasa*, for we need to be clear about what we mean by fallacy of composition, and also we need to examine real or realistic material which typically does not come with the label 'fallacy of composition' attached to it. In other words, we need to be mindful of the fact that observation is theory-laden, and that the examination of this material must be guided by some definition of what this fallacy is, and by some idea of what to do with the material under examination so as to test it for the occurrence of this fallacy.

2. Guiding Ideas: Ambiguities and Meta-arguments

The ubiquity thesis, stated above, besides generating the problem just

---

[4] Cf. Finocchiaro (1981; 1987); Woods 2013.

formulated, may also be regarded as a guiding idea for its solution, at least in the sense that it defines our task as being that of determining whether it is true.

Besides the ubiquity thesis, another guiding idea is this: there are three senses of fallacy of composition that are prima facie distinct, but often confused with each other. First, there is reasoning from premises using a term distributively to a conclusion using the same term collectively; for example, "because a bus uses more gasoline than an automobile, therefore all buses use more gasoline than all automobiles" (Copi 1968, 81). Second, there is reasoning from some property of the parts to the same property for the whole; for instance, "since every part of a certain machine is light in weight, the machine 'as a whole' is light in weight" (Copi 1968, 80). And thirdly, there is reasoning from some property of the members of a group to the same property for the entire group; the so-called tragedy of the commons can illustrate this notion, that is, "if one farmer grazes his cattle on the commons, that will be beneficial for him; therefore if all the farmers graze their cattle on the commons, that will be beneficial for all" (Govier 2009, 95).

The association of the second and third notions with each other is very common, whereas the association of all three is relatively rare. Nevertheless the three-fold association is embodied in a dictionary definition from an otherwise authoritative source, *Webster's Third New International Dictionary*: "fallacy of composition: the fallacy of arguing from premises in which a term is used distributively to a conclusion in which it is used collectively or of assuming that what is true of each member of a class or part of a whole will be true of all together" (1976 edition, p. 818).

Besides this tripartite distinction and the ubiquity thesis, there is a third guiding idea that needs to be at least mentioned and tentatively stated before we proceed. In a previous work, I criticized textbook accounts of fallacies, and on its basis I formulated a problem and advanced an hypothesis. The problem was formulated in terms of the following questions: "do people actually commit fallacies as usually understood? That is, do fallacies exist in practice? Or do they exist only in the mind of the interpreter who is claiming that a fallacy is being committed?"[5] Although these were not meant to be rhetorical questions, but rather open questions that required further investigation, it is perhaps unsurprising that some readers did view them as rhetorical questions, and concluded that I was claiming that fallacies are merely figments of critics' imagination and "are in fact an illusion."[6]

Later, I tried to be more explicit and more constructive about this issue when I elaborated a general approach to the study of fallacies. One element of that approach was connected to, and extracted from, Strawson's (1952)

---

[5] Finocchiaro 1980, 334; 1981, 15; 2005, 113.
[6] Jason 1986, 92; cf. Govier 1982.

Introduction to Logical Theory and his notion of "the logician's second-order vocabulary"; that notion was extended to include 'fallacy' terminology, "since it ordinarily occurs when someone wants to comment about some logical feature of a first-order expression of reasoning. This means that the best place to begin with in the study of fallacies, or at least a crucial phenomenon to examine, is allegations that fallacies are being committed" (Finocchiaro 1987, 264; 2005, 130). From this, some elaborated the idea that fallacies are more like theoretical entities such as quarks in physics, rather than like concrete objects such as buttercups in everyday life (Woods 1988). This elaboration was a constructive suggestion and critical appreciation, and I am far from denying its viability.

However, I now believe that the project can be articulated more clearly, incisively, and constructively in light of the notion of meta-argumentation (cf. Finocchiaro 2013b). Let us distinguish a meta-argument from a ground-level argument, and define the former as an argument about one or more arguments, or about argumentation in general. Then a ground-level argument can be defined as one about such things as natural phenomena, historical events, human actions, abstract entities, or metaphysical beings. A prototypical case of meta-argumentation is argument analysis, in which one advances and justifies an interpretive or an evaluative claim about a ground-level argument.

What I am proposing is that we search for fallacies of composition primarily in meta-argumentation rather than ground-level argumentation. However, this is not meant in the sense that we should be looking for meta-arguments that commit the fallacy of composition, but rather that we try to find meta-arguments advancing explicit conclusions that some fallacy of composition has been committed, i.e., that some ground-level argument embodies or commits a fallacy of composition. The working hypothesis is then that, at least as a first approximation, the fallacy of composition is primarily a concept of meta-argumentation, useful in the context of understanding and/or assessing ground-level argumentation. Whether this is also the case for other fallacies is not being addressed here, and is left as an open question.

3. Michels's Iron Law of Oligarchy

Let us now begin our empirical search for real or realistic material pertaining to the fallacy of composition. One of the most important discussions of the fallacy of composition I have come across is found in the field of political science. It involves one of the most famous and widely-discussed principles in that field—the so-called "iron law of oligarchy": that every bureaucratic organization has oligarchical tendencies which are impossible to overcome,

34

and that this applies even to democratic institutions, which are thus doomed to become undemocratic. This "law" was first advanced in a book published in German in 1911, translated into English in 1915, reprinted many times, and revealingly entitled *Political Parties: A Sociological Study of the Oligarchical Tendencies of Modern Democracy* (Michels 1962).

Now, an important criticism of Michels's law has been advanced by Robert Dahl, who is one of the most widely respected political scientists and the founder of the field known as democratic theory (Dahl 1956; 1989). The criticism is that Michels began by studying the workings of political parties, in particular the German Social Democratic Party; he discovered that even parties advocating democracy had insurmountable oligarchical (i.e., anti-democratic) tendencies; he concluded that what was true of political parties was also true of governmental institutions or societies as a whole; and thus he committed an error of reasoning, consisting of illegitimately inferring from parts to the whole (Dahl 1989, 275-77).

Although Dahl does not speak of "fallacy of composition," it is obvious that he is attributing this fallacy to Michels. Furthermore, if Dahl's criticism is accurate, then Michels's argument provides an example of fallacy of composition which is real, important, substantial, and interesting; again, infinitely more robust than the hackneyed and trivial examples of logic textbooks. For these reasons, it is valuable to quote Dahl's words (1989, 276):

> From the perspective of later political science, then, Michels committed an elementary mistake in generalizing from political parties to the government of a polyarchal system. His generalizations were derived from the study of a single organization, the German Social Democratic Party. His famous "iron law of oligarchy" explicitly referred to political parties ... But even if we grant that political parties are oligarchical, *it does not follow that competing political parties necessarily produce an oligarchical political system.* Business firms are among the most "oligarchical" organizations in modern societies; but as I pointed out, Michels's mentor, Pareto, writing as an economist, would never have said that these competing oligarchies produced monopolistic control over consumers and the market. Not even Marx, who saw business firms as despotic organizations, made such an elementary mistake. Quite the contrary: It was competition that *prevented* monopoly. If Michels had strictly limited his conclusions to political parties, his case would have been far stronger. But as the quotations given earlier show clearly, Michels went on to draw the unwarranted conclusion that democracy is impossible in a *political system* because it was, he believed from his study of one party, impossible in a particular *element of the system.* Had he been writing today it is inconceivable that he would have moved so casually from his observation of oligarchy in a political party to the conclusion that oligarchy is inescapable in a political system in which the political parties are highly competitive. Michels's elementary mistake reminds us that for the most part the theorists of minority domination discussed here had little or no experience with systems of competitive parties in countries with a broad suffrage

or, certainly, with systematic analysis of competitive party systems.

Here, Dahl's talk of generalization may give the impression that he is interpreting Michels's reasoning as an inductive generalization, and criticizing it as a hasty one. However, applying the principle of charity at the level of Dahl's own meta-argument, I would say that it is preferable to interpret Dahl as attributing to Michels an argument from analogy, and criticizing it as involving a weak analogy. In fact, Michels was claiming an analogy between political parties and political systems as a whole, based on similarities such as the following: (1) administration by the majority is technically impossible; (2) the better elements of the people or mass get constantly re-elected; (3) the first leaders have an advantage over newcomers; (4) the leaders control party machinery, such as the press; and (5) leaders change psychologically in their attitude due to the salary they receive, the power they exercise, their interaction with the ruling class, their age, and their attachment to their own accomplishments. Without necessarily denying such similarities, Dahl is stressing that there is an important dissimilarity, which Michels is ignoring—competition; in political systems that allow competition among political parties, the oligarchic tendencies that exist within parties are counteracted at the macro level of the whole political system.

On the other hand, whether Michels's argument is criticized as a hasty generalization, or as an incorrect analogy, in either case the criticism would be consistent with attributing to it a fallacy of composition. For Michels's argument remains an argument of composition, because it reasons from parts or elements being oligarchical to the whole system being oligarchical; and it is being criticized as incorrect or fallacious. In other words, adapting an argument by Govier,[7] I believe that arguments of composition are not a distinct kind, but can also instantiate other types, especially inductive generalizations and arguments from analogy.

Another important criticism of Michels's iron law of oligarchy also relates to the fallacy of composition. It is advanced by Seymour Martin Lipset (1962), a distinguished political sociologist who wrote the introduction to the English translation of Michels's book. Lipset's key criticism is that Michels failed to appreciate that a whole society can be democratic (i.e., anti-oligarchical) even though it is composed of institutional parts that are oligarchical (i.e., anti-democratic). Again, although Lipset does not use the term, he is attributing a fallacy of composition to Michels: that because the particular institutions of a society are oligarchic, therefore the whole society is oligarchical. Lipset can admit that Michels's argument is both compositional and analogical, as sketched above. However, Lipset questions Michels's analogy at another crucial point, thus undermining his

---

[7] Govier (2007; 2009). Cf. Finocchiaro 2013a.

36

compositional argument from analogy. For Lipset, there is one condition or property present in democratic societies, but absent in undemocratic societies and in particular institutions of democratic ones: a constitutional provision or traditional-historical practice that bans or prevents any one entity or group from exercising tyrannical or despotic power over opposing entities or groups.

This criticism strikes me as plausible and powerful. In fact, there is a tradition of political theory that regards such an anti-tyrannical or anti-despotic principle as fundamental,[8] although here Lipset does not mention any such historical precedents. However, his words in the summary of his criticism leave little doubt that he has this principle in mind, as they leave little doubt that he is charging Michels with the fallacy of composition:

> In essence, democracy in modern society may be viewed as involving the conflict of organized groups competing for support ... While most private governments, unions, professional societies, veterans' organizations, and political parties will remain one-party systems ... it is important to recognize that many internally oligarchic organizations help to sustain political democracy in the larger society and to protect the interests of their members from the encroachments of other groups. Democracy in large measure rests on the fact that no one group is able to secure a basis of power and command over the majority so that it can effectively suppress or deny the claims of the groups it opposes. [Lipset 1962, 36-37]

Dahl's and Lipset's critiques are related, insofar as competition and balance of power are substantively connected. More importantly for us here, however, their critiques are really meta-arguments, which advance the critical conclusion that Michels's argument is erroneous in its reasoning from political parties to the whole political system. These critical meta-arguments could of course be elaborated, reconstructed, analyzed, and evaluated at greater length. They strike me as cogent. But even if they were not, the relevance to the present investigation would remain, in the sense that there would be serious issues at the metalevel, rather than at the ground level, about the fallacy of composition: what we mean by fallacy of composition, what the ground-level argument is, and how accurate and fair it is to attribute this fallacy to this argument.

4. Epilogue

With regard to the fallacy of composition, the problem of how frequently it

---

[8] Hamilton, Jay, and Madison 1961, 301; Mosca 1939, 134; cf. Finocchiaro 1999, 206.

occurs is more striking than for the case of the other fallacies, because the contrast is greater and starker between the scarcity of scholarly analyses and the triviality of textbook examples on the one hand, and the widespread claims made (especially by economists) about its prevalence and importance. Thus, the empirical search for real or realistic examples is a relatively urgent task.

Such a search, however empirically minded, must also be guided by some assumptions or working hypotheses. One of these is the self-same ubiquity thesis, whose truth is being tested. Another guiding idea is that there are three distinct senses of "fallacy of composition"; these three notions may turn out to be importantly related, but they are *prima facie* different and should initially not be confused. A third key guiding idea is what I have called the meta-argumentation hypothesis: that the best places in which to search for fallacies of compositions are meta-arguments whose conclusion attributes (explicitly or implicitly) such a fallacy to some ground-level argument.

Guided by these ideas, I discussed the case of the criticism of Michels's argument for the iron law of oligarchy; that is, the argument that political parties inevitably become oligarchic even if they claim to have democratic aims; and therefore, a democratic society inevitably becomes oligarchic. Dahl objected that such reasoning fails because there is a crucial disanalogy between the parts and the whole: a democratic society allows significant competition among its parts, but a particular party does not. Similarly, Lipset objected that there is another crucial difference: a democratic society has an anti-tyrannical system of checks and balances in its written or unwritten constitution, but political parties and labor unions do not.

References

Copi, Irving M. 1968. *Introduction to Logic*, 3rd edn. New York: MacMillan.
Dahl, Robert A. 1956. *A Preface to Democratic Theory*. Chicago: University of Chicago Press.
Dahl, Robert A. 1989. *Democracy and Its Critics*. New Haven: Yale University Press.
Finocchiaro, Maurice A. 1980. *Galileo and the Art of Reasoning: Rhetorical Foundations of Logic and Scientific Method*. (Boston Studies in the Philosophy of Science, vol. 61.) Dordrecht: Reidel [now Springer].
Finocchiaro, Maurice A. 1981. Fallacies and the evaluation of reasoning. *American Philosophical Quarterly* 18: 13-22. Reprinted in Finocchiaro 2005, 109-27.
Finocchiaro, Maurice A. 1987. Six types of fallaciousness: Toward a realistic theory of logical criticism. *Argumentation* 1: 263-82. Reprinted in Finocchiaro 2005, 128-47.

Finocchiaro, Maurice A. 1999. *Beyond Right and Left: Democratic Elitism in Mosca and Gramsci*. New Haven: Yale University Press.

Finocchiaro, Maurice A. 2005. *Arguments about Arguments: Systematic, Critical, and Historical Essays in Logical Theory*. New York: Cambridge University Press.

Finocchiaro, Maurice A. 2013a. Debts, oligarchies, and holisms: Deconstructing the fallacy of composition. *Informal Logic* 33: 143-74.

Finocchiaro, Maurice A. 2013b. *Meta-argumentation: An Approach to Logic and Argumentation Theory*. (Studies in Logic, vol. 42.) London: College Publications.

Govier, Trudy. 1982. Who says there are no fallacies? *Informal Logic Newsletter*, vol. v, no. i, pp. 2-10.

Govier, Trudy. 2007. Duets, cartoons, and tragedies: Struggles with the fallacy of composition. In *Proceedings of the Sixth Conference of the International Society for the Study of Argumentation*, ed. F.H. van Eemeren, J.A. Blair, C.A. Willard, and B. Garssen, 505-11. Amsterdam: Sic Sat.

Govier, Trudy. 2009. Duets, cartoons, and tragedies: Struggles with the fallacy of composition. In *Pondering on Problems of Argumentation*, ed. F.H. van Eemeren and B. Garssen, 91-104. Dordrecht: Springer.

Hamblin, C. L. 1970. *Fallacies*. London: Methuen. Rpt., Newport News, VA: Vale Press, 1986.

Hamilton, Alexander, J. Jay, and J. Madison. 1961. *The Federalist Papers*. Ed. C. Rossiter. New York: Penguin.

Hazlitt, Henry. 1979. *Economics in One Lesson*. New Rochelle: Arlington House Publishers. 1st edn., 1946.

Jason, Gary. 1986. Are fallacies common? *Informal Logic* 8: 81-92.

Kahane, Howard. 1973. *Logic and Philosophy*, 2nd edn. Belmont, CA: Wadsworth.

Lipset, Seymour M. 1962. Introduction to Michels 1962, 15-39.

Michels, Robert. 1962. *Political Parties: A Sociological Study of the Oligarchical Tendencies of Modern Democracy*. Trans. E. Paul and C. Paul. New York: Collier.

Mosca, Gaetano. 1939. *The Ruling Class*. Trans. H.D. Kahn. Ed. A. Livingston. New York: McGraw-Hill.

Nelson, Alan. 1999. Keynes. In *Cambridge Dictionary of Philosophy*, 2nd edn., ed. R. Audi, 467-68. New York: Cambridge University Press.

Pole, Nelson. 1981. Part/whole fallacies. *Informal Logic Newsletter*, vol. 3, no. 3, June, pp. 11-13.

Samuelson, Paul A. 1955. *Economics: An Introductory Analysis*, 3rd edn. New York: McGraw-Hill.

Samuelson, Paul A., and William D. Nordhaus. 1989. *Economics*, 13th edn. New York: McGraw-Hill.

Strawson, P. F. 1952. *Introduction to Logical Theory*. London: Methuen.

Tindale, Christopher W. 2007. *Fallacies and Argument Appraisal*. New York: Cambridge University Press.

Whately, Richard. 1826. *Elements of Logic*. London: J. Mawman. Rpt., Bologna, Italy: Editrice CLUEB, 1988.

Woods, John. 1988. Buttercups, GNP's, and quarks: Are fallacies theoretical entities? *Informal Logic* 10: 67-76. Reprinted in Woods 2004, 161-70.

Woods, John. 2004. *The Death of Argument: Fallacies in Agent-Based Reasoning*. Dordrecht: Kluwer.

Woods, John. 2012. A history of the fallacies in Western logic. In *Logic: A History of Its Central Concepts*, ed. D.M. Gabbay, F.J. Pelletier, and J. Woods, 513-610. Amsterdam: North-Holland.

Woods, John. 2013. *Errors of Reasoning: Naturalizing the Logic of Inference*. London: College Publications.

Wray, L. Randall. 2006. Teaching the fallacy of composition: The federal budget deficit. At https://edi.bard.edu/research/cfeps-archive/; first consulted on October 19, 2012; later on May 25, 2023.

Chapter 3
Ubiquity, Ambiguity, and Metarationality:
Searching for the Fallacy of Composition

1. Introduction

In January 2015, on more than one occasion, the President of the United States, Barack Obama, made a proposal regarding higher education at community colleges. The idea was to enable everyone to attend for two years free of tuition charges, subject only to some requirements about good grades and progress toward graduation. The proposal was applauded by some, but criticized by others. One criticism was that the thinking underlying the proposal commits the fallacy of composition: "The spirit behind President Obama's recent proposal to make community college free is understandable, but he has fallen victim to the fallacy of composition. He has made the mistake of believing that if one person benefits from an action, then everyone else who takes the same action will also benefit" (Kelly and Kelly 2015). My aim here and now is not to discuss this particular issue or to evaluate this criticism, but rather to provide a practical motivation for scholars of logic and argumentation theory to study the fallacy of composition. That is, I firmly believe that the scholarly study of the fallacy of composition can contribute to a better understanding of such public-policy issues.

In fact, this is not an isolated example. Another illustration involves the on-going great recession affecting the whole world: on this topic, Nobel Prize economist Paul Krugman has blamed its persistence on the austerity policies that have been adopted by most countries with developed economies, and he has suggested that austerity has been the result of thinking that one can apply to a national economy the same policies that work for its constituent parts, such as households and individual firms; and this manner of thinking presumably amounts to the fallacy of composition (Krugman 2013a; 2013b). And on the issue of global warming, an author who happens to be a professional philosopher has claimed that arguments for global warming typically involve an aggregation of temperatures from particular regions of the world, and "to group and average in this way is to commit the fallacy of composition" (Haller 2002, 50).

Furthermore, lest one should think that the motivation is merely practical, let me hasten to add a theoretical one. To study the fallacy of composition is a special case of a key and well-established branch of logic and argumentation theory. In fact, with some slight but not much exaggeration, one could reconstruct the past fifty years of this field largely as a series of footnotes to Hamblin's *Fallacies* (1970), and/or as a series of developments that culminate organically with Woods's *Errors of Reasoning* (2013). And, as we shall see, the fallacy of composition is special not only in the sense of being a specific case of fallacies, but also in the sense of being especially important.

2. The Ubiquity Thesis

The fallacy of composition seems to be unique among the fallacies, insofar as its frequency and importance have been widely claimed, perhaps more than for any other fallacy. For example, in 1826, in the *Elements of Logic*, Richard Whately explicitly named and discussed this fallacy, saying among other things: "… Fallacy of Composition. There is no Fallacy more common, or more likely to deceive, than the one now before us: the form in which it is usually employed, is, to establish some truth, separately, concerning each single member of a certain class, and thence to infer the same of the whole collectively" (Whately 1826, 174-75).

Moreover, at least since the epoch-making contributions of John Maynard Keynes (who died in 1946), economists tend to regard the fallacy of composition as the single worst pitfall in economic reasoning. They also consider the exposure of it to be the greatest accomplishment of the modern science of economics. They deem the avoidance of it the most important lesson one can learn from this science. And such claims are easily found in the writings of economists of both the left and right wings of the ideological spectrum, such as Paul Samuelson and Henry Hazlitt.[1]

However, despite such attention and such claims, scholars in logic and argumentation theory seem not to have done much work on the fallacy of composition, although textbooks tend to pay lip service to it.

Sometimes this scholarly neglect of the fallacy of composition is explained and partly justified in terms of its rarity or infrequency. For example, in the 1973 edition of his textbook *Logic and Philosophy*, Howard

---

[1] See, for example, Hazlitt 1979; Nelson 1999; Samuelson 1955, 9-10, 237, 273, 350, 374, 505, 550, 693; Samuelson and Nordhaus 1989, 7-8, 183-84, 399-404, 666-67, 972, 993; and Wray 2006. Cf. Woods, Irvine, and Walton 2000, 262-83; Finocchiaro 2013a. For a revealing and emblematic piece of evidence, one may view a sculpture labeled "The Fallacy of Composition": it adorns an outside wall of the building of the Faculty of Economics at the University of Groningen, and it was created in 1988 to commemorate the 50th anniversary of the foundation of that Faculty and to celebrate Keynes's epoch-making contributions to the science of economics; cf. http://www.rug.nl/science-and-society/sculpture-project/sculpture1998?lang=en, consulted on July 24, 2012; I owe my first information about this sculpture to Govier (2007; 2009).

Kahane has a brief discussion of this fallacy together with its reverse twin, the fallacy of division. Here are his revealing words: "since non-trivial real life examples of these two fallacies … are unusual, textbook examples tend to be contrived or trivial. Thus one textbook writer gives as an example of the fallacy of composition the argument that '… since every part of a certain machine is light in weight, the machine as a whole is light in weight'."[2]

Obviously, this explanation of the scholarly neglect conflicts with the ubiquity thesis reported earlier. Thus, the question arises whether the fallacy of composition is common and important, or uncommon and unimportant. This is largely an empirical question, to be resolved by following an empirical approach.

However, such an empirical investigation cannot be conducted with a *tabula rasa*, for we need to be clear about what we mean by fallacy of composition, and also we need to examine real or realistic material which typically does not come with the label 'fallacy of composition' attached to it. In other words, we need to be mindful of the fact that observation is theory-laden, and that the examination of this material must be guided by some idea of what this fallacy means, and by some idea of what to do with the material under examination so as to test it for the occurrence of this fallacy. A brief elaboration of some of these ideas is thus in order.

3. The Ambiguity of 'Fallacy of Composition'

To begin with, it is obvious that we need some understanding of what is meant by fallacy of composition. Unfortunately, historical and contemporary writings on the topic contain three notions that are prima facie distinct, but tend to be confused with each other.

First, there is reasoning from premises using a term distributively to a conclusion using the same term collectively; for example, "because a bus uses more gasoline than an automobile, therefore all buses use more gasoline than all automobiles" (Copi 1968, 81). Second, there is reasoning from some property of the parts to the same property for the whole; for instance, "since every part of a certain machine is light in weight, the machine 'as a whole' is light in weight" (Copi 1968, 80). And thirdly, there is reasoning from some property of the members of a group to the same property for the entire group; the so-called tragedy of the commons can illustrate this notion, that is, "if one farmer grazes his cattle on the commons, that will be beneficial for him; therefore if all the farmers graze their cattle on the commons, that will be beneficial for all" (Govier 2009, 95).

---

[2] Kahane 1973, 244; cf. Copi 1972, 96-98.

Now, the association of the second and third notions with each other is very common. For example, here is how Kahane defines this fallacy: "the fallacy of composition is committed when we reason that some property possessed by every member of a class (or every part of a whole) also is possessed by that class (or whole)" (Kahane 1973, 243-44); and he is far from the only one.[3] On the other hand, the association of all three is relatively rare, but does occur. One example may be found in the following textbook definition: "The fallacy of composition consists in treating a distributed characteristic as if it were collective. It occurs when one makes the mistake of attributing to a group (or a whole) some characteristic that is true only of its individual members (or its parts), and then makes inferences based on that mistake" (Halverson 1984, 73).

4. The Metarationality Hypothesis

Besides this three-fold distinction and the ubiquity thesis, there is a third guiding idea that needs to be at least mentioned and tentatively stated before we proceed. In a previous work, I criticized textbook accounts of fallacies, and on its basis I formulated a problem and advanced an hypothesis. The problem was formulated in terms of the following questions: "do people actually commit fallacies as usually understood? That is, do fallacies exist in practice? Or do they exist only in the mind of the interpreter who is claiming that a fallacy is being committed?"[4]

Although these were not meant to be rhetorical questions, but rather open questions that required further investigation, it is perhaps unsurprising that some readers (e.g., Govier 1982) did view them as rhetorical questions. Moreover, I did express "the suspicion that logically incorrect arguments are not that common in practice, that their existence may be largely restricted to logic textbook examples and exercises."[5] Thus, some readers thought that I was claiming that fallacies are merely figments of critics' imagination, and "are in fact an illusion."[6]

Later, I tried to be more explicit and constructive about this issue when I elaborated a general approach to the study of fallacies. One element of that approach was connected to, and extracted from, Strawson's *Introduction to Logical Theory* and his notion of "the logician's second-order vocabulary" (Strawson 1952, 15); that notion was extended to include 'fallacy' terminology, "since it ordinarily occurs when someone wants to comment about some logical feature of a first-order expression of reasoning. This

[3] Cf. Cohen and Nagel 1934, 377; Salmon 2002, 371.
[4] Finocchiaro 1980, 334; 1981, 15; 2005, 113.
[5] Finocchiaro 1980, 333; 1981, 14; 2005, 111.
[6] Jason 1986, 92; cf. Govier 1982.

means that the best place to begin with in the study of fallacies, or at least a crucial phenomenon to examine, is allegations that fallacies are being committed."[7]

In this vein, some elaborated the idea that fallacies are more like theoretical entities such as quarks in physics, rather than like concrete objects such as buttercups in everyday life.[8] This elaboration was a constructive suggestion and critical appreciation, and I am far from denying its viability.

However, I now believe that the project can be articulated more clearly, incisively, and constructively in light of the notion of meta-argumentation (cf. Finocchiaro 2013b; 2013c). That is, I distinguish a meta-argument from a ground-level argument, and define the former as an argument about one or more arguments, or about argumentation in general. Then a ground-level argument can be defined as one about such things as natural phenomena, historical events, human actions, mathematical numbers, or metaphysical entities. A prototypical case of meta-argumentation is argument analysis, in which one advances and justifies an interpretive or evaluative claim about a ground-level argument.

What I am proposing is that we search for fallacies of composition primarily in meta-argumentation rather than ground-level argumentation. However, this is not meant in the sense that we should be looking for meta-arguments that commit the fallacy of composition, but rather that we try to find meta-arguments advancing explicit conclusions that some fallacy of composition has been committed, i.e., that some ground-level argument embodies or commits a fallacy of composition. The working hypothesis is then that, at least as a first approximation, the fallacy of composition is primarily a concept of meta-argumentation, useful in the context of understanding and/or assessing ground-level argumentation.

5. Hume's Critique of the Design Argument for the Existence of God

Let us now begin our empirical search for real or realistic material pertaining to the fallacy of composition. A memorable example of the fallacy of composition occurs in the design argument for the existence of God, at least according to the critique advanced in Hume's *Dialogues Concerning Natural Religion*. This charge is only one objection in the complex and multi-faceted criticism which Hume formulates; and correspondingly, it affects only one particular step of the design argument. Thus, even if cogent, this Humean meta-argument is not the end of the story; nevertheless, it is a crucial element of the over-all evaluation of the design argument.

---

[7] Finocchiaro 1987, 264; 2005, 130.
[8] Grootendorst 1987; Woods 1988.

It should be noted that Hume interprets the design argument primarily as inductive and empirical. In so doing, he is trying to abide by the principle of charity, for if one were to reconstruct the design argument as deductive and *a priori*, then according to Hume it could not even get off the ground, since it would be trying to prove a factual matter—that God exists and created the universe—from *a priori* considerations; and this for Hume is an inherently impossible task.

One version of the design argument is this: the universe was created by an intelligent designer (called God), because the universe is like a machine, and machines are made by (human) intelligent designers. This is, of course, an argument from analogy.

Now Hume questions the analogical premise. How could one show that the universe is like a machine? Well, in Hume's own memorable words, spoken through the character Cleanthes, the answer is this:

> look round the world, contemplate the whole and every part of it: you will find it to be nothing but one great machine, subdivided into an infinite number of lesser machines, which again admit of subdivisions to a degree beyond what human senses and faculties can trace and explain. All these various machines, and even their most minute parts, are adjusted to each other with an accuracy which ravishes into admiration all men who have ever contemplated them. The curious adapting of means to ends, throughout all nature, resembles exactly, though it much exceeds, the productions of human contrivance—of human design, thought, wisdom, and intelligence. [Hume 1947, 143]

This does seem to provide empirical, observational support for the claim that the universe is like a machine.

However, there are problems with this reasoning. In Hume's words, spoken through the character Philo:

> But can you think, Cleanthes, that your usual phlegm and philosophy have been preserved in so wide a step as you have taken, when you compared to the universe houses, ships, furniture, machines, and, from their similarity in some circumstances, inferred a similarity in their causes? Thought, design, intelligence, such as we discover in men and other animals, is no more than one of the springs and principles of the universe, as well as heat or cold, attraction or repulsion, and a hundred others, which fall under daily observation. It is an active cause, by which some particular parts of nature, we find, produce alterations on other parts. But can a conclusion, with any propriety, be transferred from parts to the whole? Does not the great disproportion bar all comparison and inference? From observing the growth of a hair, can we learn anything concerning the generation of a man? Would the manner of a leaf's blowing, even though perfectly known, afford us any instruction concerning the vegetation of a tree? [Hume 1947, 147]

Here, Hume is finding two things wrong with the subargument supporting the claim that the universe is like a machine. One problem is that although many parts of the universe are like machines, produced by intelligent design, many other parts (even when orderly arranged) are produced by natural causes such as attraction and heat. That is, Hume is charging that the subargument is a hasty generalization. But this is not the only problem; for even if all parts of the universe were machine-like, we could not be sure that the same would apply to the universe as a whole. In this second criticism, Hume is charging a fallacy of composition.

Hume's criticism of this subargument of the design argument is a meta-argument, and as such it is open to analysis, interpretation, and evaluation. Note, for example, that Hume's critical conclusion is based partly on an interpretation of the subargument in question, partly on a definition of the fallacy of composition, and partly on some evaluative principle. The interpretive claim is a reconstruction of this step of the design argument as transferring to the whole universe the same property which it claims to be able to observe in all (or many) of its parts; the property is that of being caused by some intelligent design. The evaluative principle is that it is illegitimate to transfer any such property from parts to whole in this case. Hume seems to give two reasons for this evaluative principle: first, the disproportion between such parts and whole is too great, presumably because the universe is infinite or indefinitely large; second, the transference from parts to the whole universe would be like reasoning from what happens to a human hair to what happens to a whole human body, or from what happens to a leaf to what happens to a whole tree. And this second reason amounts to a meta-argument from analogy, in which Hume argues that this subargument of the design argument is illegitimate because the subargument is an argument from analogy and is as illegitimate as the analogies from hair to human body or from leaf to tree.[9]

6. Concluding Remarks

My empirical and theory-laden search has found other important historical cases, which cannot be elaborated here, but which deserve a brief mention. One of these other examples is Aristotle's geocentric argument from natural motion: that the natural motion of terrestrial bodies is straight toward the center; and therefore the natural motion of the whole earth is straight toward the center. Galileo objected by arguing that if 'center' means center of the

---

[9] There is much more to be said on this aspect of the *Dialogues*, namely Hume's employment of meta-arguments from analogy to criticize or strengthen various ground-level arguments from analogy. See Barker 1989; and Finocchiaro 2013c, 201-203.

universe, Aristotle's argument begs the question; but if 'center' means center of the earth, the premise is empirically true, but the conclusion is inherently false. And the latter is a memorable counterexample that deserves further logical analysis, because it seems to undermine the formal validity of not only Aristotle's particular argument, but also of any argument from parts to whole.[10]

A third case involves Robert Michels's argument for the so-called "iron law of oligarchy": that political parties inevitably become oligarchic even if they claim to have democratic aims; and therefore, a democratic society inevitably becomes oligarchic. Political scientist Robert Dahl objected that such reasoning fails because there is a crucial disanalogy between such parts and such a whole: a democratic society allows competition among its parts, but a particular party does not. Similarly, sociologist Seymour Martin Lipset objected that there is another crucial difference: a democratic society has an anti-tyrannical system of checks and balances in its written or unwritten constitution, but political parties and labor unions do not.[11]

Such examples are certainly real and realistic. They are obviously also historically important. The ground-level arguments are clearly compositional; i.e., they are arguments of composition, if I may be allowed to introduce an obvious term for a type of argument that leaves open the question whether it is incorrect or fallacious; that is, an argument from premises with distributive terms or about parts or members to a conclusion with collective terms or about the whole or class. And the ground-level arguments are more or less inferentially incorrect: incontrovertibly and memorably so in the case of Aristotle's geocentric argument from natural motion; arguably and cogently so in the case of the compositional step of the theological argument from design; and arguably and plausibly so in the case of Michels's support for the iron law of oligarchy.

However, some qualifications are in order. First, even if we take these claims as acceptable, one important conceptual qualification needs to be kept in mind about such examples of the fallacy of composition. For these claims amount to saying that we have found important historical examples of arguments of composition that are inferentially incorrect. However, as John Woods has recently stressed,[12] the traditional concept of fallacy is that a fallacy is a common type of reasoning that appears to be correct but is actually incorrect. This conception contains five elements: frequency, generality, reasoning, apparent correctness, and actual incorrectness. Now, in my three examples, the ground-level arguments obviously meet the condition of being reasoning; they also meet the generality condition since they are

---

[10] Aristotle, *On the Heavens*, 296b7-297a1; Galilei 1997, 83-84. Cf. Finocchiaro 1980, 353-56; 2014b, 59-63; 2015, 31-32.

[11] Michels 1962; Dahl 1989; Lipset 1962. Cf. Finocchiaro 2013b; 2015, 34-36.

[12] Woods 2013; cf. Finocchiaro 2014a.

arguments from parts to whole; and they possess apparent correctness, since the exposure of the flaws of the ground-level arguments required meta-argumentation by thinkers such as Galileo, Hume, Dahl, and Lipset. But I am not sure about their common occurrence and their actual incorrectness. In fact, the same features that make these examples historically important may suggest that they are relatively uncommon; and their actual incorrectness could perhaps be questioned by questioning the critical meta-arguments of Galileo, Hume, Dahl, and Lipset. On the other hand, while such considerations would show that we have not found three examples of fallacies of compositions, they do not undermine the claim that we have found three important historical examples of seductive (i.e., apparently correct) arguments of composition. This problem required further reflection.

Another problem for future investigation concerns an issue that has received some discussion, with some promising and insightful results. The issue is that of the evaluation of the correctness of compositional arguments, and the formulation of useful evaluative principles. A key principle, which I gather from this literature (e.g., Ritola 2009), is that the evaluation of compositional arguments should not be limited to deductive evaluation, but should include inductive evaluation; for even when compositional arguments are deductively invalid, they often possess some plausibility, cogency, or inductive strength.

Another evaluative principle, advanced by van Eemeren and Grootendorst (1992, 174-83; 1999), begins by urging us to distinguish between absolute and relative properties (e.g., round vs. light, i.e., light-weight); between structured or heterogeneous and unstructured or homogenous wholes or aggregates (e.g., a team of football players vs. a heap of sand grains); and between structure-dependent and structure-independent properties (e.g., round vs. white). The principle then states that properties are transferable from parts to whole (or vice versa) if and only if the properties are absolute and structure-independent. Thus, for example, it would be correct to argue that this pile of sand is white because all its grains of sand are white; for in this case the property of being white is both absolute and structure-independent. On the other hand, in the other three possible cases the arguments would be incorrect: this pile of peas is round because the peas are all round (case of structure-dependent property); this pile of sand, from several truck loads, is light because all its grains of sand are light (case of relative property); and this football team is good because its players are good (case of relative and structure-dependent property).

These considerations and this principle are useful, but are just a start. The key problem is that, aside from simple cases, it would very difficult to determine whether a given property was or was not absolute and structure-independent; and often such a determination could not be made prior to, or independently of, knowing or determining the correctness of the corresponding compositional arguments. Thus, more work is needed to find and formulate such evaluative principles.

References

Barker, Stephen F. 1989. Reasoning by analogy in Hume's *Dialogues*. *Informal Logic* 11: 173-84.

Cohen, Morris R., and Ernest Nagel. 1934. *An Introduction to Logic and Scientific Method*. New York: Harcourt, Brace and Company.

Copi, Irving M. 1968. *Introduction to Logic*, 3rd edn. New York: MacMillan.

Copi, Irving M. 1972. *Introduction to logic*, 4th edn. New York: MacMillan.

Dahl, Robert A. 1989. *Democracy and Its Critics*. New Haven: Yale University Press.

Finocchiaro, Maurice A. 1980. *Galileo and the Art of Reasoning: Rhetorical Foundations of Logic and Scientific Method*. (Boston Studies in the Philosophy of Science, vol. 61.) Dordrecht: Reidel [now Springer].

Finocchiaro, Maurice A. 1981. Fallacies and the evaluation of reasoning. *American Philosophical Quarterly* 18: 13-22. Reprinted in Finocchiaro 2005, 109-27.

Finocchiaro, Maurice A. 1987. Six types of fallaciousness: Toward a realistic theory of logical criticism. *Argumentation* 1: 263-82. Reprinted in Finocchiaro 2005, 128-47.

Finocchiaro, Maurice A. 2005. *Arguments about Arguments: Systematic, Critical, and Historical Essays in Logical Theory*. New York: Cambridge University Press.

Finocchiaro, Maurice A. 2013a. Debts, oligarchies, and holisms: Deconstructing the fallacy of composition. *Informal Logic* 33: 143-74.

Finocchiaro, Maurice A. 2013b. The fallacy of composition and meta-argumentation. In *Virtues of Argumentation: Proceedings of the 10th International Conference of the Ontario Society for the Study of Argumentation (OSSA), 22-26 May 2013*, ed. D. Mohammed nd M. Lewiński. Windsor, ON: Ontario Society for the Study of Argumentation. ISBN: 978-0-920233-66-5.

Finocchiaro, Maurice A. 2013c. *Meta-argumentation: An Approach to Logic and Argumentation Theory*. (Studies in Logic, vol. 42.) London: College Publications.

Finocchiaro, Maurice A. 2014a. Essay-review of J. Woods's *Errors of Reasoning: Naturalizing the Logic of Inference*. *Argumentation* 28: 231-39.

Finocchiaro, Maurice A. 2014b. *The Routledge Guidebook to Galileo's Dialogue*. London: Routledge.

Finocchiaro, Maurice A. 2015. The fallacy of composition: Guiding concepts, historical cases, and research problems. *Journal of Applied Logic*, vol. 13, issue 2, part B, June, pp. 24–43. Published online 20 January 2015, DOI:10.1016/j.jal.2015.01.003.

Galilei, Galileo. 1997. *Galileo on the World Systems: A New Abridged Translation and Guide*. Trans. and ed. M. A. Finocchiaro. Berkeley: University of California Press.

Govier, Trudy. 1982. Who says there are no fallacies? *Informal Logic Newsletter*, vol. v, no. i, pp. 2-10.

Govier, Trudy. 2007. Duets, cartoons, and tragedies: Struggles with the fallacy of composition. In *Proceedings of the Sixth Conference of the International Society for the Study of Argumentation*, ed. F. H. van Eemeren, J. A. Blair, C. A. Willard, and B. Garssen, 505-11. Amsterdam: Sic Sat.

Govier, Trudy. 2009. Duets, cartoons, and tragedies: Struggles with the fallacy of composition." In *Pondering on Problems of Argumentation*, ed. F. H. van Eemeren and B. Garssen, 91-104. Dordrecht: Springer.

Grootendorst, Rob. 1987. Some fallacies about fallacies. In *Argumentation Across the Lines of Discipline: Proceedings of the Conference on Argumentation 1986*, ed. F. H. van Eemeren, R. Grootendorst, J. A. Blair, and C. A. Willard, 331-42. Dordrecht: Foris Publications.

Haller, Stephen F. 2002. *Apocalypse Soon? Wagering on Warnings of Global Warming*. Montreal: McGill-Queens University Press.

Halverson, William H. 1984. *A Concise Logic*. New York: Random House.

Hamblin, C. L. 1970. *Fallacies*. London: Methuen. Rpt., Newport News: Vale Press, 1986.

Hazlitt, Henry. 1979. *Economics in One Lesson*. New Rochelle: Arlington House Publishers. 1st edn., 1946.

Hume, David. 1947. *Dialogues concerning Natural Religion*. Ed. N. K. Smith. Indianapolis: Bobbs-Merrill. First published in 1779.

Jason, Gary. 1986. Are fallacies common?" *Informal Logic* 8: 81-92.

Kahane, Howard. 1973. *Logic and Philosophy*, 2nd edn. Belmont: Wadsworth.

Kelly, William A., and Elizabeth S. Kelly. 2015. Obama and the 'fallacy of composition'. *The Wall Street Journal*, February 4. At <http://www.wsj.com/articles/bill-kelly-and-elizabeth-sawyer-kelly-obama-and-the-fallacy-of-composition-1423095533>, consulted on March 18, 2015.

Krugman, Paul. 2013a. Austerity wrought pain, no gain. *Las Vegas Sun*, January 8, p. 3. At <http://lasvegassun.com/news/2013/jan/08/austerity-wrought-pain-no-gain/#.VHPVyW1c75E.gmail>, consulted on October 21, 2014.

Krugman, Paul. 2013b. The punishment cure. *The New York Times*, 8 December. At <http://www.nytimes.com/2013/12/09/opinion/krugman-

the-punishment-cure.html?_r=1>, consulted on October 21, 2014.

Lipset, Seymour M. 1962. Introduction to Michels 1962, 15-39.

Michels, Robert. 1962. *Political Parties: A Sociological Study of the Oligarchical Tendencies of Modern Democracy*. Trans. E. Paul and C. Paul. New York: Collier.

Nelson, Alan. 1999. Keynes. In *Cambridge Dictionary of Philosophy*, ed. R. Audi, 467-68. New York: Cambridge University Press.

Ritola, Juho. 2009. Commentary on James E. Gough and Mano Daniel's 'The fallacy of composition'. In *Argument Cultures: Proceedings of the 8th Biennial Conference of the Ontario Society for the Study of Argumentation (OSSA, 2009)*, ed. J. Ritola. Windsor, ON: Ontario Society for the Study of Argumentation. ISBN 978-0-920233-51-1.

Salmon, Merrilee. 2002. *Introduction to Logic and Critical Thinking*, 4th edn. Wadsworth Thomson Learning.

Samuelson, Paul A. 1955. *Economics: An Introductory Analysis*, 3rd edn. New York: McGraw-Hill.

Samuelson, Paul A., and William D. Nordhaus. 1989. *Economics*, 13th edn. New York: McGraw-Hill.

Strawson, P. F. 1952. *Introduction to Logical Theory*. London: Methuen.

van Eemeren, Frans H., and R. Grootendorst. 1992. *Argumentation, Communication, and Fallacies*. Hillsdale: Lawrence Erlbaum Associates.

van Eemeren, Frans H., and R. Grootendorst. 1999. The fallacies of composition and division. In *JFAK: Essays Dedicated to Johan van Benthem on the Occasion of His 50th Birthday*, ed. J. Gerbrandy, M. Marx, M. de Rijke, and Y. Venema. Amsterdam: University of Amsterdam, Institute for Logic, Language, and Computation. At <www.illc.uva.nl/j50/>, consulted on June 18, 2013.

Whately, Richard. 1826. *Elements of Logic*. London: J. Mawman. Rpt., Bologna, Italy: Editrice CLUEB, 1988.

Woods, John. 1988. Buttercups, GNP's, and quarks: Are fallacies theoretical entities? *Informal Logic* 10: 67-76. Reprinted in Woods 2004, 161-70.

Woods, John. 2004. *The Death of Argument: Fallacies in Agent-based Reasoning*. Dordrecht: Kluwer.

Woods, John. 2013. *Errors of Reasoning: Naturalizing the Logic of Inference*. London: College Publications.

Woods, John, A. Irvine, and D. Walton. 2000. *Argument: Critical Thinking, Logic, and the Fallacies*. Toronto: Prentice-Hall.

Wray, L. Randall. 2006. Teaching the fallacy of composition: The federal budget deficit. At https://edi.bard.edu/research/cfeps-archive/; first consulted on October 19, 2012; later on May 25, 2023.

Chapter 4
The Fallacy of Composition:
Guiding Concepts, Historical Cases, and Research Problems

1. Introduction

There are both theoretical and practical motivations for wanting to study the fallacy of composition.

From a theoretical point of view, such a study is a special case of a key and well-established branch of logic and argumentation theory. In fact, at least as a first approximation, one could reconstruct the past fifty years of this field largely as a series of footnotes to Hamblin's *Fallacies* (1970) and of developments culminating with Woods's *Errors of Reasoning* (2013). And, as we shall see, the fallacy of composition is special not only in the sense of being a specific case of fallacies, but also in the sense of being especially important.

On a practical level, getting clear about the fallacy of composition seems crucial if one wants to react intelligently to two of the greatest problems in the world today: global warming and the world-wide great recession. In fact, at least one philosopher has claimed that arguments for global warming typically involve an aggregation of temperatures from particular regions of the world, and "to group and average in this way is to commit the fallacy of composition" (Haller 2002, 50); thus, it would seem to be almost a civic duty for a professional in this field to try to ascertain whether he is right. And with regard to the on-going great recession, Nobel Prize economist Paul Krugman (2013a) has blamed its persistence on the austerity policies that have been adopted by most countries with developed economies, and he has suggested that austerity has been the result of thinking that one can apply to a national economy policies that work for its constituent parts, such as households and individual firms; and this manner of thinking is what logicians and argumentation theorists call the fallacy of composition, a label which he himself occasionally uses (Krugman 2013b). If Krugman is right, then such scholars have a civic duty to contribute to a clarification of this topic.

2. The Ubiquity Thesis

The fallacy of composition seems to be unique among the fallacies, insofar as its frequency and importance have been widely claimed, perhaps more than for any other fallacy. For example, in 1826, in the *Elements of Logic*, Richard Whately explicitly named and discussed this fallacy, saying among other things: "… Fallacy of Composition. There is no Fallacy more common, or more likely to deceive, than the one now before us: the form in which it is usually employed, is, to establish some truth, *separately*, concerning each single member of a certain class, and thence to infer the same of the *whole collectively*" (Whately 1826, 174-75).

Moreover, at least since the epoch-making contributions of John Maynard Keynes (who died in 1946), economists tend to regard the fallacy of composition as the single worst pitfall in economic reasoning. They also consider the exposure of it to be the greatest accomplishment of the modern science of economics. They deem the avoidance of it the most important lesson one can learn from this science. And such claims are easily found in the writings of economists of both the left and right wings of the ideological spectrum, such as Paul Samuelson and Henry Hazlitt.[1]

Additionally, in 1981, an article was published in the journal *Informal Logic*, dealing with "part/whole fallacies," of which composition may be regarded as a special case. The author argued that there is "a virtual epidemic of part/whole fallacies perpetrated on an unsuspecting public" (Pole 1981, 11).

Finally, in 2006, Trudy Govier saw it fit to devote to the fallacy of composition her keynote address to the International Society for the Study of Argumentation. In it, she followed her usual realistic and judicious approach, and thus examined some important recent examples of this fallacy, involving issues such as individual vs. national reconciliation in South Africa, and individual vs. collective actions and blame in the post-nine-eleven relations between Islam and the West.[2]

However, despite such attention and such claims, scholars in logic and argumentation theory seem not to have done much work on the fallacy of composition, although textbooks tend to pay lip service to it. For example,[3] the journal *Informal Logic* seems to have published no more articles on this fallacy in the next 32 years (i.e., through 2012), but finally published one the

---

[1] See, for example, Hazlitt 1979; Nelson 1999; Samuelson 1955, 9-10, 237, 273, 350, 374, 505, 550, 693; Samuelson and Nordhaus 1989, 7-8, 183-84, 399-404, 666-67, 972, 993; and Wray 2006. Cf. Woods, Irvine, and Walton 2000, 262-83; Finocchiaro 2013a; and <http://www.rug.nl/science-and-society/sculpture-project/sculpture1998?lang=en>, consulted on July 24, 2012.

[2] Govier (2007; 2009; 2010, 278-80); cf. Davies 2002.

[3] Besides the sources mentioned below, I can also report similarly negative results from my search of the proceedings of the conferences sponsored by the International Society for the Study of Argumentation (ISSA) and by the Ontario Society for the Study of Argumentation (OSSA). However, there are some exceptions: Davies 2002, Gough and Daniel 2009, Govier 2002, and Ritola 2009b.

following year (Finocchiaro 2013a).

Furthermore, there is no sustained discussion of it in the volume on *Fallacies and Argument Appraisal* of the Cambridge University Press series on critical reasoning and argumentation. Instead, the author only mentions it briefly in some introductory remarks on problems with language (Tindale 2007, 57-58).

And in his latest book, on *Errors of Reasoning*, even John Woods (2013) does not get around to elaborating a critique of this particular fallacy, as he does for at least thirteen others of the so-called gang of eighteen traditional fallacies. However, this is not to deny that Woods's book is full of insights and should serve as a model to emulate, both with regard to the substantive theory of fallacies and to the methodological approach of naturalism which he develops.[4] Moreover, he does give due coverage to this fallacy in his history of fallacies (Woods 2012).

Sometimes this scholarly neglect of the fallacy of composition is explained and partly justified in terms of its rarity or infrequency. For example, in the 1973 edition of his textbook *Logic and Philosophy*, Howard Kahane has a brief discussion of this fallacy together with its reverse twin, the fallacy of division. Here are his revealing words: "since non-trivial real life examples of these two fallacies … are unusual, textbook examples tend to be contrived or trivial. Thus one textbook writer gives as an example of the fallacy of *composition* the argument that '… since every part of a certain machine is light in weight, the machine as a whole is light in weight' …" (Kahane 1973, 244). Here Kahane is referring to the fourth edition of Irving Copi's *Introduction to Logic* (Copi 1972, 96-98).

Obviously, this explanation of the scholarly neglect conflicts with the ubiquity thesis reported earlier. Thus, the question arises whether the fallacy of composition is common and important, or uncommon and unimportant. This is largely an empirical question, to be resolved by following an empirical approach.

However, the investigation cannot be conducted with a *tabula rasa*, for we need to be clear about what we mean by fallacy of composition, and also we need to examine real or realistic material which typically does not come with the label 'fallacy of composition' attached to it. In other words, we need to be mindful of the fact that observation is theory-laden, and that the examination of this material must be guided by some definition of what this fallacy is, and by some idea of what to do with the material under examination so as to test it for the occurrence of this fallacy.

---

[4] In fact, it is possible to elaborate a critique of the fallacy of composition which is partly inspired by Woods (2013) and which is analogous to the critiques of other fallacies which he elaborates there; see Finocchiaro 2013a, and cf. Finocchiaro (2014a; 2014b).

3. Conceptions of the Fallacy of Composition

It ought not to be surprising that Aristotle's logical writings contain discussions that have something to do with, or are reminiscent of, the fallacy of composition.[5] Indeed, two of the Aristotelian "sophistical refutations" involve the so-called "combination" or "division" of words; and they are treated as *in dictione* fallacies, i.e., fallacies of ambiguity or equivocation. However, the term "composition" (or its Greek equivalent) is not there; and the content of this Aristotelian discussion has little to do with the part-whole relationship. For these reasons, I would not regard these discussions as belonging to the history of the notion "fallacy of composition," but at best to its pre-history.

That history seems to begin with the *Port Royal Logic*, which contains an explicit use of the term: the Latin *fallacia compositionis* in the original French edition of 1662, and the English transliteration "fallacy of composition" in the first and in the latest English translations.[6] Their definition is simply "passing from a divided sense to a composite sense" of a word (Arnauld and Nicole 1996, 199).

Interestingly, their examples all involve biblical quotations or references, and the most elaborate and explicit one is the following: "It is easy to see that we cannot pass from one of these senses to the other without committing a sophism. People reason badly, for example, who promise themselves heaven while persisting in their crimes because Christ came to save sinners, and because he says in the Gospel that women of ill repute will precede the Pharisees into the Kingdom of God. For he did not come to save sinners who remain sinners, but to make them stop being sinners."[7]

Although it is perhaps easy to see that whoever thinks in this manner is committing an error, the analysis of the error is not really easy. To explain it, I would reconstruct the argument about sinners as follows: Christ came to save sinners; I am a sinner; therefore, I shall be saved by Christ. The point is that Christ came to save sinners who repent and reform, and so the major premise is using the term 'sinners' in a "divided sense"; that is, presumably, in the sense that it is distinguishing between sinners who repent and reform from those who do not. But when a sinner says that he is a sinner, he is using the term in a "composite sense"; that is, presumably, he is mixing or combining sinners who repent and those who do not, since he is in the latter subgroup. Thus, the assertion of both premises involves passing from the "divided" sense of the first premise to the "composite" sense of the second.

---

[5] Cf. Hansen and Pinto 1995, 1-10; Woods 2012, 521-22.
[6] Arnauld and Nicole 1965, 255; 1685, 109; 1996, 199.
[7] Arnauld and Nicole 1996, 200; cf. Matthew 21: 31.

The *Port-Royal* conception of the fallacy of composition is clearly reminiscent of one of the present-day meanings of this fallacy, but equally clearly the former is not identical to the latter. That conception was echoed, modified, and refined by Whately (1826, 173-77), by John Stuart Mill (1843, 536-37), and by others (Salmon 1963, 39; 1984, 55-56) before we arrive at the following definition: "this version of the fallacy of composition turns on a confusion between the 'distributive' and the 'collective' use of general terms ... may be defined as the invalid inference that what may be truly predicated of a term distributively may also be truly predicated of the term collectively" (Copi 1968, 81). A good example is this: "because a bus uses more gasoline than an automobile, therefore all buses use more gasoline than all automobiles" (Copi 1968, 81).

Copi's definition here seems to amount to saying that one version of the fallacy of composition is an argument that goes from using a term with a distributive meaning in the premises to using it with a collective meaning in the conclusion. This corresponds to the *Port-Royal* definition insofar as the earlier talk of "passing" has now become reasoning from premises to conclusion; the earlier "divided" sense has now become "distributed" use; and the earlier "composite" sense has now become "collective" use. Obviously, now one important issue becomes that of what exactly is meant by "distributed" and "collective" meanings.

Contemporary scholars also include another meaning under the notion "fallacy of composition": reasoning from parts to the whole. For example, according to Copi, another version of the fallacy of composition may be defined as "reasoning fallaciously from the properties of the parts of a whole to the properties of the whole itself. A particularly flagrant example would be to argue that since every part of a certain machine is light in weight, the machine 'as a whole' is light in weight" (Copi 1968, 80). Copi is clear that this version of the fallacy is distinct from, although related to, the previous version. However, he is not clear that arguments from parts to whole may be correct, but gives the impression that all arguments of this type are fallacious. My own favorite example of a correct argument from parts to whole is this: all parts of this machine have weight (in the sense of mass), therefore the whole machine has weight (mass); indeed this argument is deductively valid, although not formally so.

One scholar who is clear both that this second version is distinct from the first, and that it is not always fallacious is Walton. To clarify the situation, he introduces the notion of an *argument of composition*, or as he calls it, "the argumentation scheme of composition ... All parts of X have property Y. Therefore, X has property Y" (Walton 1989, 130). For short, we might call such an argument a *compositional argument*. Then one problem or challenge becomes that of elaborating the conditions under which arguments of composition are incorrect, which he addresses in terms of the critical questions that may be asked about this type of argument.[8] However, in my view, this is not the only challenge. There is also the problem of under what conditions an incorrect argument of composition is a fallacy of composition; for a fallacy is a common type of argument that appears correct but is not really so,[9] and hence to be a fallacy an incorrect argument of composition must also be common and apparently correct. The latter two questions are largely empirical questions.

The concept of the fallacy of composition is complicated, but also made more interesting and more challenging, by the fact that there is a third meaning which is sometimes attached to the term by contemporary scholars. Once again, Copi can serve as an instructive source. In this version of the fallacy of composition, "the fallacious reasoning is from properties possessed by individual elements or members of a collection to properties possessed by the collection or totality of those elements" (Copi 1968, 80-81). However, he tends to confuse the discussion by equating this to reasoning from distributive to collective terms, and so we must look elsewhere for clear and incisive examples.

We find these in the writings of economists. Let us begin with a quaint but non-economic example, which they sometimes give: "Have you ever seen people jump up at a football game to gain a better view? They usually find that, once everybody is standing up, the view has not improved at all. Such behavior, where what is true for an individual is not necessarily true for everyone illustrates the 'fallacy of composition' " (Samuelson and Nordhaus 1989, 7-8). And from the domain of economics, one would be committing this version of the fallacy if one were to reason by disregarding the principle that "if a single individual receives more money [in wages], that person will be better off; [but] if everybody receives more money, no one will be better off" (Samuelson and Nordhaus 1989, 8).[10] Similarly, "higher prices for one

---

[8] Walton 1989, 130-31; Walton, Reed, and Macagno 2008, 112-14, 316-17.

[9] See Whately 1826, 131; Govier (1995, 172; 2010, 66, 85); Woods (2012, 514; 2013, 133-37); Finocchiaro (2013a; 2014a; 2014b); and also the discussion below (section 4). For a useful critique of this conception, see Hansen 2002.

[10] For a more recent example in a more popular context, we can find it in a column by Nobel Prize economist Paul Krugman (2013b) on the issue of whether to end unemployment benefits in the United States beyond the usual 26 weeks; he argues for continuing the benefits and criticizes arguments against: "Ask yourself how, exactly, ending unemployment benefits would create more jobs ... You might be tempted to argue that more intense competition among workers would lead to lower wages, and that cheap labor would encourage hiring. But that argument involves a fallacy of composition. Cut the wages of some workers relative to those of other workers, and those accepting the wage cuts may gain a competitive edge. Cut everyone's wages, however, and nobody gains an edge. All that happens is a general fall in income—which, among other things, increases the burden of household debt, and is therefore a net negative for overall employment." See also Krugman 2013a.

industry may benefit its members but, if the prices of everything bought and sold increased in the same proportion, no one would be better off" (Samuelson 1955, 9).

Thus far, we have seen that historical and contemporary writings on the fallacy of composition contain three notions that are *prima facie* distinct, but tend to be confused with each other: (1) reasoning from premises using a term distributively to a conclusion using the same term collectively; (2) reasoning from some property of the parts to the same property for the whole; and (3) reasoning from some property of the members of a group to the same property for the entire group.[11] The association of the second and third notions with each other is very common, as we have seen. On the other hand, the association of all three is relatively rare, but does occur. One example may found in the following textbook definition: "The fallacy of composition consists in treating a distributed characteristic as if it were collective. It occurs when one makes the mistake of attributing to a group (or a whole) some characteristic that is true only of its individual members (or its parts), and then makes inferences based on that mistake" (Halverson 1984, 73). Another instance of the three-fold association is embodied in a dictionary definition from an otherwise authoritative source, *Webster's Third New International Dictionary*: "fallacy of composition: the fallacy of arguing from premises in which a term is used distributively to a conclusion in which it is used collectively or of assuming that what is true of each member of a class or part of a whole will be true of all together" (1976 edition, p. 818).

Unfortunately, besides this internal indistinction, discussions of the fallacy of composition also exhibit a tendency to confuse it with a related error which is labeled the fallacy of division, and which is usually regarded as the exact opposite or reverse of the fallacy of composition. In the fallacy of division, one reasons from premises that attribute a property to a whole, a group, or collectively described entities to a conclusion that attributes the same property to the parts, or the individual members, or some distributively described entities. An example would be: "American Indians are disappearing. That man is an American Indian. Therefore that man is disappearing" (Copi 1968, 82). The fallacy of division so defined also embodies a conflation of three distinctions, but the issue I want to raise now is that these two fallacies are not always properly distinguished from each other.

I am not saying that these two fallacies are confused with each other. For,

---

[11] The distinction between the parts-whole relationship and the members-group relationship strikes me as intuitively obvious. However, it may be partly justified by arguing that this distinction is analogous to one needed in set theory and the foundations of mathematics; that is, the distinction between the notion of one set being a subset of another and the notion of an individual object being an element of a set; cf. Dufour 2013.

at the level of definition, these discussions are clear that one of these fallacies is the reverse or opposite of the other. Here, the key point is that the direction of reasoning is opposite in the two cases, from parts to whole in one case, and from whole to parts in the other; and the difference in direction is evident and obvious.

However, the confusion begins to emerge at the level of analysis, when both fallacies are treated as if they instantiated the same type of argument or the same type of error; as if such types depended on the same principles; and as if such principles can be formulated in terms of the relationship between the properties of wholes or groups and the properties of parts or members. Thus, the two fallacies are often not only discussed in the same breadth, but also treated as if we had just one fallacy and not two. And occasionally, the confusion is reinforced by incautious language about "the fallacy of composition and division."[12]

What is problematic here, in my opinion, is that reasoning from wholes or groups to parts or members possesses a *prima facie* plausibility which reasoning from parts or members to wholes or groups does not possess. This plausibility stems from the fact that whereas universal instantiation (all F are G, so this F is G) is deductively valid, universal generalization is not (this F is G, so all F are G). Thus the two fallacies should not be treated as involving the same principles, but rather as, at least *prima facie*, distinct.

Even when the two fallacies are clearly distinguished, the discussion is often marred by a carelessness that is symptomatic of a deeper problem. For example, a well-known and otherwise useful book defines the argument from composition, in the generic case, as going from the premise "all the parts of X have property Y" to the conclusion "X has property Y"; and it defines the argument from division, in the generic case, as going from the premise that "X has property Y" to the conclusion "all the parts of X have property Y" (Walton, Reed, and Macagno 2008, 112-14, 316-17). These definitions are clear and unobjectionable. However, in a "User's Compendium of Schemes," the same book states that the evaluation of an argument from composition depends on the critical question of whether it is the case that "when X [the whole] has property Y, then every part that composes X has property Y"; and that the evaluation of an argument from division depends on the critical question of whether it is the case that "when every part that composes X has property Y, then X [the whole] has property Y."[13] As so formulated, these

---

[12] Whately 1826, 173; Mill 1843, 536; Walton, Reed, and Macagno 2008, 112, 438. Cf. Eemeren and Grootendorst (1992, 177; 1999, 11 n. 7); Walton 1989, 131; Woods (2012, 543, 595; 2013, 5); Aberdein 2013, 15 (sect. 5).
[13] Walton, Reed, and Macagno 2008, 316-17. But on pp. 112-14 they give the correct un-reversed formulation, and so, to repeat, I think that here we have nothing more serious than carelessness about, disinterest in, or lack of appreciation of the argument and fallacy of composition.

two critical questions are being interchanged with one another: the first actually applies to arguments from division, and the second actually applies to arguments from composition. This blemish is probably just a typographical error, but the overlooking of such a typo is indicative of the muddle which I am trying to document.

My conclusion here is that there is a four-fold distinction to be made, not only among parts and wholes, individuals and groups, and distributed and collective terms, but also between reasoning from the former to the latter members of these three pairs and reasoning from the latter to the former members. As we undertake our empirical search for real examples, this distinction can be added to the ubiquity thesis to guide us in our search. That is, we are searching for important actual material whose understanding and criticism might be helped by applying, clarifying, refining, or deepening this distinction.

4. The Meta-argumentation Hypothesis

Besides the four-fold distinction and the ubiquity thesis, there is a third guiding idea that needs to be at least mentioned and tentatively stated before we proceed. This is an idea toward which a number of scholars have been groping, and it deserves to be made more explicit.

For example, in one of my first publications on this subject, I criticized textbook accounts of fallacies, and based on this criticism I formulated a problem and advanced an hypothesis. The problem was formulated in terms of the following questions: "do people actually commit fallacies as usually understood? That is, do fallacies exist in practice? Or do they exist only in the mind of the interpreter who is claiming that a fallacy is being committed?".[14] Although these were not meant to be rhetorical questions, but rather open questions that required further investigation, it is perhaps unsurprising that some readers (e.g., Govier 1982) did view them as rhetorical questions.

Moreover, a working hypothesis was being advanced when I expressed "the suspicion that logically incorrect arguments are not that common in practice, that their existence may be largely restricted to logic textbook examples and exercises."[15] However, some readers thought that I was claiming that fallacies are merely figments of critics' imagination, and "are in fact an illusion" (Jason 1986, 92).

Later, I was more explicit and more constructive about this issue when I elaborated a general approach to the study of fallacies. One element of that

---

[14] Finocchiaro 1980, 334; 1981, 15; 2005, 113.
[15] Finocchiaro 1980, 333; 1981, 14; 2005, 111.

approach was connected to, and extracted from, Strawson's (1952) *Introduction to Logical Theory* and his notion of "the logician's second-order vocabulary"; that notion was extended to include 'fallacy' terminology, "since it ordinarily occurs when someone wants to comment about some logical feature of a first-order expression of reasoning. This means that the best place to begin with in the study of fallacies, or at least a crucial phenomenon to examine, is allegations that fallacies are being committed."[16]

In this vein, other scholars elaborated the idea that fallacies are more like theoretical entities such as quarks in physics, rather than like concrete objects such as buttercups in everyday life.[17] More recently, some have pursued a linguistic and descriptive approach to argumentative norms by studying what they call the metadiscourse or the metalanguage of crucial words, such as 'argument', 'issue', 'pretext', and the French '*amalgam*'.[18]

Partly in line with the last-mentioned approach, but more directly in line with my recent work on meta-argumentation,[19] the present project can be articulated more clearly, incisively, and constructively in light of the notion of meta-argumentation. To this end, one distinguishes a meta-argument from a ground-level argument, and defines the former as an argument about one or more arguments, or about argumentation in general. Then a ground-level argument can be defined as one about such things as natural phenomena, historical events, human actions, mathematical numbers, or metaphysical entities. A prototypical case of meta-argumentation is argument analysis, in which one advances and justifies an interpretive or an evaluative claim about a ground-level argument.

The proposal here is that we search for fallacies of composition primarily in meta-argumentation rather than ground-level argumentation. However, this is *not* meant in the sense that we should be looking for meta-arguments that commit the fallacy of composition, but rather that we try to find meta-arguments advancing explicit conclusions that some fallacy of composition has been committed, i.e., that some ground-level argument embodies or commits a fallacy of composition. The working hypothesis is then that, at least as a first approximation, the fallacy of composition is primarily a concept of meta-argumentation, useful in the context of understanding and/or assessing ground-level argumentation.

Whether this is also the case for other fallacies is not being addressed here, and is left as an open question. Nevertheless, this working hypothesis is all the more promising insofar as it also corresponds to a claim found in Woods's (2013) recent account of errors of reasoning. Let us begin by noting

---

[16] Finocchiaro 1987, 264; 2005, 130.
[17] Grootendorst 1987; Woods 1988.
[18] Craig (1999; 2011); Craig and Tracy 2005; Doury (2005; 2006; 2009; 2013); Eemeren et al. 2014, 502-3; and Goodwin 2007.
[19] Finocchiaro 2013b; 2013c; 2014d.

that a main strand of his account is the claim that there is a misalignment between the traditional concept of fallacy and the traditional list of fallacies. The traditional concept is the one mentioned above, which has five elements: a fallacy is a (1) common (2) type of (3) argument that (4) appears to be correct but (5) actually is not.[20] The traditional list is what Woods has labeled the "gang of eighteen," although he points out that the number eighteen is not precise because some items can be combined or further subdivided: affirming the consequent, denying the antecedent, hasty generalization, biased statistics, gambler's fallacy, *post hoc ergo propter hoc,* faulty analogy, *ad baculum, ad hominem, ad populum, ad verecundiam, ad ignorantiam, ad misericordiam,* begging the question and circularity, many questions, equivocation, composition and division, and straw man. Woods's argument consists of examining each of these in turn, and showing that each fails to satisfy one or more of the necessary conditions of being a fallacy. Although Woods does not get around to examining a few of these argumentative practices (e.g., the fallacy of composition), he does cover at least thirteen of them, and then suggests that the same will apply to the others. And indeed, with regard to the fallacy of composition, one can argue in a similar vein (Finocchiaro 2013a) that it fails to satisfy some of the necessary conditions of the traditional conception.

However, Woods then goes on to clarify that he does not mean to say that there are no fallacies in the traditional sense—that the traditional concept is empty. In fact, he argues that sometimes fallacies in the traditional sense are committed at the meta-level when one attributes a fallacy to a reasoner at the ground level. For example, this happens when scholars like Kahneman and Tversky attribute to their experimental subjects the errors of the so-called conjunction fallacy and base-rate fallacy, and also when it is claimed that someone has committed the gambler's fallacy (Woods 2013, 478-92). The same holds when we attribute what Woods calls "Sleigh's Fallacy," which involves the misunderstanding of the scope of modal operators such as "necessarily" (Woods 2013, 485-88); when traditional scholars attribute the *ad hominem* fallacy (Woods 2013, 448); and when one is careless about the meaning of the material-implication connective and its relationship to the "if-then" of natural language, a problem which Woods labels "Powers' Paradox" (Woods 2013, 269-70, 513-14). This move to the meta-level is Woods's twist on the question of the reality of fallacies, which corresponds (without of course being identical) to my working hypothesis formulated above and to be tested below.

---

[20] However, see the useful criticism of such a historical thesis advanced by Hansen 2002. Still, I do not think his criticism undermines my main point here, partly because the target of his criticism is a much more oversimplified concept of fallacy than the one I am advocating; for example, he neglects conditions (1) and (2), and limits condition (5) to deductive invalidity or inductive weakness.

5. Aristotle's Geocentric Argument from Natural Motion

Let us now begin our empirical search for real or realistic material pertaining to the fallacy of composition. There happens to be an important and instructive example, which is sufficiently simple and clear that it can also serve as an illustration of the meta-argumentation hypothesis, useful to provide further guidance about more complicated cases. It involves an argument from Aristotle's treatise *On the Heavens* (Aristotle 296b7-297a1), which tried to show that the earth must be standing still at the center of the universe, based on what were regarded as the laws of natural motion for terrestrial bodies. This and other arguments against the earth's motion became very important and controversial during the Copernican revolution, since they had to be effectively criticized in order for the transition to succeed from a geostatic geocentric world view to a heliocentric geokinetic one. Galileo Galilei was one of these critics, and in his case, because of the involvement of the Catholic Church and the Inquisition, such arguments became a matter of liberty or imprisonment, and indeed of life and death.

The Aristotelian geocentric argument from natural motion thus occurred in the context of many other arguments for and against the earth's motion. Moreover it was itself a complex argument with several steps and strands. Nevertheless, one of its strands was the following, as reconstructed by Galileo: "who is so blind as not to see that the parts of the element earth and of the element water, being heavy bodies, move naturally downwards, namely toward the center of the universe, assigned by nature herself as the goal and end of straight downward motion ... Since this can be seen clearly, and since we are sure that the same holds for the whole as for the parts, must we not conclude that it is true and manifest that the natural motion of the [whole globe] earth is straight toward the center ... ?" (Galilei 1997, 83-84). This was an anti-Copernican argument at least in the sense that its conclusion contradicted the Copernican claim that the earth moves with daily axial rotation and annual heliocentric revolution; moreover, a further conclusion would be that once the whole earth has moved with natural motion to the center, it can do nothing but remain there.

One of Galileo's key criticisms of this argument is that it commits the fallacy of composition, although he does not use this term. However, the content of that criticism leaves no doubt. To see this, let us begin with a preliminary clarification which he makes to remove a possible equivocation. The key premise of this argument is that the parts of the earth (terrestrial bodies such as rocks and rain drops) move naturally straight downwards. In this context, "downwards" can mean either toward the center of the universe or toward the center of the earth. If it means towards the center of the universe, then it cannot be regarded as a direct observational report, and so it needs some justification, and then that justification can be criticized, in ways than need not concern us here.[21] The relevant point in this context is that if we want to consider that key premise to be an observational report, as the above quotation in part indicates, then its meaning is that heavy bodies move naturally toward the center of the earth. However, if we combine this claim with the second premise, asserting the parts-whole principle, then the conclusion we get is that the natural motion of the whole earth is straight toward its own center. Unfortunately, it is an intrinsic conceptual impossibility for a whole object to move toward its own center.[22]

---

[21] However, that version of the argument, and the Galilean criticism of it, raise other interesting issues, which happen to relate to the fallacy of *petitio principii* or begging the question; see Galilei 1997, 86-88. Cf. Arnauld and Nicole 1996, 190-92; Finocchiaro (1980, 353-56; 2014c, 59-63).

[22] Such a strong claim on my part may invite objections such as the following (which was actually raised by a referee): perhaps the phrase 'center of the earth' could be regarded as a "rigid designator" (in a sense deriving from Saul Kripke); then the center of the earth would be a particular place or point is space (which would be a viable option especially if we conceive space as absolute, along the lines of Galileo's successor Isaac Newton); and then there would be no incoherence in conceiving the whole earth as moving toward that point, which would happen to be its own center; thus the conclusion of Aristotle's argument (when so interpreted) is not necessarily false; and we have no counter-example (elegant or otherwise) to such a compositional argument. My inclination here is to regard this objection as a *reductio ad absurdum* of either the concept of rigid designator or of the judgment that 'center of the earth' is a rigid designator. For the main move in this objection seems to be the same as denying the analyticity of 'all bachelors are unmarried' because 'bachelor' could be taken to mean "human male under the age of 18," instead of "human male who is not married"; or denying the impossibility of "2+2=5," because '5' could be taken to mean "the successor of 3," instead of "the successor of 4" (in Peano's axiomatization of arithmetic); the crux is that if the whole earth were moving toward a point in absolute space "rigidly designated" as "the center of the earth," such motion would still not really be toward its own center. The only way I can think of questioning the impossibility of the whole earth moving toward its own center is along the following lines: a clear and simple distinction could be made between center of mass and geometrical center; now suppose most of the earth's mass were concentrated on one side, so that the two centers would not coincide; suppose next that the earth was undergoing external forces such that the distribution of its mass was becoming more uniform and its shape (which originally need not have been spherical) was becoming more symmetric; such a process of rearrangement could be interpreted as the earth's center of mass moving toward its geometrical center; but normally the motion of a body's center of mass defines motion for the whole body; thus in the situation described the whole earth (its center of mass) would be moving toward its own (geometrical) center. However, I am not sure this would refute Galileo's counter-example to Aristotle's argument, because the latter would have to

In other words, if we interpret this step of the Aristotelian argument as an argument of composition, then we can generate an elegant, devastating, and memorable counterexample: a situation in which the key premise is clearly and uncontroversially true, and the conclusion is clearly and uncontroversially false. I am inclined to say, if this is not a fallacy of composition, I don't know where we can find one. Thus, in Galileo's interpretation, this strand of this Aristotelian argument commits the fallacy of composition.

However, let us note that Galileo's interpretation is really a meta-argument, which advances the critical claim just formulated (that the geocentric argument from natural motion commits the fallacy of composition), and justifies this claim on the basis of various considerations. The Galilean meta-argument could of course be elaborated, reconstructed, analyzed, and evaluated at greater length.[23] It strikes me as cogent. But even if it were not, the relevance to the present investigation would remain, in the sense that there would be serious issues at the metalevel, rather than at the ground level, about the fallacy of composition: what the fallacy of composition means, what the ground-level argument is, and how accurate and fair it is to attribute this fallacy to this argument.

6. The Theological Argument from Design

A memorable example of the fallacy of composition occurs in the design argument for the existence of God, at least according to the critique advanced in Hume's *Dialogues Concerning Natural Religion*.[24] This charge is only one objection in the complex and multi-faceted criticism which Hume formulates; and correspondingly, it affects only one particular step of the design argument. Thus, even if cogent, this Humean meta-argument is not the end of the story; nevertheless, it is a crucial element of the over-all evaluation of the design argument.

It should be noted that Hume interprets the design argument primarily as inductive and empirical. In so doing, he is trying to abide by the principle of charity, for if one were to reconstruct the design argument as deductive and *a priori*, then according to Hume it could not even get off the ground, since

---

be interpreted as using 'center of the earth' in only one sense, otherwise it would be committing a fallacy of equivocation; this would yield two possible distinct interpretations of the Aristotelian argument (besides the earlier-discarded 'center of universe' interpretation); but neither one would be able to exploit motion from one center to the other, to avoid Galileo's devastating counter-example.

[23] Galilei 1997, 83-90; cf. Finocchiaro (1980, 353-56; 2014c, 59-63).

[24] Hume 1947, 143-47. Cf. Barker 1989; O'Connor 2001, 69-70; Finocchiaro 2013c, 207.

it would be trying to prove a factual matter—that God exists and created the universe—from *a priori* considerations; and this for Hume is an inherently impossible task.

One version of the design argument is this: the universe was created by an intelligent designer (called God), because the universe is like a machine, and machines are made by (human) intelligent designers. This is, of course, an argument from analogy.

Now Hume questions the analogical premise. How could one show that the universe is like a machine? Well, in Hume's own memorable words, spoken through the character Cleanthes, the answer is:

> look round the world, contemplate the whole and every part of it: you will find it to be nothing but one great machine, subdivided into an infinite number of lesser machines, which again admit of subdivisions to a degree beyond what human senses and faculties can trace and explain. All these various machines, and even their most minute parts, are adjusted to each other with an accuracy which ravishes into admiration all men who have ever contemplated them. The curious adapting of means to ends, throughout all nature, resembles exactly, though it much exceeds, the productions of human contrivance—of human design, thought, wisdom, and intelligence. [Hume 1947, 143]

This does seem to provide empirical, observational support for the claim that the universe is like a machine.

However, there are problems with this reasoning. In Hume's words, spoken through the character Philo:

> But can you think, Cleanthes, that your usual phlegm and philosophy have been preserved in so wide a step as you have taken, when you compared to the universe houses, ships, furniture, machines, and, from their similarity in some circumstances, inferred a similarity in their causes? Thought, design, intelligence, such as we discover in men and other animals, is no more than one of the springs and principles of the universe, as well as heat or cold, attraction or repulsion, and a hundred others, which fall under daily observation. It is an active cause, by which some particular parts of nature, we find, produce alterations on other parts. But can a conclusion, with any propriety, be transferred from parts to the whole? Does not the great disproportion bar all comparison and inference? From observing the growth of a hair, can we learn anything concerning the generation of a man? Would the manner of a leaf's blowing, even though perfectly known, afford us any instruction concerning the vegetation of a tree? [Hume 1947, 147]

Here, Hume is finding two things wrong with the subargument supporting the claim that the universe is like a machine. One problem is that although many parts of the universe are like machines, produced by intelligent design, many other parts (even when orderly arranged) are produced by natural causes such as attraction and heat. That is, Hume is charging that the subargument is a hasty generalization. But this is not the only problem; for even if all parts of the universe were machine-like, we could not be sure that the same would apply to the universe as a whole. In this second criticism, Hume is charging a fallacy of composition.

Again, as in the case of Galileo's criticism of Aristotle's geocentric argument from natural motion, Hume's criticism of this subargument of the design argument is a meta-argument, and as such it is open to analysis, interpretation, and evaluation. Note, for example, that Hume's critical conclusion is based partly on an interpretation of the subargument in question, partly on a definition of the fallacy of composition, and partly on some evaluative principle.

The interpretive claim is a reconstruction of this step of the design argument as transferring to the whole universe the same property which it claims to be able to observe in all (or many) of its parts. Here, the property is that of being caused by some intelligent design.

The evaluative principle is that it is illegitimate to transfer any such property from parts to whole in this case. Hume seems to give two reasons for this evaluative principle: first, the disproportion between such parts and whole is too great, presumably because the universe is infinite or indefinitely large; second, the transference from parts to the whole universe would be like reasoning from what happens to a human hair to what happens to a whole human body, or from what happens to a leaf to what happens to a whole tree. And it should be noted that with this second reason Hume is advancing a meta-argument from analogy that assesses negatively one ground-level argument from analogy (this subargument of the design argument) based on a comparison of this argument to other bad ground-level arguments from analogy (the one involving a human hair and body and the one involving a leaf and tree).[25]

7. Michels's Iron Law of Oligarchy

One of the most important discussions of the fallacy of composition I have come across is found in the field of political science. It involves one of the most famous and widely-discussed principles in that field—the so-called "iron law of oligarchy": that every bureaucratic organization has oligarchical tendencies which are impossible to overcome, and that this applies even to democratic institutions, which are thus doomed to become undemocratic. This "law" was first advanced in a book published in German in 1911, translated into English in 1915, reprinted many times, and revealingly

---

[25] Barker 1989; cf. Finocchiaro 2013c, 201-203.

entitled *Political Parties: A Sociological Study of the Oligarchical Tendencies of Modern Democracy* (Michels 1915; 1962).

Now, an important criticism of Michels's law has been advanced by Robert Dahl, who is one of the most widely respected political scientists and the founder of the field known as democratic theory (Dahl 1956; 1989). The criticism is that Michels began by studying the workings of political parties, in particular the German Social Democratic Party; he discovered that even parties advocating democracy had insurmountable oligarchical (anti-democratic) tendencies; he concluded that what was true of political parties was also true of governmental institutions or societies as a whole; and thus he committed an error of reasoning, consisting of illegitimately inferring from parts to the whole (Dahl 1989, 275-77).

Although Dahl does not speak of the "fallacy of composition," it is obvious that he is attributing this fallacy to Michels. Furthermore, if Dahl's criticism is accurate, then Michels's argument provides an example of fallacy of composition which is real, important, substantial, and interesting; again, infinitely more robust than the hackneyed and trivial examples of logic textbooks. For these reasons, it is valuable to quote Dahl's words:

> From the perspective of later political science, then, Michels committed an elementary mistake in generalizing from political parties to the government of a polyarchal system. His generalizations were derived from the study of a single organization, the German Social Democratic Party. His famous "iron law of oligarchy" explicitly referred to political parties … But even if we grant that political parties are oligarchical, *it does not follow that competing political parties necessarily produce an oligarchical political system.* Business firms are among the most "oligarchical" organizations in modern societies; but as I pointed out, Michels's mentor, Pareto, writing as an economist, would never have said that these competing oligarchies produced monopolistic control over consumers and the market. Not even Marx, who saw business firms as despotic organizations, made such an elementary mistake. Quite the contrary: It was competition that *prevented* monopoly. If Michels had strictly limited his conclusions to political parties, his case would have been far stronger. But as the quotations given earlier show clearly, Michels went on to draw the unwarranted conclusion that democracy is impossible in a *political system* because it was, he believed from his study of one party, impossible in a particular *element of the system.* Had he been writing today it is inconceivable that he would have moved so casually from his observation of oligarchy in a political party to the conclusion that oligarchy is inescapable in a political system in which the political parties are highly competitive. Michels's elementary mistake reminds us that for the most part the theorists of minority domination discussed here had little or no experience with systems of competitive parties in countries with a broad suffrage or, certainly, with systematic analysis of competitive party systems. [Dahl 1989, 276]

Here, Dahl's talk of generalization may give the impression that he is interpreting Michels's reasoning as an inductive generalization, and criticizing it as a hasty one. The extrapolation would be from one political party to all political parties, and from political parties to whole societies or political systems. However, such criticism would, I believe, be unfair because, although Michels does focus on the German Social Democratic party, his book is also filled with discussions of many other entities: other German parties; political parties in other European countries, especially Italy, but also France and England; labor unions in such European countries; and various European governments. Such evidence is impressive, and so Michels's generalization is not as hasty as Dahl makes it sound, and perhaps not hasty at all.

Moreover, I believe it is more accurate and fair to interpret Michels as advancing an argument from analogy (cf. Mosca 1912). In fact, Michels was claiming an analogy between political parties and labor unions on the one hand and whole societies and political systems on the other, based on similarities such as the following: (1) administration by the majority is technically impossible; (2) the better elements of the people or masses get constantly re-elected; (3) the first leaders have an advantage over newcomers; (4) the leaders control party machinery, such as the press; and (5) leaders change psychologically in their attitude due to the salary they receive, the power they exercise, their interaction with the ruling class, their age, and their attachment to their own accomplishments.

Nevertheless, the essence of Dahl's criticism can be adapted and applied to such an argument from analogy. Without necessarily denying such similarities, Dahl is stressing that there is an important dissimilarity, which Michels is ignoring—competition; in political systems that allow competition among political parties, the oligarchic tendencies that exist within parties are counteracted at the macro level of the whole political system.

On the other hand, whether Michels's argument is criticized as a hasty generalization, or as a faulty analogy, in either case the criticism would be consistent with attributing to it a fallacy of composition. For Michels's argument remains an argument of composition, because it reasons from parts or elements being oligarchical to the whole system being oligarchical; and it is being criticized as incorrect or fallacious. In other words, adapting an argument by Govier,[26] I believe that arguments of composition are not a distinct kind, but can also instantiate other types, especially inductive generalizations and arguments from analogy.

Another important criticism of Michels's iron law of oligarchy also relates to the fallacy of composition. It is advanced by Seymour Martin Lipset (1962), a distinguished political sociologist who wrote the introduction to the English translation of Michels's book. Lipset's key criticism is that Michels

---

[26] Govier (2007; 2009). Cf. Finocchiaro 2013a.

failed to appreciate that a whole society can be democratic (anti-oligarchical) even though it is composed of institutional parts that are oligarchical (anti-democratic). Again, although Lipset does not use the term, he is attributing a fallacy of composition to Michels: that because the particular institutions of a society are oligarchic, therefore the whole society must be oligarchical. Lipset can admit that Michels's argument is both compositional and analogical, as sketched above. However, Lipset questions Michels's analogy at another crucial point, thus undermining his compositional argument from analogy. For Lipset, there is one condition or property present in democratic societies, but absent in undemocratic societies and in particular institutions of democratic ones: a constitutional provision or traditional-historical practice that bans or prevents any one entity or group from exercising tyrannical or despotic power over opposing entities or groups.

This criticism strikes me as plausible and powerful. In fact, there is a tradition of political theory that regards such an anti-tyrannical or anti-despotic principle as fundamental.[27] Now, although here Lipset does not mention any such historical precedents, his words in the summary of his criticism leave little doubt that he has this principle in mind, as they leave little doubt that he is charging Michels with the fallacy of composition:

> In essence, democracy in modern society may be viewed as involving the conflict of organized groups competing for support ... While most private governments, unions, professional societies, veterans' organizations, and political parties will remain one-party systems ... it is important to recognize that many internally oligarchic organizations help to sustain political democracy in the larger society and to protect the interests of their members from the encroachments of other groups. Democracy in large measure rests on the fact that no one group is able to secure a basis of power and command over the majority so that it can effectively suppress or deny the claims of the groups it opposes. [Lipset 1962, 36-37]

Dahl's and Lipset's critiques are related, insofar as political competition and the anti-tyrannical principle are substantively connected, I believe, by way of the notion of the balance of power.[28] More importantly for us here, however, their critiques are really meta-arguments, which advance the critical conclusion that Michels's argument is erroneous in its reasoning from political parties to the whole political system. As was the case for Galileo's and Hume's meta-arguments, Dahl's and Lipset's meta-arguments could also be elaborated, reconstructed, analyzed, and evaluated at greater length;

---

[27] Hamilton, Jay, and Madison 1961, 301; Mosca 1939, 134; Finocchiaro 1999, 206.
[28] Traces of Dahl's and Lipset's critiques are also found in Mosca (1912), who explicitly injects the notion of balance of power into the discussion; cf. Finocchiaro 1999, 22-62.

moreover, intuitively, and as reconstructed, they strike me as cogent. But even if they were not, their relevance to the present investigation would also remain, in the sense that there would be serious issues at the metalevel, rather than at the ground level, about the fallacy of composition: what we mean by fallacy of composition, what Michels's ground-level argument is, and how accurate and fair it is to claim that his argument commits the fallacy of composition.

8. Epilogue: Conclusions and Problems

With regard to the fallacy of composition, the problem of how frequently it occurs is more striking than for the case of the other fallacies, because the contrast is greater and starker between the scarcity of scholarly analyses and the triviality of textbook examples on the one hand, and the widespread claims made (especially by economists) about its prevalence and importance. Thus, the empirical search for real or realistic examples is a relatively urgent task.

Such a search, however empirically minded, must also be guided by some assumptions or working hypotheses. One of these is the self-same ubiquity thesis, whose truth is to be tested. Another guiding idea is that there are several distinct senses of the "fallacy of composition." A brief and sketchy historical survey shows that this term refers to fallacious reasoning that goes (1) from a distributive use of a term in the premises to a collective use in the conclusion; or (2) from premises that attribute some property to the parts of a whole to a conclusion that attributes the same property to the whole; or (3) from premises that attribute some property to the members or elements of a class or group to a conclusion that attributes the same property to the group or class. These three notions may turn out to be importantly related, but they are *prima facie* different and should initially be kept distinct. A similar initial and tentative distinction should also be made between this fallacy and the fallacy of division, instead of starting their discussion by treating them as special cases of reasoning about parts and wholes, individuals and groups, and distributed and collective terms.

Another key guiding idea is what I have called the meta-argumentation hypothesis: that the best places in which to search for fallacies of composition are important meta-arguments whose conclusion attributes (explicitly or implicitly) such a fallacy to some ground-level argument. This hypothesis may be regarded as a more promising, more judicious, and more concrete twist on previous claims such as the following: that in general fallacies exist only in the minds of critics; or that they come into being primarily through Strawson's second-order logical vocabulary; or that they are theoretical entities like quarks; or that they are best studied in terms of the evaluative

72

metalanguage used by ordinary arguers; or that they are committed by experimenters like Kahneman and Tversky when they attribute the conjunction and base-rate fallacies to their experimental subjects, rather than by these subjects themselves.

Guided by these ideas, I presented three cases. The first is a criticism of Aristotle's geocentric argument from natural motion: that the natural motion of terrestrial bodies is straight toward the center; and therefore the natural motion of the whole earth is straight toward the center. Galileo objected by arguing that if "center" means center of the universe, Aristotle's argument begs the question; but if center means center of the earth, the premise is empirically true, but the conclusion is inherently false. And the latter is a memorable counterexample that deserves further logical analysis, because it seems to undermine the *formal* validity of not only Aristotle's particular argument, but also of any compositional argument from parts to whole.

My second example involves one of Hume's criticisms of a subargument of the design argument for the existence of God. The subargument is the justification of the claim that the universe is like a machine, which claim is then used in an argument from analogy to reach the main conclusion that the universe was created by God. The justification is that many parts of the universe are like machines. Hume objects that the inference from parts to the whole universe is faulty because in this case there is too great a disproportion between parts and whole.

My third case involves some criticisms of Michels's argument for the iron law of oligarchy: that political parties inevitably become oligarchic even if they claim to have democratic aims; and therefore, a democratic society inevitably becomes oligarchic. Dahl objected that such reasoning fails because there is a crucial disanalogy between such parts and such a whole: a democratic society allows competition among its parts, but a particular party does not. Similarly, Lipset objected that there is another crucial difference: a democratic society has an anti-tyrannical system of checks and balances in its written or unwritten constitution, but political parties and labor unions do not.

These examples are certainly real and realistic. They are obviously also historically important. The ground-level arguments are clearly compositional; i.e., they are arguments of composition. And the ground level arguments are more or less inferentially incorrect: incontrovertibly and memorably so in the case of Aristotle's geocentric argument from natural motion, arguably and cogently so in the case of the compositional step of the theological argument from design, and arguably and plausibly so in the case of Michels's support for the iron law of oligarchy.

However, some qualifications are in order, leading to a number of future research problems. First, even if we take these claims as acceptable, one important conceptual qualification needs to be kept in mind about these three examples of the fallacy of composition. For these claims amount to saying that we have found three important historical examples of arguments of composition that are inferentially incorrect. But as mentioned earlier, conceptually speaking, a fallacy is a common type of argument that appears to be correct but is not so. This conception contains five elements: frequency, generality, reasoning, apparent correctness, and actual incorrectness. Now, in my three examples, the ground-level arguments obviously meet the condition of being reasoning; they also meet the generality condition since they are arguments from parts to whole; and they *appear* to be correct, since the exposure of the flaws of the ground-level arguments required meta-argumentation by thinkers such as Galileo, Hume, Dahl, and Lipset. But I am not sure about their common occurrence and their actual incorrectness. In fact, the same features that make these examples historically important may suggest that they are relatively uncommon; and their actual incorrectness could perhaps be questioned by questioning the critical meta-arguments of Galileo, Hume, Dahl, and Lipset. On the other hand, while such considerations would show that we have not found three examples of *fallacies* of composition, they do not undermine the claim that we have found three important historical examples of seductive (i.e., apparently correct) arguments of composition. This problem required further reflection.

Another problem for future investigation concerns an issue which I have not mentioned at all, but which has received some discussion in the literature, with some promising and insightful results. The issue is that of the evaluation of the correctness of compositional arguments, and the formulation of useful evaluative principles. A key principle which I gather from this literature (e.g., Ritola 2009b) is that the evaluation of compositional arguments should not be limited to deductive evaluation, but should include inductive evaluation; for even when compositional arguments are deductively invalid, they often possess some plausibility, cogency, or inductive strength. Another principle urges us to distinguish between absolute and relative properties (e.g., square vs. heavy) and between structured or heterogeneous and unstructured or homogeneous wholes or aggregates; and it claims that properties are transferable from parts to whole (or vice versa) only if the properties are absolute and the wholes are unstructured.[29] However, the 'only if' in this formulation should be taken literally and strictly, as not including an 'if', that is, the principle at best states necessary but not sufficient conditions for transferability; thus, more work is needed to find and formulate sufficient conditions.

Thirdly, we need more analysis and clarification of the distinction drawn above among three subtypes of compositional arguments, and consequently

---

[29] Eemeren and Grootendorst (1992, 177; 1999). Cf. Gough and Daniel 2009; Ritola 2009b.

three subtypes of fallacies of composition. For example, we noted earlier that the concepts of distributive and collective meanings need explicit definition and more clarification, insofar as the first conception of the fallacy of composition speaks of reasoning from premises using a term in a distributive sense to a conclusion using the same term in a collective sense. In discussions of this conception (e.g., Salmon 1984, 54-57), one gets the impression that the concept of distribution being presupposed here is the same as the one prevalent in the theory of categorical propositions and syllogisms, namely, that in a categorical proposition, a term is distributed if and only if it says something about each and every entity designated by that term; and this yields that a term is distributed when it is the subject of a universal proposition (whether affirmative or negative) or the predicate of a negative proposition (whether universal or particular). However, even if we take this to be the meaning of 'distributed sense' in the definition of the first version of the fallacy of composition, the meaning of 'collective sense' obviously cannot be equated to 'undistributed sense'. On the other hand, if we define the collective sense of a term as being the one that refers to the group or class which it designates, then the first version would approach or reduce to the third version of the fallacy of composition. Perhaps that is the case, and the first is a semantical formulation, and the third an ontological formulation, of the same idea. Add to this the fact that the historical cases revealed by our search above are all instances of the second version of the fallacy of composition, involving reasoning from parts to the whole; this suggests that the first and third versions perhaps share another feature, namely unreality, i.e., empirical unreality, so to speak. And then we begin to feel the depth or weight of this problem of the relationship among the three conceptions of this fallacy.

However, there is perhaps an even deeper, fourth, problem. We saw above, in the discussion of the argument from design, that the subargument for the universe being like a machine could be criticized not only as an erroneous argument of composition, but also as a biased inductive generalization; that is, as generalizing from examples of intelligently-designed order and illegitimately ignoring examples where order is produced by natural causes like attraction and heat. Moreover, in the discussion of Michels's iron law of oligarchy, we saw that his argument could be interpreted not only as a compositional one, but also as an inductive generalization about human organizations, and as an argument from analogy between political parties and political societies or systems. In connection with the latter discussion, I pointed out that this pluralism of interpretations seemed to be in accordance with a general thesis advanced by Govier, to the effect that arguments of compositions are often susceptible of such alternative interpretations. However, such pluralism seems to be a way of diminishing the importance or relevance of compositional arguments, and hence of deconstructing the concept of the fallacy of composition (so to speak), as I myself have argued elsewhere (Finocchiaro 2013a). On the other hand, I am now inclined to think that 'deconstruction' is perhaps too strong a word, and that instead we could now exploit the full power of the meta-argumentation hypothesis being explored here. Doing so means that the important point is not whether a given argument "really" is compositional, analogical, or generalizing. Instead the point becomes *whether* it can be interpreted in these ways and *whether* it can then be criticized as erroneous or fallacious; and not just "whether" but also "why," namely how we can justify claiming that the given argument has one of these forms, and that it commits some particular error. Now, such justifications of interpretive or evaluative claims are obviously meta-arguments, and so main thing to worry about is that our own meta-argumentation is accurate, fair, and correct.[30]

Besides such mostly conceptual and philosophical problems, there is no lack of problems that are mostly of an empirical and historical sort. In fact, the cases presented here do not by any means exhaust the empirical material available to study the fallacy of composition.

One reason is that there is another area of the social sciences which I believe can be fruitfully searched for material relating to the fallacy of composition. This is the controversy that goes under such names as holism vs. individualism, or reductionism vs. anti-reductionism, which generates the fifth research problem in our present list. Individualism claims that all properties at the macro or social level can be linguistically defined, and/or causally explained, in terms of properties at the micro or individual level; whereas holism denies one or both of these claims. Similarly, reductionism claims that all macro or social properties can be "reduced" (semantically and/or causally) to micro or individual properties. However, philosophers of the social sciences (cf. Jones 2003; 2010) typically do not try to relate this controversy to the problem of the nature and frequency of compositional arguments and fallacies. And scholars in logic and argumentation theory are usually unaware of this controversy, although some of Govier's work (2007; 2009) may be viewed as an attempt to address this problem. In my view, such material simply cries out to be analyzed from the point of view of the fallacy of composition.

Sixth, another non-negligible source of potentially relevant material involves the so-called problem of aggregation, as Gough and Daniel (2009, 7-8) call it, following an analysis advanced by Haller (2002, 48-52). The problem relates to ecological reasoning and the question of how to properly extrapolate from details known about various regions of the world to general

---

[30] I thank a referee for having made a suggestion along these lines, namely that there is a problem about the pluralism of interpretations, and that the meta-argumentation hypothesis points the way toward a possible solution.

conclusions about the global system as a whole. When one of such details and conclusions is about global warming or climate change, the importance of the issue becomes obvious.

Moreover, with regard to global warming, some of these discussions may be potentially instructive in another way, in a negative way, so to speak. That is, as alluded to earlier (section 1), there exists at least one meta-argument by a philosopher which explicitly advances the conclusion that typical ground-level arguments for global warming "commit the fallacy of composition" (Haller 2002, 50). His reasoning is that arguments for global warming usually involve an aggregation of temperatures from particular regions of the world. However, such regional evidence only shows that "the predicted warming will most likely be manifested in a reduction of the diurnal temperature range (the difference between maximum and minimum daily temperatures), with the warming taking place mostly at night and mostly in winter."[31] However, claims about global warming do not differentiate between such warming and warming in which both maximum and minimum temperatures would increase; and "each deserves its own risk assessment" (Haller 2002, 50). By failing to make the differentiation, such arguments allegedly commit the fallacy of composition.

Such arguments certainly deserve careful scrutiny. But so does Haller's own meta-argument. And my hunch is that here we are not faced with fallacies of composition, because the ground-level arguments (whether correct or incorrect) are not compositional. In this case, the ground-level arguments, as reported by Haller, seem to start from premises that attribute to the regions of the world the property that minimum daily and seasonal temperatures are increasing; and they seem to infer (or at least suggest) the conclusion that the whole terrestrial globe is experiencing an increase of temperature (in the general sense of all temperatures, minimum, maximum, and mean). Insofar as there is a significant difference between a temperature increase consisting of an increase of minimum temperatures and a temperature increase consisting of an increase of all temperatures, then such ground-level arguments seem to be equivocating between two relevant meanings of the same term (temperature increase); but this raises issues related to the fallacy of equivocation, rather than composition.

Finally (our seventh problem), the fallacy of composition in economic thinking urgently needs and deserves more critical scrutiny by philosophers. We need not uncritically accept the claims of economists, mentioned above; but their claims are too authoritative, frequent, important, and widespread for us to dismiss them without a serious examination of their supporting arguments. Their supporting arguments are, of course, meta-arguments concluding that some ground-level arguments commit the fallacy of

---

[31] Haller 2001, 50; cf. Balling 1992, xxiv, 101-4, 118.

composition; and so such critical scrutiny would be essentially an exercise in argument analysis at the metalevel.

In this regard, it is encouraging that a relatively recent textbook (Woods, Irvine, and Walton 2000) has seen it fit to have a whole chapter discussing "economic reasoning" in general, and the fallacies of composition and division in particular. However, unfortunately, their pioneering effort remains an isolated one.

Thus, it may be fitting to end here by echoing a point alluded to at the beginning of this essay. Recall Krugman's (2013a; 2013b) explanation of the persistence of the great recession as resulting from a fallacy of composition that extrapolates austerity programs from the micro to the macro level. Here, we need not uncritically accept Krugman's own meta-argument, whose reconstruction and evaluation are part of the agenda being proposed here. Instead, I believe one can endorse the empirical claim of the prevalence of the ground-level argument about budgets, deficits, and debts, which assumes that what holds at the private or personal level also holds at the national or public level. In fact, here is a particularly incisive example, which I quote from a letter to the editor of a local daily newspaper, published on January 7, 2013; it was written by someone who is apparently a layman, and who duly signed the letter but need not be identified here:

> To the editor:
> What does the next "fiscal cliff"—the debt ceiling—look like, and what is a possible solution?
> U.S. tax revenue in fiscal year 2012: $2,450,000,000,000.
> Federal spending in fiscal year 2012: $3,500,000,000,000.
> New debt: $1,050,000,000,000.
> Current national debt: $16,400,000,000,000.
> "Fiscal cliff" budget cuts: $12,000,000,000.
> For the sake of argument and clarity, let's remove eight zeros and pretend these numbers are a typical household budget:
> Family income: $24,500.
> Family spending: $35,000.
> New debt on credit card: $10,500.
> Outstanding balance on credit card: $164,000.
> Total budget cuts: $120.
> Another way to look at the debt ceiling: Let's say you come home from work or a day out and find there has been a major sewer backup in your neighborhood, and your home is flooded with sewage all the way to the ceiling.
> What do you do? Raise the ceiling or remove the sewage?
> [*Las Vegas Review-Journal*, 7 January 2013, p. 5B; at: <http://www.reviewjournal.com/opinion/letters/if-you-ran-your-budget-washington>]

References

Aberdein, Andrew. 2013. Fallacy and argumentational vice. In Mohammed and Lewiński 2013.

Arnauld, Antoine, and P. Nicole. 1685. *Logic; or, the Art of Thinking*. Trans. by several hands. London: H. Sawbridge.

Arnauld, Antoine, and P. Nicole. 1965. *La logique ou l'art de penser*. Critical edition by P. Clair and F. Girbal. Paris: Presses Universitaires de France.

Arnauld, Antoine, and P. Nicole. 1996. *Logic or the Art of Thinking*. Trans. J.V. Buroker. Cambridge: Cambridge University Press.

Balling, Robert C., Jr. 1992. *The Heated Debate: Greenhouse Predictions versus Climate Reality*. San Francisco: Pacific Research Institute for Public Policy.

Barker, Stephen F. 1989. Reasoning by analogy in Hume's *Dialogues*. *Informal Logic* 11: 173-84.

Copi, Irving M. 1968. *Introduction to Logic*, 3rd edn. New York: MacMillan.

Copi, Irving M. 1972. *Introduction to Logic*, 4th edn. New York: MacMillan.

Craig, Robert T. 1999. Metadiscourse, theory, and practice. *Research on Language and Social Interaction* 32: 21-29.

Craig, Robert T. 2011. The uses of 'argument' in practical meta-discourse. In *Reasoned Argument and Social Change*, ed. R.C. Rowland, 78-86. Washington, DC: National Communication Association.

Craig, Robert T., and K. Tracy. 2005. The 'issue' in argumentation practice and theory. In van Eemeren and Houtlosser 2005, 11-28.

Dahl, Robert A. 1956. *A Preface to Democratic Theory*. Chicago: University of Chicago Press.

Dahl, Robert A. 1989. *Democracy and Its Critics*. New Haven: Yale University Press.

Davies, Jacqueline M. 2002. In response to: Trudy Govier's 'Collective responsibility and the fallacies of composition and division'. In Hansen et al. 2002.

Doury, Marianne. 2005. The accusation of *amalgame* as a meta-argumentative refutation. In van Eemeren and Houtlosser 2005, 145-161.

Doury, Marianne. 2006. Evaluating analogy: Toward a descriptive approach to argumentative norms. In *Considering Pragma-Dialectics. A Festschrift for Frans H. van Eemeren on the Occasion of his 60th Birthday*, ed. P. Houtlosser and A. van Rees, 35-49. Mahwah (NJ) / London: Lawrence Erlbaum Associates.

Doury, Marianne. 2009. Argument schemes typologies in practice: The case of comparative arguments. In van Eemeren and Garssen 2009, 141-55.

Doury, Marianne. 2013. The virtues of argumentation from an amoral analyst's perspective. *Informal Logic* 33: 486-509.

Dufour, Michel. 2013. Commentary on: Maurice Finocchiaro's 'The fallacy of composition and meta-argumentation'. In Mohammed and Lewiński 2013.

Finocchiaro, Maurice A. 1980. *Galileo and the Art of Reasoning: Rhetorical Foundations of Logic and Scientific Method*. (Boston Studies in the Philosophy of Science, vol. 61.) Dordrecht: Reidel [now Springer].

Finocchiaro, Maurice A. 1981. Fallacies and the evaluation of reasoning. *American Philosophical Quarterly* 18: 13-22. Reprinted in Finocchiaro 2005, 109-27.

Finocchiaro, Maurice A. 1987. Six types of fallaciousness: Toward a realistic theory of logical criticism. *Argumentation* 1: 263-82. Reprinted in Finocchiaro 2005, 128-47.

Finocchiaro, Maurice A. 1999. *Beyond Right and Left: Democratic Elitism in Mosca and Gramsci*. New Haven: Yale University Press.

Finocchiaro, Maurice A. 2005. *Arguments about Arguments: Systematic, Critical, and Historical Essays in Logical Theory*. New York: Cambridge University Press.

Finocchiaro, Maurice A. 2013a. Debts, oligarchies, and holisms: Deconstructing the fallacy of composition. *Informal Logic* 33: 143-74.

Finocchiaro, Maurice A. 2013b. The fallacy of composition and meta-argumentation." In Mohammed and Lewiński 2013.

Finocchiaro, Maurice A. 2013c. *Meta-argumentation: An Approach to Logic and Argumentation Theory*. (Studies in Logic, vol. 42.) London: College Publications.

Finocchiaro, Maurice A. 2014a. Essay-review of J. Woods's *Errors of Reasoning: Naturalizing the Logic of Inference*. *Argumentation* 28: 231-39.

Finocchiaro, Maurice A. 2014b. Review of J. Woods's *Errors of Reasoning: Naturalizing the Logic of Inference*. *Notre Dame Philosophical Reviews*, online journal at: http://ndpr.nd.edu/news/45997-errors-of-reasoning-naturalizing-the-logic-of-inferenc/; posted on February 4, 2014.

Finocchiaro, Maurice A. 2014c. *The Routledge Guidebook to Galileo's Dialogue*. London: Routledge.

Finocchiaro, Maurice A. 2014d. Ubiquity, ambiguity, and metarationality: Searching for the fallacy of composition." In *Proceedings of the Eighth Conference of the International Society for the Study of Argumentation*, ed. A.F. Snoeck Henkemans, B. Garssen, D. Godden, and G. Mitchell, 426-34. Amsterdam: Sic Sat.

Galilei, Galileo. 1997. *Galileo on the World Systems: A New Abridged Translation and Guide*. Trans. and ed. M. A. Finocchiaro. Berkeley: University of California Press.

Goodwin, Jean. 2007. What, in practice, is an argument? In Hansen et al. 2007.

Gough, James E., and M. Daniel. 2009. The fallacy of composition. In Ritola

80

2009a.

Govier, Trudy. 1982. Who says there are no fallacies? *Informal Logic Newsletter*, vol. v, no. i, pp. 2-10.

Govier, Trudy. 1995. Reply to Massey. In Hansen and Pinto 1995, 172-80.

Govier, Trudy. 2002. Collective responsibility and the fallacies of composition and division. In Hansen et al. 2002.

Govier, Trudy. 2007. Duets, cartoons, and tragedies: Struggles with the fallacy of composition. In *Proceedings of the Sixth Conference of the International Society for the Study of Argumentation*, ed. F. H. van Eemeren, J.A. Blair, C.A. Willard, and B. Garssen, 505-11. Amsterdam: Sic Sat.

Govier, Trudy. 2009. Duets, cartoons, and tragedies: Struggles with the fallacy of composition. In van Eemeren and Garssen 2009, 91-104.

Govier, Trudy. 2010. *A Practical Study of Argument*, 7th edn. Belmont: Wadsworth.

Grootendorst, Rob. 1987. Some fallacies about fallacies. In *Argumentation Across the Lines of Discipline: Proceedings of the Conference on Argumentation 1986*, ed. Frans H. van Eemeren, R. Grootendorst, J.A. Blair, and C.A. Willard, 331-42. Dordrecht: Foris Publications.

Haller, Stephen A. 2002. *Apocalypse Soon? Wagering on Warnings of Global Warming*. Montreal: McGill-Queens University Press.

Halverson, William H. 1984. *A Concise Logic*. New York: Random House.

Hamblin, C. L. 1970. *Fallacies*. London: Methuen. Rpt., Newport News: Vale Press, 1986.

Hamilton, Alexander, J. Jay, and J. Madison. 1961. *The Federalist Papers*. Ed. C. Rossiter. New York: Penguin.

Hansen, Hans V. 2002. The straw thing of fallacy theory: The standard definition of 'fallacy'. *Argumentation* 16: 133-55.

Hansen, Hans V., and R.C. Pinto, eds. 1995. *Fallacies: Classical and Contemporary Readings*. University Park: Pennsylvania State University Press.

Hansen, Hans V., C.W. Tindale, J.A. Blair, R.H. Johnson, and D.M. Godden, eds. 2007. *Dissensus and the Search for Common Ground*. Windsor: Ontario Society for the Study of Argumentation. CD-ROM. ISBN 978-0-9683461-5-0.

Hansen, Hans V., C.W. Tindale, J.A. Blair, and R.H. Johnson, and R.C. Pinto, eds. 2002. *Argumentation and Its Applications*. Windsor: Ontario Society for the Study of Argumentation. CD-ROM. ISBN: 0-9683461-2-X.

Hazlitt, Henry. 1979. *Economics in One Lesson*. New Rochelle: Arlington House Publishers. 1st edn., 1946.

Hume, David. 1947. *Dialogues Concerning Natural Religion*. Ed. N. K. Smith. Indianapolis: Bobbs-Merrill. First published in 1779.

Jason, Gary. 1986. Are fallacies common? *Informal Logic* 8: 81-92.

Jones, Todd. 2003. The failure of the best arguments against social reduction (and what that failure doesn't mean. *Southern Journal of Philosophy* 41: 547-81.

Jones, Todd. 2010. *What People Believe when They Say That People Believe: Folk Sociology and the Nature of Group Intentions*. Lanham: Lexington Books.

Kahane, Howard. 1973. *Logic and Philosophy*, 2nd edn. Belmont: Wadsworth.

Krugman, Paul. 2013a. Austerity wrought pain, no gain. *Las Vegas Sun*, January 8, p. 3. At <http://lasvegassun.com/news/2013/jan/08/austerity-wrought-pain-no-gain/#.VHPVyW1c75E.gmail>, consulted on October 21, 2014.

Krugman, Paul. 2013b. The punishment cure. *The New York Times*, 8 December. At <http://www.nytimes.com/2013/12/09/opinion/krugman-the-punishment-cure.html?_r=1>, consulted on October 21, 2014.

Lipset, Seymour M. 1962. Introduction to Michels 1962, 15-39.

Michels, Robert. 1915. *Political Parties: A Sociological Study of the Oligarchical Tendencies of Modern Democracy*. Trans. E. Paul and C. Paul. Glencoe: The Free Press.

Michels, Robert. 1962. *Political Parties: A Sociological Study of the Oligarchical Tendencies of Modern Democracy*. Trans. E. Paul and C. Paul. New York: Collier.

Mill, John S. 1843. *A System of Logic: Ratiocinative and Inductive*. Rpt., London: Spottiswoode, 1961.

Mohammed, Dima, and M. Lewiński, eds. 2013. *Virtues of Argumentation: Proceedings of the 10th International Conference of the Ontario Society for the Study of Argumentation (OSSA), 22-26 May 2013*. Windsor, ON: Ontario Society for the Study of Argumentation. CD ROM, ISBN: 978-0-920233-66-5.

Mosca, Gaetano. 1912. La sociologia del partito politico nella democrazia moderna. *Il pensiero moderno* 1: 310-16. Reprinted in G. Mosca, *Partiti e sindacati nella crisi del regime parlamentare*, 26-36 (Bari: Laterza, 1949).

Mosca, Gaetano. 1939. *The Ruling Class*. Trans. H.D. Kahn. Ed. A. Livingston. New York: McGraw-Hill.

Nelson, Alan. 1999. Keynes. In *Cambridge Dictionary of Philosophy*, 2nd edn., ed. R. Audi, 467-68. New York: Cambridge University Press.

O'Connor, David. 2001. *Routledge Philosophy Guidebook to Hume on Religion*. London: Routledge.

Pole, Nelson. 1981. Part/whole fallacies. *Informal Logic Newsletter*, vol. 3, no. 3, June, pp. 11-13.

Ritola, Juho, ed. 2009a. *Argument Cultures: Proceedings of the 8th Biennial Conference of the Ontario Society for the Study of Argumentation (OSSA,*

2009). Windsor, ON: Ontario Society for the Study of Argumentation. CD-ROM, ISBN 978-0-920233-51-1.

Ritola, Juho. 2009b. Commentary on James E. Gough and Mano Daniel's 'The fallacy of composition'. In Ritola 2009a.

Salmon, Wesley C. 1963. *Logic*. Englewood Cliffs, NJ: Prentice-Hall.

Salmon, Wesley C. 1984. *Logic*, 3rd edn. Englewood Cliffs: Prentice-Hall.

Samuelson, Paul A. 1955. *Economics: An Introductory Analysis*, 3rd edn. New York: McGraw-Hill.

Samuelson, Paul A., and W.D. Nordhaus. 1989. *Economics*, 13th edn. New York: McGraw-Hill.

Strawson, P. F. 1952. *Introduction to Logical Theory*. London: Methuen.

Tindale, Christopher W. 2007. *Fallacies and Argument Appraisal*. New York: Cambridge University Press.

van Eemeren, Frans H., and B. Garssen, eds. 2009. *Pondering on Problems of Argumentation*. Dordrecht: Springer.

van Eemeren, Frans H., B. Garssen, E. C. W. Krabbe, A. F. Snoeck Henkemans, B. Verheij, and J. H. M. Wagemans. 2014. *Handbook of Argumentation Theory*. Dordrecht: Springer.

van Eemeren, Frans H., and R. Grootendorst. 1992. *Argumentation, Communication, and Fallacies*. Hillsdale: Lawrence Erlbaum Associates.

van Eemeren, Frans H., and R. Grootendorst. 1999. The fallacies of composition and division. In *JFAK: Essays Dedicated to Johan van Benthem on the Occasion of His 50th Birthday*, ed. J. Gerbrandy, M. Marx, M. de Rijke, and Y. Venema. Amsterdam: University of Amsterdam, Institute for Logic, Language, and Computation. At <www.illc.uva.nl/j50/>, consulted on June 18, 2013.

van Eemeren, Frans H., and P. Houtlosser, eds. 2005. *Argumentation in Practice*. Amsterdam: John Benjamins.

Walton, Douglas N. 1989. *Informal Logic*. Cambridge: Cambridge University Press.

Walton, Douglas, C. Reed, and F. Macagno. 2008. *Argumentation Schemes*. Cambridge: Cambridge University Press.

Whately, Richard. 1826. *Elements of Logic*. London: J. Mawman. Rpt., Bologna, Italy: Editrice CLUEB, 1988.

Woods, John. 1988. Buttercups, GNP's, and quarks: Are fallacies theoretical entities? *Informal Logic* 10: 67-76. Reprinted in Woods 2004, 161-70.

Woods, John. 2004. *The Death of Argument: Fallacies in Agent-Based Reasoning*. Dordrecht: Kluwer.

Woods, John. 2012. A history of the fallacies in Western logic. In *Logic: A History of Its Central Concepts*, ed. D.M. Gabbay, F.J. Pelletier, and J. Woods, 513-610. Amsterdam: North-Holland.

Woods, John. 2013. *Errors of Reasoning: Naturalizing the Logic of*

Inference. London: College Publications.

Woods, John, A. Irvine, and D. Walton. 2000. *Argument: Critical Thinking, Logic, and the Fallacies*. Toronto: Prentice-Hall.

Wray, L. Randall. 2006. Teaching the fallacy of composition: The federal budget deficit. At https://edi.bard.edu/research/cfeps-archive/; first consulted on October 19, 2012; later on May 25, 2023.

Chapter 5
Economic Reasoning and Fallacy of Composition, Part I: The Problem

1. Introduction

Let us begin by summarizing some terminological clarifications and stipulations, which I gather from the relevant theoretical literature, and which I have found useful when researching the present topic.[1]

Economic reasoning refers to argumentation by laypersons or professional economists about topics such as money, jobs, budgets, debts, deficits, etc. By fallacy of composition I mean an argument of composition that commits a fallacy. An argument of composition is one which concludes that a whole or group has a certain property because the parts of the whole or members of the group have that property. An argument of composition may also be called a compositional argument. A fallacy is a common type of argument that appears to be correct but is actually incorrect.

It is important to distinguish between arguments of composition and fallacies of composition because not all compositional arguments are incorrect, let alone fallacious; rather, some are correct, indeed deductively valid, although not formally valid. My favorite example is the following: all the parts of this automobile have weight; therefore, the whole automobile has weight.

Note also that I am distinguishing between incorrect arguments and fallacious arguments. In order to be fallacious, namely to be a fallacy, an argument must meet other conditions besides incorrectness: it must *seem* to be correct; it must be an instance of a *general type*; and it must occur *commonly* or *frequently*. Thus, although all fallacious arguments are incorrect, not all incorrect arguments are fallacious.

Furthermore, it should be noted that I have said nothing about the fallacy of division, or arguments of division, or divisional arguments. Such fallacies and arguments are often defined as being just the reverse of the fallacy and argument of composition. Then both composition and division are discussed under the same heading, with the pretext that they both involve reasoning about parts and wholes, or groups and members; thus, composition would be the special case when one reasons from parts or members to wholes or

---

[1] Cf. Bar-Hillel 1964, Broyles 1975, Cole 1965, Davies 2002, van Eemeren and Garssen 2010, van Eemeren and Grootendorst 1999, Finocchiaro (2013a; 2013b; 2014; 2015a; 2015b), Gough and Daniel 2009, Govier (2002; 2007; 2009), Pole 1981, Ritola 2009b, Rowe 1962, Woods 2013, and Woods and Walton 1977.

groups, and division would be the special case when one reasons from wholes or groups to parts or members.

There are several reasons for wanting to distinguish, even by way of introduction, between arguments and fallacies of composition on the one hand and arguments and fallacies of division on the other. One reason is that composition is reminiscent of (although not identical to) universal generalization, which is deductively invalid, whereas division is reminiscent of universal instantiation, which is deductively valid; thus, we may expect composition to be problematic in ways in which division is not. Moreover, as we shall see, arguments and fallacies of composition are common and important in ways that have no counterpart for the case of division.

In short, please note that I will be talking about arguments and fallacies of composition, but not about arguments and fallacies of division (except when necessary). Still less, will I be talking about "the fallacy of composition and division," in the singular.

Finally, it is useful to distinguish between meta-argumentation (which may also be called metalevel argumentation) and ground-level argumentation (which may also be labeled object-level, or target, or ground, or object argumentation). A meta-argument is simply an argument about another argument or about argumentation in general. This distinction is not absolute but contextual or relative or nominalistic, in the sense that it depends on the content or subject matter and not on the structure or form of the reasoning. Thus, all meta-arguments are automatically also arguments, although not all argument are meta-arguments; and a meta-argument can easily become a ground-level argument in a context where it (the meta-argument) becomes in turn the target or object of interpretation, evaluation, and analysis, and of the argumentation supporting these.

2. The Woods-Walton Thesis

Let me now begin my substantive discussion by calling attention to a 1977 article by John Woods and Douglas Walton entitled "Composition and Division." That article is primarily a historical account of the origin of these concepts and an attempt to elaborate a formal analysis of their logical structure. However, there is also a short section dealing with the "importance of these fallacies," and concluding that "from a point of view of significant errors and pitfalls of actual argumentation, composition and division are indeed fallacies of some genuine importance—easy enough to commit and mischievous enough to avoid committing" (Woods and Walton 1977, 117).

A footnote to this passage brings us closer to our present topic. They note that the importance claim just made is "a perspective that non-philosophers can also share" (Woods and Walton 1977, 280 n. 6). And as an illustration, they quote from a 1973 economics textbook by Maurice Archer entitled *Introductory Macroeconomics: A Canadian Analysis*. The passage reads as follows: "The study of economic problems can be fascinating. However, ... there are several pitfalls ... These pitfalls can be listed under the following headings: preconceptions; self-interest; problems of definition; fallacy of composition; and false analogy ... By fallacy of composition we mean the mistake of assuming that what is true for part of a group must necessarily be true for the group as a whole. Thus, whereas an individual farmer may be better off by increasing his production, farmers as a whole may be worse off" (Archer 1973, 45-46).

This easily missed detail is all that Woods and Walton say about this topic in their 1977 article. However, in their textbook entitled *Argument*, whose later editions are co-authored with Andrew Irvine, there is a whole chapter dealing with "Economic Reasoning." This chapter contains a significant elaboration of their 1977 footnote, besides containing discussions of other topics relevant to economic reasoning, such as decision theory, expected utility, minimax principles, Pareto optimality, and the prisoner's dilemma. Let us examine that elaboration dealing with the fallacy of composition in economic reasoning.

In that elaboration, Woods and Walton advance a thesis that has several parts. One claim is that economic reasoning is of "obvious importance ... for personal, domestic, regional, national and international affairs" (Woods and Walton 1982, 203). A second claim is that economic reasoning "is inherently liable to the fallacy of composition" (Woods, Irvine, and Walton 2004, 251). Thirdly, this liability is connected with the fundamental division between microeconomics and macroeconomics and the problematic relationship between the two. The fourth claim is a qualification to the second: this liability does not mean that economics is not a science, or "that economists commit the fallacy of composition more often than other thinkers" (Woods, Irvine, and Walton 2004, 251). On the contrary, fifthly, as I would put it, one could say that professional economists are thinkers who have mastered the art of avoiding the fallacy of composition in economic reasoning, and the art of exposing this fallacy when it is committed by laypersons, or even by other economists.

In advancing this multifaceted thesis, Woods, Irvine, and Walton (2004, 250) explicitly point out that they are echoing claims advanced by economists themselves. In fact, by way of illustration and substantiation, they quote a passage from a 1978 book by economist Leonard Silk entitled *Economics in One Lesson*. The passage reads as follows:

> THE FALLACY OF COMPOSITION: It is often mistakenly assumed that what is true for the parts of a system is true for the system as a whole. If you stand up at a football game, you can see better, but if everybody stands up nobody can see better.

In economics, if you, as an individual, decide to save more out of your income, you will increase your wealth. But if everyone in the nation tries to save more out of income, this may reduce national wealth—by reducing, in succession, sales, the production of goods, the incomes of producers and their employees, and ultimately national savings and investment.

If you, as an individual, are able to raise your prices, this may be a good thing for your business. But if every business does the same, the obvious result will be inflation, a bad thing for the nation.

Balancing the budget so that outgo does not exceed income may be a sound rule for you and your family. But budget balancing does not always make sense for the national government; for the government to do so during a business slump when unemployment is rising would worsen the slump and increase unemployment.

Cutting wage rates may enable one employer to hire more workers; but cutting the wages of all workers may lead to fewer, not more, jobs—since workers would have less to spend on goods.

Thus, when we shift from micro- to macroeconomics, some key concepts change. [Silk 1978, 83-84]

3. Argumentation Scholars on Economic Reasoning and Fallacy of Composition

In this paper I want to pursue this thesis about the susceptibility of economic reasoning to the fallacy of composition. Before I do that, however, I want to briefly explore to what extent this underlying topic has been studied by scholars of informal logic, argumentation theory, and critical thinking.

To begin with, it is disappointing to find that, as far as I can tell, Woods and Walton themselves have not pursued the project, neither jointly nor separately. Of course, I don't need to remind the reader here that they have not been idle, but rather have worked hard in this field and produced, separately, an impressive number and range of works. However, let me simply add an impression I have gotten from Woods's latest book on fallacies, an impression that is something of a constructive suggestion.

I am referring to the book published by Woods in 2013, entitled *Errors of Reasoning: Naturalizing the Logic of Inference*. A key strand of this book concerns the so-called "gang of eighteen" fallacies, namely affirming the consequent, denying the antecedent, hasty generalization, biased statistics, gambler's fallacy, *post hoc ergo propter hoc*, faulty analogy, *ad baculum, ad hominem, ad populum, ad verecundiam, ad ignorantiam, ad misericordiam*, begging the question and circularity, many questions, equivocation, composition and division, and straw man. Woods examines them one by one, and argues that each fails to satisfy one or more of the necessary conditions of being a fallacy. He does this for at least thirteen of them, suggesting that the same will apply to the others. The fallacy of composition happens to be one of the few which are not explicitly examined for this purpose. Now, my conjecture is that this non-examination of the fallacy of composition is no accident, and perhaps it is unlike the others and special in some way. This is what I am taking here as a constructive encouragement to pursue the present project.

Let us now look at other potentially relevant works in the scholarly literature. For this purpose, I have consulted a large number of works, and in each case I have tried to determine five things. The main question was whether or not a given work contains some discussion or even an awareness of the fallacy of composition in economic reasoning. To contextualize this question to some extent, I also checked whether or not each work discussed the fallacy of composition *per se* and economic reasoning *per se*. Two other related questions were whether or not the given work discusses the fallacy of division, and whether or not it could be regarded to have an orientation that focuses seriously on actual argumentation. It will be useful to discuss the results separately for the cases of textbooks and for scholarly books and articles.

Of the thirty-one textbooks examined, none, other than the three editions of the textbook by Woods and Walton, discuss the fallacy of composition in economics. This is so despite the fact that four out of the other textbooks do cover economic reasoning, and ten mention the fallacy of composition; that is, these two subsets of four and ten are disjoint. Even greater are the numbers of textbooks that mention the fallacy of division (eleven) and that have some focus on actual argumentation (sixteen). These results are presented in tabular form in Table I.

The results for scholarly works are similar. To be specific, out of twenty-four works examined, the focus on actual argumentation is relatively high (twelve works), but the inclusion of economic reasoning is less so (only five works). A high proportion (seventeen) do mention the fallacy of composition, and yet only four connect it to economic reasoning. These are the 1977 article by Woods and Walton, the essay by Trudy Govier stemming from her 2006 keynote address at ISSA, a paper by James Gough and Mano Daniel presented at the 2008 OSSA conference, and Ritola's commentary on that paper; but even these four works discuss the issue in an incidental or secondary manner. Table II summarizes these results.

4. Pursuing the Project

Thus, it seems that the pioneering effort of Woods and Walton has been largely ignored. I find such a neglect unfortunate, but rather than letting such a situation depress me, I want to derive some extra motivation to pursue the problem further. For I am convinced that the topic is an extremely important one, that is, the topic of the susceptibility of economic reasoning to the fallacy of composition. This conviction is based, not on the writings of philosophers and argumentation scholars (as we have just seen), but on the writings of economists, who constantly harp on this fallacy. In fact, this situation creates an opportunity that is simply too promising to be missed.

That is, the project of pursuing a further study of the fallacy of composition in economics fits very well with the approach to argumentation studies which I have followed for a long time. Let me explain. This project exemplifies an empirical historical approach to argumentation theory which I have previously practiced to good effect many times (cf. Finocchiaro 2005). Moreover, it instantiates an approach that studies meta-argumentation (arguments about arguments) and has been similarly successful in the past (cf. Finocchiaro 2013b). Specifically, it studies the fallacy of composition by focusing on actual meta-arguments claiming that some ground-level argument commits this fallacy. Finally, this connects with economic reasoning in various ways: insofar as professional economists frequently claim that common people tend to commit this fallacy when thinking about topics like debts and deficits, and that a knowledge of economic science can free them from such pitfalls; and insofar as in controversial contexts, economists sometimes accuse one another of committing the fallacy of composition.

5. Economists on the Fallacy of Composition

We have seen above that, as reported by Woods and Walton, economists Archer and Silk are keen to point out the susceptibility of economic reasoning to the fallacy of composition. But they are not the only such economists, by any means. They are advancing a claim that is widely shared among economists, and indeed they are probably echoing the views of the distinguished and famous economist Paul Samuelson, Nobel laureate in economics in 1970.

5.1 Pedagogical Contexts

In fact, the concern expressed by Archer and Silk is found in a textbook by Samuelson, which was the most successful and popular economics textbook of the twentieth century. The first edition of Samuelson's textbook was published in 1948, and there were many other editions, the latest being the nineteenth, published in 2010, and co-authored with his former student and himself distinguished economist William Nordhaus.

For example, in the third edition, Samuelson (1955, 9) has an introductory chapter in which one of several sections is entitled "the whole and the part: the 'fallacy of composition'." In it, he starts by giving seven examples of paradoxical-sounding statements that are nevertheless true, like those later echoed by Archer and Silk. Samuelson then claims that these statements can be easily and clearly shown to be true, as he actually does at various points in the book, when the various particular topics come up for detailed discussion. And then comes the connection with the present topic: "many of the above paradoxes hinge upon one single confusion or fallacy, called by logicians the 'fallacy of composition'. In books on logic, this is defined as follows: '*A fallacy in which what is true of a part is, on that account alone, alleged to be also true of the whole*' " (Samuelson 1955, 10). After this preliminary discussion in the introductory chapter, later chapters discuss in detail about a dozen examples of fallacies of composition, at various points when the substantive topics become relevant. Especially incisive are the discussions of individual banks vs. the banking system, private debt vs. public debt, and the connection between commodity prices and land rents (Samuelson 1955, 273, 350-52, 504-505).

Another pedagogical discussion of the fallacy of composition is found in an economics textbook available on the internet from an organization called "Study.com." Entitled *Introduction to Macroeconomics*, the book has sixteen chapters, each subdivided into a number of sections, for a total of 164 sections. The third chapter, dealing with "Demand, Supply and Market Equilibrium," has twelve sections, the last one of which is on "The Fallacy of Composition in Economics: Definition and Examples."[2]

Its definition is a typical one: "The fallacy of composition arises when an individual assumes something is true of the whole just because it is true of some part of the whole." However, its introductory example is somewhat more interesting: "Have you ever been at a sporting, musical, or community event and thought to yourself, 'If we leave a few minutes early, we can beat all the traffic?' You might discover that everyone else was thinking the same thing, and it still ends up taking a long time to get out of the parking lot. You'll only manage to beat traffic when just a few people are thinking that way, but not when everyone at the event has the same idea." Such an example is also mentioned by economist Paul Krugman (2009, 35-36), to illustrate a similar point, although in that context he does not use the term fallacy of composition.

Moreover, this internet textbook advances a helpful explanation of the occurrence of this economic fallacy: "Why does this fallacy exist, and why do we think this way sometimes? The answer is that we usually reason and draw conclusions from our own situation and individual experiences. It is easiest to examine our situation, and then reason that the same actions would have the same results for society and the economy as a whole. Although this

---

[2] http://study.com/academy/lesson/the-fallacy-of-composition-in-economics-definition-examples.html, consulted on March 1, 2016.

may be true in some circumstances, it is not always. Sometimes, it may simply be reasoning that results from not having all the necessary facts and information. You may only know what you have experienced yourself." And again, this explanation is reminiscent of a similar thesis advanced by the famous economist Henry Hazlitt, in a book entitled *Economics in One Lesson*, but without the fallacy-of-composition terminology.[3]

Finally, a third pedagogically noteworthy discussion is an essay entitled "Teaching the Fallacy of Composition: The Federal Budget Deficit," authored by L. Randall Wray, professor of economics at the University of Missouri, Kansas City, and published online by the Center for Full Employment and Price Stability at the same university. This discussion is significant because it focuses on the issue of deficits, which is probably the most urgent and controversial economic problem in the world today.

Wray (2006, 1) begins with the definition that "one of the most important concepts to be taught in economics is the notion of the fallacy of composition: what might be true for individuals is probably not true for society as a whole." After giving some relatively simple examples, he moves "on to a more important fallacy of composition. We hear politicians and the media arguing that the current federal budget deficit is unsustainable. I have heard numerous politicians refer to their own household situation: if my household continually spent more than its income year after year, it would go bankrupt. Hence, the federal government is on a path to insolvency, and by implication, the budget deficit is bankrupting the nation" (Wray 2006, 4). Then Wray (2006, 6) goes on to argue in detail why this is a "fallacy of composition. It ignores the impact that the budget deficit has on other sectors of the economy."

5.2 Professional Technicalities

Let us now move from the pedagogical context of textbooks to the research context of articles in professional journals. An instructive example is provided by a 1992 article entitled "A Fallacy of Composition," published by an economist named Ricardo Caballero in the *American Economic Review*, the official journal of the American Economic Association.

Substantively speaking, the article discusses the relationship between microeconomics and macroeconomics with regard to the pricing of commodities. The main question is whether there exists an asymmetry between the increase and the decrease of prices, with upward movements being much more common than downward movements.

The article begins by quoting the definition of the fallacy of composition given by Samuelson, which I myself quoted above. Then Caballero (1992, 1279) explicitly tells us that "in this paper I attempt to isolate the mechanism

---

[3] Hazlitt 1979, 17; cf. Finocchiaro 2013a, 163-66.

underlying the course of several *fallacies of composition*." The main one of these fallacies is described with these words: "the basic insight developed in this paper shows that asymmetric policies at the firm level do not necessarily imply asymmetries in upward and downward adjustments of the aggregate price level" (Caballero 1992, 1279). In other words, it is fallacious to argue that just because individual firms have a strong tendency to raise prices but not to lower them, in the economy as a whole there is the same (level of) tendency for prices to increase but not to decrease.

The reason for the incorrectness of such inferences involves technical details in the mathematics of probability theory. In other words, the premises in Caballero's own meta-argument are technical, mathematical, and probabilistic. Nevertheless, his own qualitative summaries give us a glimpse of the key problem. In the introductory section, he tells us that "I argue that the essence of these fallacies relies on the fact that direct microeconomic arguments do not consider the strong restrictions that probability theory puts on the joint behavior of many units that are less than fully synchronized" (Caballero 1992, 1279). And in the concluding section, after some qualifications to the effect that he is not saying that microeconomics is irrelevant to macroeconomics, he clarifies that "the paper does say, however, that *direct application of microeconomic explanations to aggregate data can be seriously misleading, since they typically do not consider the natural probability forces that tend to undo such explanations*" (Caballero 1992, 1292).

Let us now examine a more recent but less technical article, published in 2002 in a journal entitled *The World Economy*, by an economist named Jörg Mayer, affiliated with the United Nations Conference on Trade and Development (UNCTAD). The article bears a very ambitious title, namely "The Fallacy of Composition: A Review of the Literature." However, as might be expected from the position of the author and the title of the journal, the substantive topic is international trade and the behavior of various countries in the context of the evolution of the world economy. It may be summarized as follows.

Consider world economic development since World War II. During an initial period, several developing countries (e.g., South Korea, Taiwan, Hong Kong, and Singapore) experienced great economic progress by exporting cheaply manufactured goods to developed countries. On the basis of this experience, many other countries (especially in East and South Asia) started manufacturing and exporting cheap goods to developed countries. The thinking underlying such policies could be claimed to involve the fallacy of composition.

In fact, many of the second-phase exporting countries did not experience the anticipated economic progress comparable to the earlier exporting countries. There were two reasons for this (relative) failure. One was that as the supply of manufactured goods exported by all developing countries increased, their prices tended to decrease. The second reason was that the developed countries importing such goods started instituting protective tariffs against the cheap imports.

These reasons help us understand why it was wrong (fallacious?) to argue that what had happened to some developing countries, and what could happen to any one particular country, could happen to all.

However, the situation was dynamic and more complicated. In fact, other developments started taking place. One was that among developing countries, some (especially those with a longer history of exports) started focusing on products of higher quality, requiring greater labor skills, more technology, and more capital investment. Such products did not suffer from the competition of those produced by the second wave of exporting developing countries. That is, a division of labor arose among developing countries between two main subgroups, one at a relatively higher stage of economic development, the other at a relatively lower stage.

The second dynamic complication was that developed countries started undergoing an additional level of development, to counteract the competition experienced by their own industries and emanating from the cheap imports. The developed countries started moving more and more away from manufacturing and toward services, and eventually toward computerization and information processing.

Where does this leave the compositional problem in international trade? It seems that compositional arguments about international trade provide good examples of the fallacy of composition. However, the considerations that generate this fallaciousness in any particular case are subject to change, in part because of the perception of this fallaciousness. When such changes happen, the risk of committing the fallacy of composition does not completely disappear, but merely affects other aspects of the situation.

To get a flavor of this kind of discussion, the following quotation will have to suffice:

> The fallacy of composition—sometimes also called the 'adding-up problem'—means that what is viable for one small exporter acting in isolation may not be viable for a group of exporters acting at the same time … Bhagwati (1958) first discussed the fallacy of composition in the context of immiserising growth. Since then, at least four distinct versions of the fallacy of composition have been presented in the literature, namely (i) an early version pioneered by Cline (1982) who emphasizes protectionist policies in developed countries—beyond some critical level of import penetration, exports from developing countries will face rapid escalation of protective barriers in developed countries—(ii) a more recent version used by Faini, Clavijo and Senhadji-Semlali (1992) who focus on the elasticity of export demand from a partial equilibrium point of view—the elasticity of export demand for a group of countries is smaller in absolute value

than the corresponding elasticity for an individual country—(iii) a version identified by Havrylyshyn (1990) and first tested by Martin (1993) that highlights the general equilibrium nature of the fallacy of composition ... a further (iv) version of the fallacy of composition argument is whether manufactured exports—both on aggregate and from specific manufacturing sectors—from developing countries have been falling in price compared to those of developed countries. [Mayer 2002, 875-77]

5.3 Public-issue Discussions

Let us now examine some examples of economic reasoning from a different context: that is, policy discussions by columnists aimed at intelligent and thoughtful laypersons. In this regard, the columns of Paul Krugman are very instructive.[4] Krugman is, of course, the recipient of the 2008 Nobel Prize in economics and a columnist for the *New York Times*.

In December 2013, the American Congress was debating whether to extend unemployment benefits; the Democratic Party was in favor, and the Republican Party against. On December 9, Krugman published a column entitled "The Punishment Cure." He advanced several criticisms of the Republicans, one of which was the following:

> the G.O.P. answer to the problem of long-term unemployment is to increase the pain of the long-term unemployed: Cut off their benefits, and they'll go out and find jobs. How, exactly, will they find jobs when there are three times as many job-seekers as job vacancies? ... You might be tempted to argue that more intense competition among workers would lead to lower wages, and that cheap labor would encourage hiring. But that argument involves a fallacy of composition. Cut the wages of some workers relative to those of other workers, and those accepting the wage cuts may gain a competitive edge. Cut everyone's wages, however, and nobody gains an edge. All that happens is a general fall in income — which, among other things, increases the burden of household debt, and is therefore a net negative for overall employment. [Krugman 2013b]

Needless to say, such fallacy charges require analysis and evaluation, in the sense that we want to know exactly what the argument being criticized is, what the meta-argument being advanced is, and whether the latter is correct. However, for the moment I cannot pursue such analysis and evaluation. Instead I want to present some more empirical historical material.

Now, it turns out that, on at least one occasion, Krugman himself has been charged with committing a fallacy of composition. This fallacious reasoning allegedly happened in a *New York Times* blog entitled "Small Is Beautiful," posted on February 25, 2011. The substantive topic was the connection between the stimulus spending which the American government

---

[4] Besides the works explicitly cited below, other relevant writings are Krugman (2012a; 2012b; 2013a; 2015).

enacted in 2009-2010 and unemployment, and, more specifically, the existence and national effects of cross-state differences. Krugman was commenting on the views of several other economists, and was advancing other arguments besides the one to be quoted presently. The problematic passage is the following: "more federal spending in a given state or county creates more jobs. And the burden of proof should always have been on the stimulus critics to explain why this doesn't mean that stimulus spending creates jobs at the national level too" (Krugman 2011).

In a blog entitled "Small Is Irrelevant (in Macro)," posted the same day (February 25), economist Scott Sumner criticized this argument as follows: "it's a near perfect example of the fallacy of composition. Every single anti-stimulus model would predict exactly the same finding at the micro level. If the federal government builds a billion dollar military base in Fargo, North Dakota, I think all economists agree that the number of jobs increases—in Fargo, North Dakota. Does the number of jobs increase at the national level? Very possibly yes, but nothing in … [Krugman's argument] addresses that question" (Sumner 2011). And, connecting this issue to the distinction between microeconomics and macroeconomics, Sumner (2011) added that "micro studies can't tell us whether fiscal stimulus works. Micro studies can't tell us whether monetary stimulus works … Micro studies can't tell us anything about macro. That's why macro is a different field."

Let us now look at a more complicated case, more complicated not because of intrinsic complexities, but because the discussion includes some analysis and evaluation. That is, in this case, the material I found for our own reflection itself contains the sort of thing which earlier I postponed to a subsequent stage of this investigation.

This case involves a fallacy charge made by Krugman in a blog posted on September 3, 2010, entitled "Paradoxes of Deleveraging and Releveraging." The substantive topic was, again, the fiscal stimulus of 2009-2010, but now in the context of a general economic problem, namely the new debt generated by such spending. Krugman claimed the following, where I have inserted in brackets some labels:

> Whenever the issue of fiscal stimulus comes up, you can count on someone chiming in to say, "Only a moron could believe that the answer to a problem created by too much debt is to create even more debt." It sounds plausible—but it misses the key point: [a] there's a fallacy of composition here. [b] When everyone tries to pay off debt at the same time, the result is contraction and deflation, which ends up making the debt problem worse even if nominal debt falls. On the other hand, [c] a strong fiscal stimulus, by expanding the economy and creating moderate inflation, can actually help resolve debt problems. [Krugman 2010]

Then proposition [b] is supported with the historical evidence that [d] "from 1929 to 1933, everyone was trying to pay down debt — and the debt/GDP ratio skyrocketed thanks to contraction and deflation" (Krugman 2010). And proposition [c] is supported with the historical evidence that [e] "during and immediately after WWII, there was massive borrowing — but GDP grew faster than debt, and the debt burden ended up falling" (Krugman 2010). The whole argument is: [a] because [b] and [c]; [b] because [d]; and [c] because [e].

This argument was criticized by an economist named William Anderson, in a blog dated September 5, 2010, entitled "Fallacy of Composition, or a Non Sequitur?" Anderson argues that Krugman's own argument is a non sequitur partly because during World War II the economic growth (the growth of the GDP) was not caused by the government's massive borrowing; here, in [e], Krugman is presumably confusing correlation with causation. Moreover, Anderson claims that such massive borrowing was not accompanied by economic prosperity. In short, presumably, Krugman's conclusion [a] does not follow from his own evidence.[5]

Finally, it will be useful to present another example, not merely or primarily to increase *quantitatively* the amount of evidence presented here, but also and primarily to add *variety* to such evidence. Here the desirable variety is the diversity stemming from the distinction between the right (or conservative, or traditionalist) and left (or liberal, or progressive) wings of the political and ideological spectrum. With all due caution and nuances in distinguishing between these two wings,[6] it is not just liberal economists such as Krugman (cf. Krugman 2007) who have a penchant for charging and exposing the fallacy of composition. In fact, even in the evidence presented above we have seen that sometimes such charges are advanced by Krugman's critics, who are presumably conservatives, at least approximately. However, charges of fallacy of composition are also advanced by right-wingers in discussions of public issues where they are not merely responding to other critics, but rather analyzing some policy problem or responding to policy proposals by politicians.

In January 2015, the President of the United States, Barack Obama, made a proposal regarding higher education at community colleges. The plan was

---

[5] This exchange elicited a number of blog responses, including one by "Anonymous" dated April 4, 2011, which is of some interest in the present context: "Really? You are so good that you are at F[rostburg] State [University, Maryland] trying to challenge a Nobel prize winning economist, a professor at Princeton and London School — with an MIT PhD. Sorry, nice try but you aren't in the same league. And it's obvious" (http://krugman-in-wonderland.blogspot.com/2010/09/fallacy-of-composition-or-non-sequitur.html). In the present context, I would ask: is this an *ad hominem* fallacy, a plausible inductive argument, or a weak inductive argument?
[6] For a critical analysis, see Finocchiaro 1999, especially pp. 201-222.

to enable everyone to attend for two years free of tuition charges, subject only to some requirements about good grades and progress toward graduation. This proposal was later also advocated by Bernie Sanders, during his 2015-2016 campaign for nomination by the Democratic Party to be its candidate in the presidential election of November 2016. Needless to say, the proposal has been applauded by some, but criticized by others.

One striking criticism was made soon after President Obama's original proposal. It is contained in an opinion piece by economists William A. Kelly and Elizabeth Sawyer Kelly, published in *The Wall Street Journal*, on February 4, 2015. They argued that the thinking underlying the proposal commits the fallacy of composition. In their own words:

> The spirit behind President Obama's recent proposal to make community college free is understandable, but he has fallen victim to the fallacy of composition. He has made the mistake of believing that if one person benefits from an action, then everyone else who takes the same action will also benefit. Economics teaches us otherwise.
>
> Although getting an associate degree or some college education at a community college may benefit any one person, in the aggregate a policy that increases the supply of people with associate degrees can backfire unless it has been designed to fill an existing excess demand. Otherwise such a policy will merely exacerbate an existing excess supply of labor with that level of educational attainment.
>
> That looks likely to happen here. The Bureau of Labor Statistics has projected the percentage of new job openings (actual new jobs plus turnover of existing jobs) that will require "an associate degree or some college" through the year 2022. The BLS answer is that 17% of these new job openings will require this level of degree. Meanwhile, data from the Census Bureau tell us what percent of the existing workforce has "an associate degree or some college," and their figure is 28% of the workforce.
>
> This discrepancy means that getting "an associate degree or some college" is like buying a lottery ticket for a job that requires this level of education, with a 39% chance of losing the lottery: $[(28\%-17\%)/28\%] (100\%) = 39\%$. A plainer way to express this idea is that we already have a large oversupply of people in the workforce with "an associate degree or some college." [Kelly and Kelly 2015]

In short, they recommend, "let's not spend $60 billion to demonstrate the folly of a policy based on the fallacy of composition" (Kelly and Kelly 2015).

6. Questions

This survey seems to confirm the susceptibility of economic reasoning to the fallacy of composition—perhaps with a vengeance. That is, it is not just laypersons who have such a tendency, but also economists and businessmen involved in pricing policies and in international trade, as well as distinguished economists of the caliber of Paul Krugman. However, other questions need to be asked and answered.

One question is to determine what exactly is the concept of fallacy of composition which such economic discussions are operating with. Despite Samuelson's reference to logicians and logic textbooks, it may or may not be the case that their concept coincides with the one in such economic discussions.

Another question is, exactly what is the structure of such critical meta-arguments. Consider the following sequence of increasing complexity:

(M1) *Meta-argument 1:*
  (M1a) argument A is an argument of composition, because ...;
  (M1b) therefore, argument A is a fallacy of composition.
(M2) *Meta-argument 2:*
  (M2a) argument A is an argument of composition because ...;
  (M2b) argument A is incorrect, because ...;
  (M2c) therefore, argument A is a fallacy of composition.
(M3) *Meta-argument 3:*
  (M3a) argument A is an argument of composition because ...;
  (M3b) argument A is incorrect, because ...;
  (M3c) argument A appears to be correct, because ...;
  (M3d) therefore, argument A is a fallacy of composition.
(M4) *Meta-argument 4:*
  (M4a) argument A is an argument of composition because ...;
  (M4b) argument A is incorrect, because ...;
  (M4c) argument A appears to be correct, because ...;
  (M4d) argument A is a common or frequent type, as shown by ...;
  (M4e) therefore, argument A is a fallacy of composition.

Although it might be excessively pedantic to require critiques like (M4), clearly (M1) is inadequate. Indeed (M1) is itself incorrect, since, as mentioned in the Introduction, some compositional arguments are valid. Moreover, (M1) may be a fallacy; that would depend, in part, on how common (M1) is in these discussions.

Similar remarks apply to (M2). However, one of its issues is intrinsically important, independently of its connection with other issues; that is, it is important to determine whether or not the ground-level compositional argument is correct, independently of its fallaciousness. In this regard, a plausible-sounding general principle proposes that arguments from the properties of parts or members to the properties of wholes or aggregates are correct if and only if the properties are absolute and structure-independent.[7] Unfortunately, as far as I can tell, in economic reasoning the properties in question are usually relative and structure dependent. Thus, although I don't think it would be proper to abandon the search for such general principles of evaluation, it seems they have to be grounded on the study of real, realistic, and relevant examples like the ones presented here.

These are some of the many questions that need to be asked and answered about the problem of the susceptibility of economic reasoning to the fallacy of composition.[8]

---

[7] van Eemeren and Grootendorst (1992, 174-83; 1999); van Eemeren and Garssen 2010.

[8] A much shorter version of this paper was presented at the conference sponsored by the Ontario Society for the Study of Argumentation (OSSA), University of Windsor, Ontario, Canada, May 18-21, 2016.

Table I: Textbooks on Fallacy of Composition in Economics

Work	Fall. Comp.	Fall. Div.	Actual Argtn.	Econ. Reas.	Fall. Comp. Econ.
Angell 1964	No	Yes	Yes	No	No
Beardsley 1966	No	No	No	No	No
Beardsley 1967	No	No	Yes	Yes	No
Cederblom & Paulsen 2012	No	No	No	No	No
Chaffee 2009	No	No	Yes	No	No
Cohen & Nagel 1934	Yes	Yes	Yes	No	No
Copi, IL, 1986	No	No	Yes	No	No
Copi & Cohen 1994, 9th edn	Yes	Yes	No	No	No
Damer 1980	Yes	Yes	No	No	No
Epstein 2002	No	No	No	No	No
Fisher 1988	No	No	Yes	Yes	No
Fogelin 1982	No	No	Yes	No	No
Freeman 1988	No	No	No	No	No
Govier 2010	Yes	Yes	No	No	No
Groarke & Tindale 2008	No	No	Yes	No	No
Hintikka & Bachman 1991	No	No	No	No	No
Hurley 2003	Yes	Yes	No	No	No
Johnson & Blair 2006	No	No	Yes	No	No
Kahane 1971	No	No	Yes	No	No
Kahane 1973	Yes	Yes	No	No	No
Kelley 1990	No	No	No	No	No
Moore & Parker 1998	Yes	Yes	Yes	No	No
Salmon 2002	Yes	Yes	No	No	No
Scriven 1976	No	No	Yes	Yes	No
Thomas 1981	No	No	Yes	No	No
Toulmin Rieke & Janik 1979	Yes	Yes	Yes	Yes	No
Vaughn 2008	Yes	Yes	Yes	No	No
Woods Irvine Walton 2000	Yes	Yes	Yes	Yes	Yes
Woods Irvine Walton 2004	Yes	Yes	Yes	Yes	Yes
Woods & Walton 1982	Yes	Yes	Yes	Yes	Yes
Wright 2001	No	No	Yes	No	No

Table II: Scholarship on Fallacy of Composition in Economics

Work	Fall. Comp.	Fall. Div.	Actual Argtn.	Econ. Reas.	Fall. Comp. Econ.
Bar-Hillel 1964	Yes	No	No	No	No
Blair 2012	No	No	Yes	No	No
Broyles 1975	Yes	Yes	No	No	No
Cole 1965	Yes	No	No	No	No
Davies 2002	Yes	Yes	Yes	No	No
Eemeren & Garssen 2010	Yes	Yes	No	No	No
Eemeren&Grootendorst 1999	Yes	Yes	No	No	No
Eemeren&Grootendorst 2004	Yes	Yes	No	No	No
Eemeren et al 2014	Yes	Yes	No	No	No
Gough & Daniel 2009	Yes	No	Yes	Yes	Yes
Govier 2002	Yes	Yes	Yes	No	No
Govier 2007/2009	Yes	No	Yes	Yes	Yes
Hamblin 1970	Yes	Yes	No	No	No
Johnson 2000	No	No	No	No	No
Paul 1990	No	No	Yes	Yes	No
Perelman & O-T 1958	Yes	Yes	Yes	No	No
Pole 1981	Yes	Yes	Yes	Yes	No
Ritola 2009b	Yes	No	Yes	Yes	Yes
Rowe 1962	Yes	Yes	No	No	No
Toulmin 1958	No	No	No	No	No
Weinstein 2013	No	No	Yes	No	No
Wohlrapp 2014	No	No	Yes	No	No
Woods 2013	No	No	No	No	No
Woods & Walton 1977	Yes	Yes	(Yes)	(Yes)	Yes

References

Anderson, William L. 2010. Fallacy of composition, or a non sequitur? At http://krugman-in-wonderland.blogspot.com/2010/09/fallacy-of-composition-or-non-sequitur.html; consulted on December 14, 2015.

Angell, Richard B. 1964. *Reasoning and Logic*. New York: Appleton.

Archer, Maurice. 1973. *Introductory Macroeconomics: A Canadian Analysis*. Toronto: Macmillan.

Bar-Hillel, Yehoshua. 1964. More on the fallacy of composition. *Mind* 73: 125-26.

Beardsley, Monroe C. 1966. *Thinking Straight: Principles of Reasoning for Readers and Writers*, 3rd edn. Englewood Cliffs, NJ: Prentice-Hall.

Beardsley, Monroe C., ed. 1967. *Modes of Argument*. Indianapolis: Bobbs-Merrill.

Bhagwati, Jagdish. 1958. Immiserizing growth: A geometrical note. *Review of Economic Studies* 25: 201-205.

Blair, J. Anthony. 2012. *Groundwork in the Theory of Argumentation*. Dordrecht: Springer.

Broyles, James E. 1975. The fallacies of composition and division. *Philosophy and Rhetoric* 8: 108-113.

Caballero, Ricardo J. 1992. A fallacy of composition. *American Economic Review* 82: 1279-92.

Cederblom, Jerry, and D. W. Paulsen. 2012. *Critical Reasoning*, 7th edn. Boston: Wadsworth, Cengage Learning.

Chaffee, John. 2009. *Thinking Critically*, 9th edn. Boston: Houghton Mifflin.

Cline, William R. 1982. Can the East Asian model of development be generalized? *World Development* 10: 81-90.

Cohen, Morris R., and E. Nagel. 1934. *An Introduction to Logic and Scientific Method*. New York: Harcourt, Brace and Company.

Cole, Richard. 1965. A note on informal fallacies. *Mind* 74: 432-33.

Copi, Irving M. 1986. *Informal Logic*. New York: MacMillan.

Copi, Irving M., and C. Cohen. 1994. *Introduction to Logic*, 9th edn. New York: MacMillan.

Damer, T. Edward. 1980. *Attacking Faulty Reasoning*. Belmont, CA: Wadsworth.

Davies, Jacqueline M. 2002. In response to: Trudy Govier's 'Collective responsibility and the fallacies of composition and division'. In Hansen et al. 2002.

Epstein, Richard L. 2002. *Critical Thinking*, 2nd edn. Belmont, CA: Wadsworth.

Faini, Riccardo, F. Clavijo, and A. Senhadji-Semlali. 1992. The fallacy of composition argument: Is it relevant for LDCs' manufactures exports? *European Economic Review* 36: 865-82.

Finocchiaro, Maurice A. 1999. *Beyond Right and Left: Democratic Elitism in Mosca and Gramsci*. New Haven: Yale University Press.

Finocchiaro, Maurice A. 2005. *Arguments about Arguments: Systematic, Critical, and Historical Essays in Logical Theory*. New York: Cambridge University Press.

Finocchiaro, Maurice A. 2013a. Debts, oligarchies, and holisms: Deconstructing the fallacy of composition. *Informal Logic* 33: 143-74.

Finocchiaro, Maurice A. 2013b. *Meta-argumentation: An Approach to Logic and Argumentation Theory*. London: College Publications.

Finocchiaro, Maurice A. 2014. Essay-review of J. Woods's *Errors of reasoning: Naturalizing the logic of inference*. *Argumentation* 28: 231-39.

Finocchiaro, Maurice A. 2015a. The fallacy of composition: Guiding concepts, historical cases, and research problems. *Journal of Applied Logic*, vol. 13, issue 2, part B, June 2015, pp. 24–43.

Finocchiaro, Maurice A. 2015b. Ubiquity, ambiguity, and metarationality: Searching for the fallacy of composition. In *Reflections on Theoretical Issues in Argumentation Theory*, ed. Frans H. van Eemeren and B. Garssen, 131-41. Dordrecht: Springer.

Fisher, Alec. 1988. *The Logic of Real Arguments*. Cambridge: Cambridge University Press.

Fogelin, Robert J. 1982. *Understanding Arguments: An Introduction to Informal Logic*, 2nd edn. New York: Harcourt Brace Jovanovich.

Freeman, James B. 1988. *Thinking Logically*. Englewood Cliffs, NJ: Prentice-Hall.

Gough, James E., and M. Daniel. 2009. The fallacy of composition. In Ritola 2009a.

Govier, Trudy. 2002. Collective responsibility and the fallacies of composition and division. In Hansen et al. 2002.

Govier, Trudy. 2007. Duets, cartoons, and tragedies: Struggles with the fallacy of composition. In *Proceedings of the Sixth Conference of the International Society for the Study of Argumentation*, ed. Frans H. van Eemeren, J.A. Blair, C.A. Willard, and B. Garssen, 505-11. Amsterdam: Sic Sat.

Govier, Trudy. 2009. Duets, cartoons, and tragedies: Struggles with the fallacy of composition. In *Pondering on Problems of Argumentation*, ed. Frans H. van Eemeren and B. Garssen, 91-104. Dordrecht: Springer.

Govier, Trudy. 2010. *A Practical Study of Arguments*, 7th edn. Belmont, CA: Wadsworth.

Groarke, Leo A., and C.W. Tindale. 2008. *Good Reasoning Matters! A Constructive Approach to Critical Thinking*. Don Mills, Ontario: Oxford University Press.

Hamblin, C. L. 1970. *Fallacies*. London: Methuen. Rpt., Newport News, VA:

104

Vale Press, 1986.

Hansen, Hans V., C.W. Tindale, J.A. Blair, and R.H. Johnson, and R.C. Pinto, eds. 2002. *Argumentation and Its Applications.* Windsor: Ontario Society for the Study of Argumentation. CD-ROM. ISBN: 0-9683461-2-X.

Havrylyshyn, O. 1990. Penetrating the fallacy of export composition. In *North-South Trade in Manufactures,* ed. Hans W. Singer, N. Hatti, and T. Tandon. New Delhi: Indus Publishing Co.

Hazlitt, Henry. 1979. *Economics in One Lesson.* New Rochelle: Arlington House Publishers. 1st edn., 1946.

Hintikka, Jaakko, and J. Bachman. 1991. *What If ...? Toward Excellence in Reasoning.* Mountain View, CA: Mayfield Publishing Co.

Hurley, Patrick J. 2003. *A Concise Introduction to Logic,* 8th edn. Belmont, CA: Wadsworth.

Johnson, Ralph H. 2000. *Manifest Rationality: A Pragmatic Theory of Argument.* Mahwah, NJ: Lawrence Erlbaum Associates.

Johnson, Ralph H., and J. A. Blair. 2006. *Logical Self-Defense.* New York: International Debate Education Association.

Kahane, Howard. 1971. *Logic and Contemporary Rhetoric.* Belmont, CA: Wadsworth.

Kahane, Howard. 1973. *Logic and Philosophy,* 2nd edn. Belmont, CA: Wadsworth.

Kelley, David. 1990. *The Art of Reasoning,* expanded edn. (with symbolic logic). New York: Norton.

Kelly, Jr., William A., and Elizabeth S. Kelly. 2015. Obama and the 'fallacy of composition'. *The Wall Street Journal,* February 4. At http://www.wsj.com/articles/bill-kelly-and-elizabeth-sawyer-kelly-obama-and-the-fallacy-of-composition-1423095533; consulted on March 18, 2015.

Krugman, Paul. 1996. A country is not a company. *Harvard Business Review,* January-February, pp. 40-51.

Krugman, Paul. 2007. *The Conscience of a Liberal.* New York: Norton.

Krugman, Paul. 2009. *A Country Is Not a Company.* Boston: Harvard Business Press. Rpt. of Krugman 1996.

Krugman, Paul. 2010. Paradoxes of deleveraging and releveraging. At http://krugman.blogs.nytimes.com/2010/09/03/paradoxes-of-deleveraging-and-releveraging/; consulted on December 17, 2015.

Krugman, Paul. 2011. Small is beautiful. Posted on February 25, 2011. At http://krugman.blogs.nytimes.com/?s=small+is+beautiful; consulted on December 15, 2015.

Krugman, Paul. 2012a. *End This Depression Now!* New York: Norton.

Krugman, Paul. 2012b. Nobody understands debt. *New York Times,* January 2, p. A21. At http://www.nytimes.com/2012/01/02/opinion/krugman-nobody-understands-debt.html?_r=0; consulted on December 15, 2015.

Krugman, Paul. 2013a. Austerity wrought pain, no gain. *Las Vegas Sun*, January 8, p. 3. At http://lasvegassun.com/news/2013/jan/08/austerity-wrought-pain-no-gain/#.VHPVyW1c75E.gmail.

Krugman, Paul. 2013b. The punishment cure. *The New York Times*, December 9. at http://www.nytimes.com/2013/12/09/opinion/krugman-the-punishment-cure.html?_r=0; consulted on December 15, 2013.

Krugman, Paul. 2015. Boehner ends era of budget blackmail, but madness lives on. *Las Vegas Sun*, October 4, p. 5.

Martin, Will. 1993. The fallacy of composition and developing country exports of manufactures. *The World Economy* 16: 159-72.

Mayer, Jörg. 2002. The fallacy of composition: A review of the literature. *The World Economy* 25: 875-94.

Moore, Brooke N., and R. Parler. 1998. *Critical Thinking*, 5th edn. Mountain View, CA: Mayfield Publishing Co.

Paul, Richard W. 1990. *Critical Thinking*. Ed. A. J. A. Binker. Rohnert Park, CA: Center for Critical Thinking and Moral Critique, Sonoma State University.

Perelman, Chaim., and L. Olbrechts-Tyteca. 1969. *The New Rhetoric: A Treatise on Argumentation*. Tr. J. Wilkinson and P. Weaver. Notre Dame: University of Notre Dame.

Pole, Nelson. 1981. Part/whole fallacies. *Informal Logic Newsletter*, vol. 3, no. 3, June, pp. 11-13.

Ritola, Juho, ed. 2009a. *Argument Cultures: Proceedings of OSSA 09*. Windsor, ON: Ontario Society for the Study of Argumentation. CD-ROM, ISBN 978-0-920233-51-1.

Ritola, Juho. 2009b. Commentary on: James E. Gough and Mano Daniel's 'The Fallacy of Composition'. In Ritola 2009a.

Rowe, William L. 1962. The fallacy of composition. *Mind* 71: 87-92.

Salmon, Merrilee. 2002. *Introduction to Logic and Critical Thinking*, 4th edn. Wadsworth Thomson Learning.

Samuelson, Paul A. 1955. *Economics: An Introductory Analysis*, 3rd edn. New York: McGraw-Hill.

Samuelson, Paul A., and W. D. Nordhaus. 2010. *Economics: An Introductory Analysis*, 19th edn. Boston: Irwin/McGraw-Hill.

Scriven, Michael. 1976. *Reasoning*. New York: McGraw-Hill.

Silk, Leonard. 1978. *Economics in Plain English*. New York: Simon and Schuster.

Sumner, Scott. 2011. Small is irrelevant (in macro). Posted February 25, 2011. At http://www.themoneyillusion.com/?p=9056; consulted on December 15, 2015.

Thomas, Stephen N. 1981. *Practical Reasoning in Natural Language*, 2nd edn. Englewood Cliffs, NJ: Prentice-Hall.

Toulmin, Stephen E. 1958. *The Uses of Argument*. Cambridge: Cambridge

University Press.

Toulmin, Stephen, R. Rieke, and A. Janik. 1979. *Introduction to Reasoning.* New York: MacMillan.

van Eemeren, Frans H., and B. Garssen. 2010. Linguistic criteria for judging composition and division fallacies. In *Perspectives on Language Use and Pragmatics: A Volume in Memory of Sorin Stati*, ed. A. Capone, 35-50. Munich: Lincom Europa.

van Eemeren, Frans H., B. Garssen, E. C. W. Krabbe, A. F. Snoeck Henkemans, B. Verheij, and J. H. M. Wagemans. 2014. *Handbook of Argumentation Theory*. Dordrecht: Springer.

van Eemeren, Frans H., and R. Grootendorst. 1992. *Argumentation, Communication, and Fallacies*. Hillsdale: Lawrence Erlbaum Associates.

van Eemeren, Frans H., and R. Grootendorst. 1999. The fallacies of composition and division. In *JFAK: Essays Dedicated to Johan van Benthem on the Occasion of His 50th Birthday*, ed. J. Gerbrandy, M. Marx, M. de Rijke, and Y. Venema. Amsterdam: University of Amsterdam, Institute for Logic, Language, and Computation. At www.illc.uva.nl/j50/; consulted on June 18, 2013.

van Eemeren, Frans H., and R. Grootendorst. 2004. *A Systematic Theory of Argumentation: The Pragma-dialectical Approach*. Cambridge: Cambridge University Press.

Vaughn, Lewis. 2008. *The Power of Critical Thinking: Effective Reasoning About Ordinary and Extraordinary Claims*. New York: Oxford University Press.

Weinstein, Mark. 2013. *Logic, Truth and Inquiry*. London: College Publications.

Wohlrapp, Harald R. 2014. *The Concept of Argument. A Philosophical Foundation*. Berlin: Springer.

Woods, John. 2013. *Errors of Reasoning: Naturalizing the Logic of Inference*. London: College Publications.

Woods, John, A. Irvine, and D. Walton. 2000. *Argument: Critical Thinking, Logic and the Fallacies*. Toronto: Prentice-Hall.

Woods, John, A. Irvine, and D. Walton. 2004. *Argument: Critical Thinking, Logic and the Fallacies*, 2nd edn. Toronto: Prentice-Hall.

Woods, John, and D. N. Walton. 1977. Composition and division. *Studia Logica* 36: 381-406. Reprinted in Woods and Walton 1989, 93-119, 279-81.

Woods, John, and D. N. Walton. 1982. *Argument: The Logic of Fallacies*. Toronto: McGraw-Hill Ryerson Limited.

Woods, John, and D. N. Walton. 1989. *Fallacies: Selected Papers 1972-1982*. Dordrecht: Foris Publications.

Wray, L. Randall. 2006. Teaching the fallacy of composition: The federal budget deficit. At https://edi.bard.edu/research/cfeps-archive/; first consulted on October 19, 2012; later on May 25, 2023..

Wright, Larry. 2001. *Critical Thinking*. New York: Oxford University Press.

Appendix, by John Woods
Economic Reasoning and Fallacy of Composition,
Part II: Comments on Maurice Finocchiaro's Paper

1. The Empirical Turn in Logic

Maurice Finocchiaro is a pioneering figure in the naturalistic and empirically sensitive approach to real-life reasoning and argument. In taking this turn, he finds himself in the tradition of Dewey, Toulmin and Scriven. It is a turning to which I myself am drawn and one I'm happy to recommend to the rest of us. Another distinctive feature of the Finocchiaran way of dealing with argument is the emphasis placed on the role of meta-argument, and the skill with which Finocchiaro illuminates its uses, as with his meta-argument 4 in section 6 of his paper, about which more in my parting words at the end of this exchange.

Finocchiaro does a masterly job of following his own advice. His review of the empirical record – in the first instance of the attention paid by logic textbooks to the composition fallacy in economic contexts, and in the second of the attention paid to it by economists – is exemplary, and not a little embarrassing to us textbook writers. Especially valuable is the wealth of examples from the economics literature. I regard this as a major improvement on how composition has so far been dealt with by theorists of argument. For anyone who's interested in fallacies or in compositional reasoning in its own right, these surveys are important data-sets, and admonitory ones at that, as we will see. They tell us something important. They help us see how difficult compositionality is to pin down.

2. The Elusiveness of Compositionality

We might say that the Finocchiaro examples are negatively instructive. They are presented for information, and not necessarily with Finocchiaro's own endorsement. We learn, for example, how fatal it would be to confuse the part-whole relation with the property-instantiation relation. If P is a part of a whole W, it has the property Q of being one of W's parts. But being one of W's parts is not itself a part of W. Similarly, if P is a part of W, W bears the property Q* of having P as one of its parts. But Q* is not a part of W, or of P either. Whenever something W is a thing of parts, it will have the property Q′ of having all those parts. But if W had Q′ as a part, parthood would be reflexive on W. This, we may assume, cannot be so. Whatever the logical structure of the P-W relation in fine, we can safely say that it is irreflexive and antisymmetrical. (Transitivity might have a shot, but I wouldn't bet on it.)

Let me now borrow a phrase from Quine and say that in "canonical notation" a composition claim is a statement in the form

CNC: Since all parts P of the whole W have the property Q, W likewise has it.

When *CNC* holds for some P, W and Q, Q is a property of each of W's parts and, on that account, is a property of W too. Q, then, is a *composable* property for those P and that W. It is supported by the P-W relation but is not a part of either of its relata. The question that now presses is "What is it about those P and that W that makes Q composable on W?" It is not an easy question, no doubt in part (no pun) because of the elusiveness of the concept of part.

Consider Finocchiaro's favourite example: Since all parts of the whole car have weight, the car itself has weight. I'm not so sure. At the top end of the 2016 E-series Mercedes, each car has been set up with thirty million lines of code. By any fair measure, they are parts of the car, and by no fair measure do they have weight. In any case, the code lines are certainly covered by the Benz parts warranty. If this is right, the E-series sedan disinstantiates the premiss-set of Finocchiaro's favourite example. Of course, this does nothing to disturb the truth of that conditional, but it does place some pressure on the question of what it takes to be a part of a whole. As I say, compositionality has a mercurial nature, inherited in part from the elusiveness of parthood.

Here is an example of my own. You've just made yourself a cake from your grandmother's favourite recipe. It is a wonderful cake, thanks to the way the recipe regulates its ingredients. When it comes time to serve the cake, you take care to divide it into six equal parts, one piece each for each of the assembled party. No one doubts that your cake was made from things that aren't cake, for example, from some baking powder, which won't work properly unless properly sifted. Is the sifted baking powder part of the cake? Are the servings you've prepared for guests parts of it too? What about the elements of the periodic table? One might start thinking that the parthood is a property that lacks quiddity.

As a related preliminary, we should also note that a divisional argument is *not* the structural converse of its compositional ancestor. In those cases in which it is correct to observe that W has P because all its parts have it, it is frequently not the case that all the parts of W have it because W itself has it. If W is a 2016 E 550 Mercedes, it has a compression ratio of 0.5:1, but hardly any of its parts do, never mind all. Let's note in passing that these same considerations disable the corresponding composition argument. If all parts of the Mercedes cost less than CAN $74,000 then that lesser number can't be the selling price of the car.

These are telling difficulties. The tale they tell is that the compositionality of a conditional depends on properties of the right kind. Hasty generalization is somewhat like this. It is empirically discernible that on those occasions when we generalize from small samples, most of the time we get it right. That would be impossible except for our good record in sussing out generalizable small-sample properties. The same might be true of compositional inferences. But for an adeptness at spotting composable properties, our compositional reasoning would be the disaster that informal logicians mistakenly ascribe to hasty generalization.

Of course, this is not to say that composition mistakes never, or hardly ever, occur. The same is true of hasty generalization errors. What matters in each case are the factors of attractiveness, universality, and higher than normal recidivism rates. I am unable to see in the examples collected by Finocchiaro anything discernible as high levels of fulfilment of these conditions. Besides, when the householder reasons that if high consumer debt loads are bad household economics how could it not also be bad government economics, his failure (if there is one) arises from his not knowing how differently structured national economies are from the way in which household economies work. The mistake lies in the faulty assumption that national economies are analogues of household ones, only much bigger. Thinking so is a mistake, but it is not a mistake of premiss-conclusion reasoning. He may be ignorant, but he needn't be stupid. Mind you, it bears repeating that in advancing these examples from economics Finocchiaro stands mute on the question of their compositional integrity.

Before continuing with economics, here are a few more words about how not to think of composition and division. When composition goes wrong, it has nothing to do with misapplications of the universal generalization law: From $\ulcorner \Phi \delta \urcorner$ to infer $\ulcorner \forall \nu \, \Phi \nu \urcorner$, wherein δ is an arbitrary singular term. It is certainly true that if any individual whatever has Φ, all of them have it too. Note well, however, that the rule makes no mention of wholes and their parts. The same is true of divisionality. The universal instantiation law has it that from $\ulcorner \forall \nu \, \Phi \nu \urcorner$ to infer $\ulcorner \Phi \alpha \urcorner$, without any regard to considerations of wholeness and parthood. Finocchiaro is careful *not* to say that composition and division errors are violations of the quantifier rules. However, he sees them as "reminiscent." I wonder why. Finocchiaro, by the way, thinks that universal generalization is invalid. Unless he means by this *formally* invalid, I think he is mistaken. The law is valid, but would not be formally so if the specification clause "where δ is arbitrary" were not itself formally renderable.

3. Economics

As noted in section 1, there is hardly a more abundant source of the elusiveness of compositionality than the rich writings of economists who aren't paying attention. Consider Maurice Archer's non-canonical characterization of the composition fallacy as the mistake of assuming that what is true for *a* part of a group must necessarily be true for the group as a whole. If a member of the U.S. Democratic Party lives in Palo Alto, who would ever dream of saying that this is where the Party itself is domiciled? Similarly, the prominent example of standing up in a football game to get a better view of things – also found in one variation or another in Silk, Samuelson and Krugman – lies markedly askew from compositionality's canonical structure. If a *few* of the people in the stadium who aren't seeing very well get to their feet, they'll have a better view of things. But if *everyone* with an impoverished view gets to his feet, *none* of them will attain a better one. Schematize this (crudely) as "If some *x* who has P stands up, *x* will have not-P". This is not an inaccurate example of the type of case in question, but it is an unexpectedly instructive one all the same. The syntactic structure of this conditional shows it as reasoning from particulars to particulars in a way that replaces properties in antecedent-position with their complements in consequent-position. It is an interesting structure, but in and of itself tells us nothing about compositionality. Let's now switch the example to something schematizable as "If everyone with an unsatisfactory view got to his feet, he'd still have an unsatisfactory view." It is a perfectly good general-to-general bit of reasoning, but this time preserving in the consequent the property flagged in the antecedent. Here, too, we get no whiff of compositionaliy. Even if we strung the two schemata together, compositionality in the sense announced by these authors is nowhere to be found. Once again, the economists are simply not paying attention. I mean by this that they aren't paying attention to canonical notation. They violate one of Finocchiaro's most important metaphilosophical rules: Give heedful attention to the relevant empirically discernible facts.

These shortcomings are also instructive. The greater the difficulty in matching examples to what they try to exemplify, the greater the elusiveness of the examplificandum. I'd like now, in this same spirit, to move briefly to some remarks about one of the more interesting and lastingly important realities of post-war international trade. When I was a boy in the aftermath of the surrender of Japan's imperial forces in August 1945, I started noticing at the corner store very inexpensive boxes of matches bearing the stamp "Made in occupied Japan". Little did I realize that this marked the start-up of a powerful post-war economy, far outstripping the one that preceded it. In short order, other developing countries followed suit, and like Japan, made striking strides by selling goods to developed countries at lower than homeland prices. It soon became apparent that if an undeveloped country with similar ambitions didn't move very quickly, it would be too late to catch this wave. The successes to date either caused or motivated countervailing forces that weren't present in the initial stages of Japan's and South Korea's economic miracle. Finocchiaro reports economists as thinking that what we have here is a compositionality problem. Late-comers made the mistake of supposing that "what could happen to any one particular country, could happen to all." (Note again the absence of canonical notation.) I must say that since there is no indication of it recognizable in the facts that this paper reports, no one in the late-comer community made a composition mistake. On the facts presented here, the difficulties the late-comers fell into was overlooking the difference between the start-up conditions for Japan and conditions that pertained later. It is the mistake of not paying attention. If we put our minds to it, perhaps we could construe the late-comers' thinking as a misbegotten by-parity-of-reasoning argument. But what really matters here is that compositionality has no presence in those international-trade examples. This might take some of the steam out of Finocchiaro's conviction that "the topic of the susceptibility of economic reasoning to the fallacy of composition" … "is an extremely important one".

On the other hand, it can't simply be ruled out that the significance of Finocchiaro's economic examples lies not in their compositionality but rather in the fact that they lack the structure that economists claim for them. If that were so, it would be well worth knowing. It would show that their claim is true with such little frequency as to make it an error in the general case and, moreover, one that economists are much drawn to and at ease with. That would be a kind of fallacy about compositionality, but of course it wouldn't be the fallacy of composition.

A final comment on the economic side. Finocchiaro's careful discussion of how economists tend to see the move from microeconomic premises to macroeconomic conclusions as a composition fallacy inclines me to a contrary view. It is clear that even fallacy-attributing economists don't think that such arguments are intrinsically fallacies. When Alberta flew high on $100 oil, the prosperity of Canada increased but did not boom. Now that Alberta is in the dumps, the Canadian economy has worsened but not collapsed. It is no good saying that micro-to-macro thinking is *sometimes* fallacious. That is little more than saying that micro-to-macro reasoning is always fallacious except when it isn't. Economists invite this confusion in their failure to recognize that compositionality requires a move from *all* the parts of a thing to the thing itself. Micro-to-macro reasoning doesn't tick this box. It doesn't tick the box of canonical notation. The reason, again, is the elusiveness of the concept of parthood.

4. Jury Decisions in Criminal Trials

I'd like now to move from economics to the criminal law. A jury is constituted by its (usually) twelve members. Each juror has a sworn duty to consider the total evidence, that is to say, all that he sees and hears in court – and in the jury room too – open-mindedly, impartially and patiently, and to obey the judge's instructions on matters of law. Each has a sworn duty to arrive at a choice of two outcomes: the accused is guilty beyond a reasonable doubt of the offence he's been charged with, or he is not. No juror convicts or acquits an accused. No plurality or even large majority of them does. Only the jury *itself* does. If each juror votes for conviction then the jury has convicted the accused and, if it convicts him, each of the jurors will have voted for it. The reasoning here is perfectly good. But it is sometimes said that convictions are wrought by *aggregating* the twelve individual votes to convict. Thinking so is a misconception. No juror's vote carries verdictifiable weight. When a juror votes to convict, no glove has been laid on the presumption of innocence. When three more jurors vote for conviction, the innocence presumption is as unruffled as it was at the beginning. When all twelve vote for conviction, that makes it the case that the jury has voted for conviction. It is secured by unanimity. But unanimity is not an additive measure. The "all" required for unanimity is not a measure of that kind.

It is interesting to examine the etiology of these intelligent-agent interactions. Each juror has identically the same duties, one of which is to arrive at his or her decision having taken due and heedful note of the total evidence. This inclines some people to think that for twelve people to arrive at a unanimous view of the case they must share a common view of the evidence. There is scant chance of that ever being true. Even at the testimonial level, it is a virtual certainty that the evidence will be inconsistent. The adversarial character of trials at common law virtually guarantees it. I mean, of course, logically inconsistent; from which it follows that no verdict would be secure if based upon it. It is therefore widely supposed that what jurors must (and do) do is put their minds to all consistent subsets of the inconsistent total evidence. It turns out that no juror can do this. Beings like us can't even run truth functional consistency checks. They massively outreach our computational capacities.

It is known from interviews with American jurors (such interviews are unlawful in Canada) that when jurors are able to achieve unanimity, they are unanimous about the verdict, but often nothing close to unanimous about the *reasons* for their individual findings. There is nothing especially odd about this. Jury deliberations are negotiations about conflicted matters of existential importance, informed by contradictory evidence, and subject to the harsh and frankly not very realistic demand to arrive at a unanimous finding of guilt or innocence. It is characteristic of successful negotiations that parties settle for different – often very different – reasons. Parties are also legally required to bargain in good faith in union-management contract talks. This means, among other things, that the parties' opening offers cannot be their final ones. In collective bargaining contexts, parties are bound by law to strive for contracts that split the differences between their opening offers. But since jurors have no differences to split between all-in for guilty and all-in for not guilty, the only place they can find them is in their reasons for voting as they do. However an individual juror manages to find his or her way to a consistent subset of the total evidence, it is highly unlikely – indeed known not to be true – that each of the others will have proceeded from that same subset. What is more, it is possible in principle for each juror to operate with a subset that none of the others have selected. Indeed, the greater the number of consistent subsets, the greater the likelihood of inter-subset inconsistency. At the limit of what's possible, the jury's verdict is a logical construction of individual findings based on twelve different subsets of the total evidence, each of which is pairwise inconsistent. Here too aggregation gets no credible purchase. If juror #1's reasons for conviction are aggregated with juror #12's reasons for the same outcome, the likelihood is high that *in the aggregate* there is no good reason to convict.

Where, then, does this leave us? It leaves us oddly positioned. On the one hand, each juror has reasoned consistently in arriving at the verdict that the others have also arrived at. On the other hand, by construction of the case the opposite is true of the jury *itself*. The jury arrived at *its* verdict inconsistently. To the best of my knowledge, everyone who writes about such things assumes otherwise. In so doing, all the boxes of fallacy are ticked. We might take it that what we have here is a perfect example of the composition fallacy in conditions of real-life reasoning about a disputed matter of pressing importance. It is a pure example of compositional reasoning, and a pure example of fallacious reasoning. It deserves a name. Let's call it the Consistent Verdict fallacy.

I have long thought that the best part of the 1977 paper is its discussion of the part-whole relation and the two supporting Appendices. Our finding then was that the relation we sought is not capturable in abstract set theory, and it is not well-handled in Leśniewski's mereology or in the Noll-Suppes theory of bodies. We came to a better view of Tyler Burge's theory of aggregates. The point of my discussing the jury problem here is to observe that – sad to say – it is *not* to be solved in aggregate theory, notwithstanding its unmissable compositional features. Aggregate theory won't work for compositionality, after all.

Chapter 6
Economic Reasoning and Fallacy of Composition, Part III: Response to John Woods's Comments

1. Introduction

Woods's comments strike me as perceptive, thoughtful, and mostly favorable. Thus, they do not require a lengthy defensive reply. However, they are also insightful and provocative, and so they certainly invite and elicit some further reflections.

2. Method

Woods properly begins by calling attention to the empirical character of my approach to logic and argumentation theory. I agree that this approach is in the tradition of Dewey, Toulmin, and Scriven, and that Woods himself shares such an orientation to some extent.[1] And I certainly welcome his general recommendation that this approach should be followed by others. I have little to add here, except for two clarifications, which are occasioned by his commentary, but which, I believe, are no news to Woods himself and are offered here for the benefit of other potential practitioners.

The empirical approach should *not* be taken to limit itself to description and interpretation and to avoid evaluation and normative prescriptions. My paper may give that impression because its discussion of what economists say and think about the fallacy of composition is primarily descriptive and non-evaluative. On the other hand, in his comments on the central part of my paper, Woods (section no. 3) engages primarily in criticism of economists and seems to use such criticism to undermine my conclusion about the importance of studying the fallacy of composition in economic reasoning. The details of these issues will be discussed below. For the moment, I merely want to clarify that there is no methodological disagreement between us on this issue, and that my own empirical approach is not meant to be purely descriptivist. It should be clear that my paper's avoidance of the evaluation of economists' views was temporary and a matter of sequence of investigation.

In fact, my paper gives hints of this clarification. For example, in the context of my first example of a public-issue discussion (in section 5.3), I

---

[1] Cf. Dewey 1910, Toulmin 1958, Scriven (1976; 1987), Woods 2013, and Finocchiaro (2005, 1-18; 2013b, 4-17).

report Paul Krugman advancing a charge of fallacy of composition. There, the reader should not ignore the following qualification on my part: "Needless to say, such fallacy charges need analysis and evaluation, in the sense that we want to know exactly what the argument being criticized is, what the meta-argument being advanced is, and whether the latter is correct. However, for the moment I cannot pursue such analysis and evaluation. Instead I want to present some more empirical historical material." And in the last section (number 6) of my paper, it is no accident that the first question which I say needs to be asked and answered is: "Despite Samuelson's reference to logicians and logic textbooks, it may or may not be the case that their concept coincides with the one in such economic discussions." This may be taken to anticipate some of Woods's criticism, as it will emerge in detail below.

Another common misinterpretation of the empirical approach is to view it as "empiricist," in the sense of pretending that the reporting and describing of the empirical material is being done without any theoretical assumptions, with a *tabula rasa*, so to speak. This is *not*, of course, a misinterpretation perpetrated by Woods; and so it is probably no accident that before discussing my empirical material (in his section no. 3), he discusses some theoretical issues (in his section no. 2). This clarification may be explicitly seen in my paper from the fact that it begins (my section no. 1) with a discussion of a series of theoretical issues.

3. Theoretical Issues

One of the theoretical assumptions in my paper is the brief claim that not all arguments of composition are incorrect, but rather some are even deductively valid, although not formally valid. Woods seems to agree with this, and to elaborate it further. Since this point is often misunderstood in the literature, it may be useful to amplify it even more.[2]

Woods begins the substantive part of his comments (section 2) by arguing that although the part-whole relation may be transitive, it is irreflexive and antisymmetrical. One of his supporting considerations is this: "If P is a part of a whole W, it has the property Q of being one of W's parts. But being one of W's parts is not itself a part of W." I take this as an elegant counter-example to the formal validity of compositional arguments.

However, formal invalidity is not the same as deductive invalidity. To justify this claim, in my paper I appealed to my favorite example: "all the parts of this automobile have weight; therefore, the whole automobile has weight." This argument is deductively valid, although not formally valid.

---

[2] Cf. the clarifications by Bar-Hillel (1964), who also refers to Carnap (1952).

116

Here, by way of elaboration, I can also appeal to the basic definitions of deductive validity and of formal validity. That is, an argument is deductively valid iff it is impossible for its premises to be true and its conclusion false; in other words, such that if its premises are true then its conclusion must also be true. However, an argument is formally valid iff it is deductively valid by virtue of its logical form; in other words, such that it has a logical form all instances of which are also deductively valid.

Moreover, needless to say (and easily implied by the definitions just formulated), validity (deductive and/or formal) is a property of arguments that is distinct from the truth of their premises. Thus, even if an argument has false premises, it may still be deductively valid, if the truth of the conclusion follows necessarily from the truth of the premises. For example, even if the premise in my "favorite example" of a deductively valid argument of composition were false (as Woods otherwise claims), that would not affect its validity.

And this brings us to what may be a small point of disagreement with Woods, involving his counterexample of the "2016 E-Series Mercedes." If I understand him correctly, Woods seems to be objecting to my "favorite example" insofar as not all parts of all automobiles have weight: "At the top end of the 2016 E-series Mercedes, each car has been set up with thirty million lines of code. By any fair measure, they are parts of the car, and by no fair measure do they have weight" (section 2). I would question whether lines of code created to build an automobile are really "parts" of it; they may be parts of *the process* of building an automobile, but they are no more parts of the automobile than the laws of thermodynamics are, just because these laws are necessary to the design of an automobile, and even for the proper functioning of an already-manufactured automobile.

Another "theoretical" issue on which Woods and I seem to agree it the relationship between compositional and divisional arguments. He amplifies my slight elaboration of this point in my paper. For example, he rightly point out that there is no correlation between the correctness or incorrectness of arguments in one direction of the parts-whole divide, and the correctness or incorrectness of arguments in the opposite direction.

In this context, Woods makes an additional point which I had not touched upon, but which I find plausible. The correctness of arguments of composition "depends on properties of the right kind" (section 2). That is, some properties are such that the corresponding compositional arguments are correct, and some properties yield incorrect arguments of composition.

Moreover, Woods goes on to make an analogy between compositional arguments and generalization arguments, which I find acceptable only in part. Woods claims that there is an important similarity between these two kinds of arguments, for it is also the case that generalization arguments are correct depending on whether the properties in question are *generalizable* from

117

sample to population; on this I agree. And I also agree with Woods's next point, which is that normally even common people know which properties are generalizable and which are not, so as to avoid the so-called fallacy of "hasty generalization," which can thus be declared to be just another non-fallacy.

However, then Woods advances the following (meta)argument from analogy: "The same is true of compositional inferences. But for an adeptness at spotting composable properties, our compositional reasoning would be the disaster that informal logicians mistakenly ascribe to hasty generalization" (section 2). And here I would question whether common people are normally that skillful in determining which properties are composable, namely at formulating correct arguments of composition, and thus avoiding the fallacy of composition. For example, I would point out that if professional economists are right, normal people (who have not studied and learned the science of economics) are terrible about composable properties in economic situations. And I would point to the corroborating fact that the science of economics arose relatively late in human history, in the eighteenth century, and even within this science it was not until the twentieth century that there was an appreciation of the distinction between microeconomics and macroeconomics. Thus, this particular issue certain requires more investigation.

This also brings us to the details of economic reasoning both in my paper and in Woods's commentary. But before I examine that, there is one last theoretical issue which he discusses and deserves some attention. It involves the relationship between compositional argumentation and universal generalization.

In my paper (section 1), I had claimed that "composition is reminiscent of (although not identical to) universal generalization, which is deductively invalid, whereas division is reminiscent of universal instantiation, which is deductively valid." And I had given this as a reason to keep arguments of composition and arguments of division separate. As we have just seen, Woods shares the conclusion (about separation) just stated. But he also seems to object that the reason in this argument of mine is not true and that it is irrelevant.

Woods's objection to the truth of my premise focuses on the clause claiming that universal generalization is deductively invalid. As he points out, in almost all systems of natural deduction, there is a rule labeled "universal generalization" which is sound (valid); but one must be sure to formulate the rule with the proper conditions attached to it. The rule says that a universal generalization, '$(\forall x)\Phi x$', is derivable from a particular instance, 'Φa', provided that the derivation of 'Φa' does not utilize any sentence in which 'a' occurs, and provided that one takes as premises from which the generalization follows all the premises from which the instance followed.

Stated in this way, which I believe is equivalent to the formulation given by Woods, universal generalization is indeed deductively valid. However, the contrast I wanted to make was the following. The rule of universal instantiation stipulates that a particular instance, 'Φa', is derivable from a universal generalization, '$(\forall x)\Phi x$', without any further conditions attached to it. Thus, it seems to me that there is a useful contrast here. Woods suggests that perhaps I should formulate my point by saying that universal generalization is *formally* invalid, although deductively valid. If one accepts this suggestion, then universal instantiation would be both formally valid and deductively valid, and the contrast would remain.

With regard to the connection between compositional reasoning and universal generalization, up to a certain point, I agree with Woods. That is, in saying that "when composition goes wrong, it has nothing to do with misapplications of the universal generalization law" (section 2), Woods is saying something that is *literally* correct. However, this claim is somewhat misleading insofar as it suggests that composition and generalization have nothing to do with each other. Moreover, it does not undermine what I claimed in my paper. When I said that "composition is reminiscent of (although not identical to) universal generalization" (section 1), the term 'reminiscent' was meant to suggest similarity rather than identity. The similarity is that composition involves arguing from all the parts having a property to the whole having the same property, and universal generalization involves arguing from some one (arbitrarily chosen) part having a property to the whole class having the same property. The similarity is even more striking for the version of composition that involves arguing from all the members of a class having a property to the whole class having the same property. Another similarity would emerge with regard to inductive generalization, since the latter argues from a part (the sample) exhibiting a certain property to the whole (the population) possessing the same property; and this is a similarity which Woods himself exploits for another reason, as we saw earlier. Such similarities often generate confusion, as we shall see below when we examine some details of economic reasoning.

In any case, my main point on this particular issue was to support a contrast with arguments of division. These are also similar to, or reminiscent of, without being identical to, other argument types, with which they can be confused. However, in this case, the other argument types are less problematic, since they are universal instantiations, which are afflicted by fewer difficulties than generalizations.

Finally, none of my clarifications, amplifications, or disagreements about the various theoretical issues examined in this section are meant to undermine Woods's claim about, as he phrases it, "the elusiveness of compositionality"; or as I would put it, the claim that compositional arguments are especially challenging and problematic. On the contrary, it should be obvious that I also

119

hold this claim. Indeed, I believe that my critical elaboration here reinforces this claim.

4. Data Analysis and Evaluation

Let us now go on to what is after all the central topic, namely economic reasoning, which Woods examines in section no. 3 of his comments. By and large, he is critical of economists' claims involving the fallacy of composition, as I report and describe them (without criticism) in my paper. And based on his critiques, he feels entitled to conclude that, as he says more than once, "economists are not paying attention"; he also suggests that, consequently, the topic of the susceptibility of economic reasoning to the fallacy of composition may not be as important as I think it is.

With regard to Woods's criticism of economists, basically I agree. For example, he objects to Archer's definition of the fallacy of composition, as reasoning from what is true of "a" part to the same thing being true of the whole. Woods is right that this is not the logicians' concept, which is rather that the reasoning proceeds from what is true of "all" parts.

Strengthening his criticism, I would point out that Samuelson's definition (quoted in my paper) seems misconceived in the same way. On the other hand, it is useful to note that Silk's definition does properly speak of "the parts," thus suggesting all the parts.

Woods also finds problems with economists' favorite example of the fallacy of composition, about the behavior of spectators in a football or baseball game. That is, it is obvious that if a particular person is having difficulties seeing the players due to the obstruction of the other spectators seated in front of him, he could have a better view if he stood up; but it is equally obvious that if all spectators were to stand up, hardly anyone would have a better view; thus it would be fallacious to think otherwise, namely to reason that because one spectator can improve his view by standing up, all spectators can improve their views by standing up. Of course, this is a non-economic example, but there is no question that it is very popular among economists, so much so that it almost performs the function of an ostensive definition of what *they* mean by fallacy of composition. Woods argues that this is not a genuine example of compositional argument.

Again, I agree. I find Woods's own meta-argument plausible and intriguing. And I would add that my own inclination would be to disqualify this example in another way. I would first interpret the target argument as an inductive generalization reasoning from what is true of some members of a class to the same thing being true of all members of the class; this would open the way to faulting the inference in the usual way, on the grounds of the sample being unrepresentative and/or insufficiently large and/or

120

insufficiently varied. It would also be interesting to explore the possibility of interpreting the example as a deductive argument, attempting to ground a universal generalization on what is true of an arbitrarily chosen individual; here I believe that the invalidity would stem from the fact that in the target argument the individual described in the premises is not really arbitrarily chosen, which is required by the sound and valid rule of deductive universal generalization (as we saw above);[3] instead, it is an individual who does something (standing up) while the others do not.

With regard to the example of international trade, Woods argues that the target reasoning is not a fallacy of composition because the target argument is not a compositional argument. Rather, he is inclined to regard it as "a misbegotten by-parity-of-reasoning argument" (section 3). I believe that what Woods calls parity of reasoning here is argumentation by analogy.[4] In fact, the reasoning being exposed by economists of international trade is primarily an argument that would have been given during the second wave of economic development by leaders in countries such as Thailand, trying to imitate what countries such as South Korea had done during the first wave: that is, just as South Korea made great economic progress by manufacturing cheap goods and exporting them to developed countries, the same thing can happen to Thailand. However, there are significant disanalogies here: as previously discussed, during the second wave the world market was saturated with cheap goods manufactured in developing countries, but during the first wave it was not; moreover, during the second wave, developed countries were instituting tariffs on cheap imports, but this had not yet happened during the first wave.

It is apparent from my reconstruction just given, that I find considerable plausibility in such an alternative interpretation of international-trade arguments, as arguments from analogy, rather than as compositional arguments. Indeed, it is often the case that alleged fallacies of composition can be viewed as weak arguments from analogy, as I have myself argued elsewhere (Finocchiaro 2013a). And this also corresponds to Woods's criticism (in section 2) of the argument from the undesirability of private debt to the undesirability of government debt as being more a faulty analogy than a fallacious composition.

Moreover, and perhaps more importantly, it is significant that sometimes

---

[3] The arbitrary selection of an individual from a class can be difficult and problematic, even in deductive reasoning. This is well illustrated by a notorious argument in geometry that seemingly shows that all triangles are isosceles; the flaw is that the apparently arbitrary diagram drawn to construct the pseudo-proof involves a triangle with peculiar properties, not shared by all triangles; for details, see Maxwell 1959, 13-14, 24-32.

[4] For a discussion of parity of reasoning, see Woods and Hudak 1989 and Finocchiaro 2013b, 81-83.

economists themselves recognize that, instead of dealing with fallacies of composition, they are really dealing with weak or incorrect inductive generalizations or arguments from analogy. For example, consider the article by Cline (1982), which is discussed by Mayer (2002) as a pioneering critique of the fallacy of composition in international trade. A careful examination reveals that, although Cline occasionally (twice) and incidentally pays lip service to the terminology of fallacy of composition, he is more explicitly and substantively focused on exposing the illegitimacy of the generalization and/or of the analogy. The very title of the article hints at both of these criticisms, by the use of the terms 'generalized' and 'model': "Can the East Asian Model of Development Be Generalized?" (Cline 1982, 81). The abstract of the article highlights these two points, as well as the lip service to the fallacy of composition:

> advocates of the model frequently illustrate its merits by pointing to the remarkable success of its most prominent practitioners, the East Asian "Gang of Four" (Hong Kong, Korea, Singapore and Taiwan). This study explores a possible limitation of the model, known as the fallacy of composition: while the model may work well if pursued by a limited number of countries, it may break down if a large majority of developing countries seeks to pursue it at the same time, because the resulting outpouring of manufactured exports might be more than Western markets could absorb. Protectionist response might be the result of attempts to generalize the East Asian export model of growth. [Cline 1982, 81]

And throughout the article, Cline is clear and persistent that he is pointing out the limitations of the generalization and/or emulation of the East Asian economic strategy.

For another example, consider Wray's critique of the argument against federal budget deficits, mentioned in my paper. While paying lip service to the fallacy of composition, he himself more than once speaks as if he were dealing with a weak argument from analogy. In fact, in the essay's "Summary," Wray interprets the target argument by saying that "if a household were to continually spend more than its income, it would eventually face insolvency; it is thus claimed that government is in a similar situation" (Wray 2006, 1); and his criticism reduces to explaining how "careful examination of macroeconomic relations will show that this analogy is incorrect" (Wray 2006, 1). This also corresponds to the essay's ending, which reads as follows: "the purpose of this particular note is to explain why we cannot aggregate up from the individual household situation to the economy as a whole. The US government's situation is not in any way similar to that of a household because its deficit spending is exactly offset by private sector surpluses; its debt creates equivalent net financial wealth for the private sector" (Wray 2006, 7).

Woods's last criticism of economists relates to their views about how the fallacy of composition relates to the problem of the relationship between microeconomics and macroeconomics. Here, I find this criticism relatively obscure. As I understand it, he is perhaps saying the following. Some economists speak as if any argument from microeconomic premises to macroeconomic conclusions is a fallacy of composition; and this claim is certainly incorrect To refute this, Woods gives an example from recent economic history in Canada.

If this is what Woods means, again, I would agree: some of the economists quoted in my paper seem to hold such a claim about micro and macroeconomics; and his Canadian counterexample seems decisive and effective. In that case, I would also amplify his criticism in my own way as follows.

In one of the examples discussed in my paper, economist Sumner criticizes Krugman by accusing him of committing a fallacy of composition when he (Krugman) advances the following argument: that because "more federal spending in a given state or county creates more jobs … stimulus spending creates jobs at the national level too" (Krugman 2011). Sumner (2011) thinks that this is "a near perfect example of the fallacy of composition."

I would object to Sumner that Krugman's argument is a near perfect example of an *argument of composition*, but that this is one of those compositional argument that are correct; for in this case the macroeconomic conclusion does derive, by a kind of straightforward addition, from the microeconomic premise. Now, one way of understanding Sumner's criticism is to point out that he seems to be presupposing that all compositional arguments are fallacious. And this, of course, generates a criticism of Sumner's criticism to the effect that he fails to understand that although some compositional arguments are incorrect, some are correct. This is a point which I make at the beginning of my paper, and which Woods reinforces at the beginning his section no. 2.

However, we also need to consider the conclusion that Woods seems to want to draw from his criticism. When that conclusion is stated by saying that "economists are not paying attention," this formulation is perhaps mild enough and vague enough to be acceptable. However, I don't think we can draw the further conclusion that the topic of the susceptibility of economic reasoning to the fallacy of composition may not be as important as I think it is. I would argue as follows.

There is no question that economists constant harp on this fallacy. Perhaps obsession is too strong a word, but they seem to be almost obsessed with avoiding and with exposing this fallacy, and with the problem in general. Now, perhaps they are wrong to focus so much attention on this topic. But if so, their own error or errors need to be exposed. This is especially true for those logicians and argumentation theorists who have seriously studied the nature of errors of reasoning (e.g., Woods 2013). It would be "nice," so to speak, that is, it would be theoretically fruitful if the error(s) of the economists would fit in some recognizable or definable pattern. In that case, we might even be justified in attributing to *them* some fallacy, which they commit in their thinking about the fallacy of composition. After all, this would not be the first time that fallacy chargers are the ones who commit a fallacy, although of course not the one which they are attributing to the subjects of their criticism. Indeed, Woods himself (2013, 478-92) has argued that this happens when experimental psychologists Kahneman and Tversky attribute to their subjects the errors of the so-called conjunction fallacy and base-rate fallacy, and also frequently when it is claimed that someone has committed the gambler's fallacy.

In fact, some patterns have begun to emerge already, as a result of Woods's comments and my reaction to them so far. One pattern seems to be that of thinking that all compositional arguments are fallacious. This is reflected both in economists' general definitions of the fallacy of compositions and in particular applications of the concept to concrete issues. The other pattern seems to be a confusion or equivocation between compositional arguments and other types, especially generalization arguments and arguments from analogy. This is reflected both in economists' favorite example of viewers' behavior at spectator sports, and in their frequent discussions of concrete issues (e.g., international trade) involving generalization and analogy, but under the label of fallacy of composition.

These patterns could be interpreted as meta-arguments of the type which I mentioned at the end of my paper. And such economists' meta-arguments would frequently or typically have incorrect interpretive premises or evaluative premises. That is, the incorrect interpretive premises would be claims such as that the target argument being criticized is compositional, when in fact it is better interpreted as a generalization or as analogical; and the evaluative premises would be claims such as that all compositional arguments are fallacious, when in fact only some are incorrect.

Here, then, we have an hypothesis about the (meta)arguments which economists advance when they criticize the (ground-level) arguments of others as committing the fallacy of composition. Obviously, this hypothesis needs further testing, which could yield disconfirmation as well as confirmation.

An alternative (and more charitable) hypothesis would be the following. Let us focus on the arguments typically criticized by economists as committing the fallacy of composition. Let us assume, partly in accordance with the criticism of economists' meta-arguments elaborated in Woods's commentary and in my considerations above, that the ground-level arguments being criticized are not exactly simple and clear instances of compositional arguments, in the standard logicians' sense defined at the beginning of my paper and shared by Woods. Let us add that those ground-level arguments sometimes have elements of generalization and/or analogical arguments. The challenge is to try to define a type of argument which those ground-level arguments instantiate. Another challenge would be to formulate some evaluative principle(s) that would help us determine the correctness or incorrectness of such arguments. Perhaps no such interpretive or evaluative principles will be found, but the attempt should be made. The desirability of such a project can be grounded on the empirical (*cum* theoretical, *cum* normative) approach to logic and argumentation theory: for it suggests that the preoccupation with the "fallacy of composition" on the part of economists cannot be a gigantic accident, a collective hallucination, mere thoughtlessness, or sheer ignorance.

5. Law

In the last section (number 4) of his comments, Woods discusses an example from criminal law. This is an arrestingly elegant case that bears witness to the depth of his recent work in the philosophy of law (cf. Woods 2015). Legal reasoning is arguably no less important than economic reasoning. Woods's approach to it is apparently no less realistic and empirical-oriented than the one I am practicing in the study of economic reasoning. And his theoretical acuity is unsurpassable.

The example involves a jury convicting a defendant as a result of each juror's vote in favor of conviction. Now, if we examine the reasoning underlying such voting and such a conviction, it is very common and tempting to argue as follows: each juror reasons consistently in arriving at a decision to vote "guilty"; therefore, the jury arrived at its verdict consistently. Here, the premise is true in the sense that, although the total evidence presented is normally inconsistent, each juror normally selects a consistent subset of that total, which he can use to arrive at his decision; but the conclusion is false because normally each juror's subset of evidence is inconsistent with the subsets of most or all other jurors; and the argument form is strictly compositional. Thus, as Woods says, "here is a perfect example of the composition fallacy in conditions of real-life reasoning about a disputed matter of pressing importance."

References

Bar-Hillel, Yehoshua. 1964. More on the fallacy of composition. *Mind* 73: 125-26.

Carnap, Rudolf. 1952. Meaning postulates. *Philosophical Studies: An International Journal for Philosophy in the Analytic Tradition* 3: 65-73.

Cline, William R. 1982. Can the East Asian model of development be generalized? *World Development* 10: 81-90.

Dewey, John. 1910. *How We Think*. Lexington, MA: Heath. Rpt. Buffalo, NY: Prometheus, 1991.

Finocchiaro, Maurice A. 2005. *Arguments about Arguments: Systematic, Critical, and Historical Essays in Logical Theory*. New York: Cambridge University Press.

Finocchiaro, Maurice A. 2013a. Debts, oligarchies, and holisms: Deconstructing the fallacy of composition. *Informal Logic* 33: 143-74.

Finocchiaro, Maurice A. 2013b. *Meta-argumentation: An Approach to Logic and Argumentation Theory*. London: College Publications.

Krugman, Paul. 2011. Small is beautiful. Posted on 25 February 2011. At http://krugman.blogs.nytimes.com/?s=small+is+beautiful; consulted on December 15, 2015.

Maxwell, E. A. 1959. *Fallacies in Mathematics*. Cambridge: Cambridge University Press.

Mayer, Jörg. 2002. The fallacy of composition: A review of the literature. *The World Economy* 25: 875-94.

Scriven, Michael. 1976. *Reasoning*. New York: McGraw-Hill.

Scriven, Michael. 1987. Probative logic. In *Argumentation: Across the Lines of Disciplines*, ed. Frans H. van Eemeren, R. Grootendorst, J. A. Blair, and C. A. Willard, 7-32. Dordrecht: Foris Publications.

Sumner, Scott. 2011. Small is irrelevant (in macro). Posted February 25, 2011. At http://www.themoneyillusion.com/?p=9056; consulted on December 15, 2015.

Toulmin, Stephen E. 1958. *The Uses of Argument*. Cambridge: Cambridge University Press.

Woods, John. 2013. *Errors of Reasoning: Naturalizing the Logic of Inference*. London: College Publications.

Woods, John. 2015. *Is Legal Reasoning Irrational? An Introduction to the Epistemology of Law*. London: College Publications.

Woods, John, and B. Hudak. 1989. By parity of reasoning. *Informal Logic* 11: 125-39.

Wray, L. Randall. 2006. Teaching the fallacy of composition: The federal budget deficit. At https://edi.bard.edu/research/cfeps-archive/; first consulted on October 19, 2012; later on May 25, 2023.

Appendix, by John Woods
Economic Reasoning and Fallacy of Composition, Part IV: Some Parting Words

1. Over-abstraction

Parting words are sometimes final, but these ones of mine are not. They are an invitation to keep on thinking about the matters to which Finocchiaro has engagingly directed our attention. One of the things that our present discussion helps make clear is the disoriented state in which we find the present literature on composition, in both logic and economics alike. Also much appreciated are Finocchiaro's clarifications of some of the points I was confused about in my commentary, and for the further occasion they've given me to sort out my own thoughts about the matters under review here. Finocchiaro's examples disclose two significant omissions, one on the part of logicians and the other on the part of economists. Logicians of the present day who take the occasion to mention composition arguments rarely trouble to negotiate the interrelations among the variables P, W and Q of composition claims in canonical notation. Notably absent are analyses of the underlying part-whole relations that deliver a property of all the parts to the whole of which they are its parts, notwithstanding the efforts otherwise of the 1977 paper. Economists, on one hand, simply will not address the compositionality in the terms in which it is presented in canonical notation. Finocchiaro is right to emphasize that his economics examples are presented for our consideration, not necessarily – or even for the most part – with his endorsement. But, upon consideration, they are strikingly informative examples, perhaps surprisingly so.

To take an example close to my heart, one of the virtues of Finocchiaro's inspection of the logic textbook literature is its exposure of difficulties with the textbook treatments of Woods-Walton (and later Irvine) treatment of economically compositional contexts in the three editions of *Argument*. In the 2004 edition, it is claimed that economic reasoning "is inherently liable to the fallacy of composition" (p. 251), and that – to quote Finocchiaro's paraphrase – "this liability is connected with the fundamental division between microeconomics and macroeconomics and the problematic relationship between the two." On the basis of Finocchiaro's data-sets, I find that I have changed my mind about these claims, or at least lessened the confidence with which I first advanced them. At the heart of it all is the compositionality property in canonical notation: "Every part P of the whole W has property Q. So W has Q too". The plain fact that compositionality claims in the economics literature are so rarely in canonical notation suggests (to me) that composition thus rendered holds little interest for economists. Suppose that this were so. Why would it be? It would be because the complexities of economics are seldom renderable in so stripped-down an idiom as "from all parts of W to W itself." For one thing, it is surprisingly difficult to see in the structure of a functioning economic relationship anything as simplified as this one. It is not for nothing that economics is the plaything of statisticians, real number theorists and the purveyors of differentiations and integration, and more recently biologists and physicists. Structures in the form "All P have Q. So W has Q" are too abstract for economic reality.

A related example of over-abstraction is the habit of theorists of *abductive inference* to choose the schema

1. If H then E
2. E
3. Hence H

as canonical for abduction, for requisite interpretations of H, E, "if … then" and "hence". Of course, it is an all but useless schema, in which all the weight is placed on the *unschematized* "if … then" and "hence". It is a schema that breaks away from the gravitational pull of the very idea of abduction. It carries a helpful quite general reminder. It tells us that it is one thing to talk the talk of canonical notation and another thing entirely to walk it. (Quine himself talked it wonderfully, but walked it wobbly.)

I began my remarks at the OSSA session with a threefold expression of thanks to my colleague Maurice Finocchiaro. I thanked him for his plug of the 1977 paper. I thanked him for his data-sets. And I thanked him for having re-awakened my dormant interest in compositionality. In his reply, Maurice (I think that first names are now *de rigeur* at this parting stage) points out that in my *Errors of Reasoning* (2013), I leave untested the claim that none of the traditional examples exemplifies the traditional conception of fallacy in the logician's sense of an error of reasoning that is commonly and confidently committed and subject to unusually high levels of recidivism. Consider hasty generalizations again. If hasty generalization really is an error of reasoning, it is a damnably difficult one to stop committing. The composition fallacy was one of those untested examples. Maurice wonders why. Was there, perhaps, some particular reason, beyond the size of an already large book, to omit it from consideration? The answer, as I am now led to believe, is not that an analysis of composition would have disturbed my thesis that none of the traditional examples instantiates the traditional concept of fallacy, but rather that composition corroborates it with emphatic effect. The problem, again is that hardly any grown-up reasoning about entities of any interesting complexity is formulable in the canonical notation that logicians have mandated for compositionality, least of all in economics.

2. Complex Systems

Consider for example the hot-button issue of the economics of hot-climate mitigation. Usually considered as complements of cap-and-trade regimes, command and control prices imply that decision-makers have the tetrabytes of information on hand, together with the means to process it, on the basis of which it can be determined "whether shutting down natural gas for homes and pushing gasoline cars off the road create more benefits than costs. But [carbon-pricers have already] adopted cap and trade precisely because [they] don't have that information."[1]

Of course, Watson's point is that economies are too complex to be left to the command of centralized control centres. Notoriously, their complexity is not even yet a well-understood relation. It is partly a part-whole relationship, but is massively underdetermined by it. Complex systems are now the subject of sprawling research programmes. A leading researcher proposes that the "kernel" of the concept of a complex system can be captured as follows.

- A complex system must contain *many* subunits, whose number is left unspecified.
- Subunits must be *independent* at least *some* of the time.
- The interactions among these subunits must be nonlinear at least *some* of the time.
- Individual subunits modify their properties and behaviour with respect to a changing environment, resulting in the generation of new systemic properties that 'reflect' the change that the environment has undergone.
- In the case of self-organizing systems, subunits modify their own properties and behaviour in light of the system they jointly determine – in other words, there is 'downwards causation' operating from the systemic properties to the subunits' properties.[2]

In this large volume of 936 pages, there is but one mention of part-whole relations in which there is nothing reflected in what I've been calling canonical notation. The same is true, only more so, of its almost as large companion volume *Philosophy of Economics* (2012) edited by Uskali Mäki, in which there is no indexical mention of parts, wholes, composition or division. Fallacies merit twelve references, none having to do with the ones on offer here. Apart from Aristotle, no fallacy theorist makes the index of names, nor is Aristotle cited for either *Parts of Animals*[3] or his contributions

---

[1] William Watson, "How not to do cap and trade", *Financial Post* (Toronto), May 26, 2016, FP9.

[2] Dean Rickles, "Econophysics and the complexity of financial markets," in *Philosophy of Complex Systems*, ed. Cliff Hooker, pp. 531-564 (vol. 10 of the *Handbook of the Philosophy of Science*, ed. Dov M. Gabbay, Paul Thagard and John Woods. Amsterdam: North-Holland, 2011).

[3] Arguably the best book from antiquity on the part-whole relation was written by the founder of systematic logic, and yet no reference to parts and wholes is to be found in Aristotle's logical discourses in the *Organon*, including the treatment of the enthymeme in the *Rhetoric*. *Parts of Animals* is a wonderful book on natural

129

to fallacy theory. The moral? Compositionality in canonical notation is not a load-bearing concept in economics. It is hard to see how it would be in logic either.

3. Thermodynamic Costs

Before quitting this part, it might repay us to tarry awhile over William Watson's reference to the tetrabytes of information that centralized carbon pricers would have to process in arriving at their decisions. At once questions arise. Where would such information come from and how would it be processed? Information theory is dominated by theoretical wrangles and high levels of polysemy. Even so, there is a body of opinion backing the idea that consciousness is a massive suppressor of information, a thermodynamically costly state to be in. It is estimated that the information in the sensorium – the site were information from the five senses converges – is ≈ 11 million bits, most of which is lost when admitted to consciousness – only ≈ 40 bits make that cut. Worse still is the transition from consciously possessed information and its linguistic expression. Only ≈ 16 bits survive that transformation. To put it over-simply, no system demanding tetrabytes of information can conceivably function on consciously held and/or linguistically formulated information. If we make the plausible assumption that human cognition is an information-thirsty phenomenon, then we have it quite straightforwardly that whatever cognitive command we may ever achieve of the economics of carbon mitigation will be the product of information flow-throughs that are processed unconsciously.[4] In his paper, Maurice touches on the (contested) view that, in their nervousness about debt, it is typical of conservative economists to be more vigilant about the composition fallacy than their liberal colleagues whose macro-principles take

---

history, positively brimming with the myriad ways in which connections are wrought and maintained in the animal kingdom. To the best of my knowledge, no logician writing on part-whole fallacies has seen reason to consult this work. Certainly Walton and I didn't in 1977. While on the subject of Aristotle, I might add that for him the combination and division of words fallacies are errors dependent on language. Depending on whether the words "can sit while walking" are taken in their combined or divided sense, it is true or not that Socrates can walk while sitting. In the divided sense, the claim is true. Even a seated Socrates has the power to stop sitting and start walking. However, things go wrong in the combined sense. Not even Socrates can manage to walk and sit at the same time. It is easy to see how different the modern fallacies are from these old ones. Part-whole fallacies are never construed as dependent on language, but rather are given the *extra dictionem* classification. See, for example, Irving M. Cohen and Carl Cohen, *Introduction to Logic,* 8th edition, New York: Macmillan, 1970; pp. 17-20.
[4] There is a larger development of these points in *Errors of Reasoning* at pages 204-226.

much of the sting out of macro-debt. (When I say that the view is contested, as Maurice points out, I mean that part of it that describes compositional nervousness as *typical* of conservatives.) I have come to a somewhat different view. It is driven by the thesis that information-rich cognitive ecologies must be consciously impoverished. If that is so then in the context of carbon-mitigation economies, free-marketers have a clear advantage over carbon-pricing bureaucracies. There may be some question as to whether command and control bureaucracies are conscious, but there is none at all about whether free markets are. They aren't, period. This stirs the possibility that free-market economists are more attuned to thermodynamic realities of information-processing than their command and control rivals. The point of more immediate importance is that there is, in this rivalry about how carbon-mitigation is to be handled, little that pivots on part-whole relations in canonical notation.

Perhaps I might be forgiven for a small tip of the hat to the Woods-Walton effort to get to the bottom of the part-whole relation. As noted in my comments on Maurice's paper, all the candidates we examined in 1977 are inadequate. This is both good news and bad, at once a setback and an energetic motivator of a wide-open research programme in the logic of human reasoning. Unless I am mistaken, bringing this project to a successful conclusion will add welcome flesh to Finocchiaro's meta-argument schema 4:

     (M4a) Argument A is an argument of composition because …;

     (M4b) Argument A is incorrect because …;

     (M4c) Argument A appears to be correct because …;

     (M4d) Argument A is a common or frequent type, because …;

     (M4e) Therefore, argument A is a fallacy of composition.

To make real progress here, we may have to give up the talk of canonical notation and learn to walk the talk of complex systems. I regard the fulfilment conditions on M4 as the *sine qua non* of a tenable account of the fallacy of composition. There only remains the challenge of finding them.

Chapter 7
Samuelson on the Fallacy of Composition in Economics:
A Woodsian Critique

1. Introduction

There is a monument at the University of Groningen, in North Holland, dedicated to the subject matter of this essay. I am referring to a sculpture named "The Fallacy of Composition," on the building of the Faculty of Economics. It was created in 1988 by artists Trudi van Berg and Jos Steenmeijer, and its purpose was to commemorate the 50th anniversary of the foundation of that Faculty, as well as to celebrate Keynes's epoch-making contributions to the science of economics. This purpose is explained in the website of the University of Groningen with the following words: "this work ... was inspired by an economic concept. The work of John M. Keynes led to valuable insights, including the fact that macro-economy—the behaviour of aggregated variables—is very different to micro-economy, or the behaviour of individuals. The whole behaves very differently to the sum of its parts. This is known as 'the fallacy of composition'. In 1998 the Faculty of Economics celebrated its 50th anniversary ..."[1]

This cultural tourist attraction may be fruitfully connected to a cultural curiosity that happened a few years ago at the other side of the world. On 7 January 2013, a daily newspaper in my home town (*Las Vegas Review-Journal*) published the following letter to the editor by a local resident:

> To the editor:
> What does the next "fiscal cliff"—the debt ceiling—look like, and what is a possible solution?
> U.S. tax revenue in fiscal year 2012: $2,450,000,000,000.
> Federal spending in fiscal year 2012: $3,500,000,000,000.
> New debt: $1,050,000,000,000.
> Current national debt: $16,400,000,000,000.
> "Fiscal cliff" budget cuts: $12,000,000,000.
> For the sake of argument and clarity, let's remove eight zeros and pretend these numbers are a typical household budget:
> Family income: $24,500.
> Family spending: $35,000.

---

[1] Cf. http://www.rug.nl/science-and-society/sculpture-project/sculpture1998?lang=en; consulted on July 24, 2012. I owe my first information about this sculpture to Govier (2007; 2009); cf. my Finocchiaro 2013a.

New debt on credit card: $10,500.
Outstanding balance on credit card: $164,000.
Total budget cuts: $120.
Another way to look at the debt ceiling: Let's say you come home from work or a day out and find there has been a major sewer backup in your neighborhood, and your home is flooded with sewage all the way to the ceiling.
What do you do? Raise the ceiling or remove the sewage?[2]

This letter can be easily interpreted as containing primarily the following argument: the economic policies of the national government in the USA, regarding deficit spending and accumulated debt, are wrong or irresponsible because it would obviously be wrong or irresponsible for any family to incur a relatively comparable level of deficits and debt. This argument, in turn, could be interpreted as a compositional argument (or argument of composition); that is, based on the fact that something is true of the individual parts of a national economy, it concludes that the same thing is true of the whole system. And then one could criticize this argument as a fallacy of composition, namely as a common type of argument that appears to be correct but is actually erroneous. As we shall soon see, I believe this would be the typical reaction of professional economists to such an argument (although I myself do not share their critical interpretation).

Despite the unpretentiousness of this letter, and independently of the logical or scientific correctness of its content, together with the Groningen monument, it provides an eloquent and revealing introduction to the subject of the present investigation. In fact, the two references just given and their connection may be quaint, accidental, and personalistic, but they point toward a problem whose theoretical and practical significance and seriousness are difficult to overestimate; that is, the problem of the fallacy of composition in economic reasoning. As I have explicitly pointed out on several occasions, professional economists tend to harp on this fallacy, and this tendency seems to occur in many different contexts: in textbooks and pedagogical situations,[3] in research and academic contexts,[4] and in editorial discussions of current events.[5]

In this paper, I undertake a critical examination of the conception and the examples of the fallacy of composition in Paul Samuelson's textbook

---

[2] *Las Vegas Review-Journal*, January 7, 2013, p. 5B; at:
https://www.reviewjournal.com/opinion/letters/if-you-ran-your-budget-like-washington/.
[3] See Archer 1973, Silk 1978, Wray 2006; cf. Finocchiaro 2016a, 22-24.
[4] See Caballero 1992, Cline 1982, Mayer 2002; cf. Finocchiaro 2016a, 24-26.
[5] See Anderson 2010, Boudreaux 2018, Epstein 2018, Kelly and Kelly 2015, Krugman (2010; 2013a; 2013b), Sumner 2011; cf. Finocchiaro 2016a, 26-30.

Economics. Samuelson (1915-2009) was, of course, one of the most distinguished and influential economists of the twentieth century. A professor at the Massachusetts Institute of Technology, he received the Nobel Prize in economics in 1970, the second year that the prize was awarded.[6] His textbook *Economics* was first published in 1948, went through at least 19 editions (as of 2010), and was translated into 41 languages; hence, it is the best-selling economics textbook of all time,[7] and perhaps the most popular textbook ever in any discipline. Indeed, from a global, cultural, and historical point of view, it could be regarded as one of the most influential books ever written, perhaps on a par with Euclid's *Elements* and the like.

What concerns me here is the fact that in his textbook, Samuelson regards the fallacy of composition as one of the main pitfalls of (untutored) economic reasoning, so that one of the main things to learn in the study of economic science is how to avoid this fallacy when thinking about economic matters. In the past,[8] I have had occasion to examine some of what Samuelson says about this fallacy; specifically, in the edition of the textbook which was used when I took a university course on the subject (and which I still own), and also in the latest edition which I could find in my university library (and which happened to be the 13th edition, of 1989). Moreover, previously my attitude has been primarily descriptive and interpretive, namely focused on trying to understand Samuelson's points.

What I would like to do now is to expand the historical horizon to cover the entire history of the textbook (1948-2010): partly to get an overview, and partly to detect possible modifications and revisions from one edition to another. Moreover, as befits the philosophical conception of argumentation theory, in addition to the interpretive attitude of understanding what Samuelson says, I want to adopt an evaluative and critical attitude aiming to determine several things: whether his definition (which he attributes to "logicians" and "logic textbooks") is conceptually adequate; whether his economic examples fit his own conception; whether his examples are really arguments of composition and/or errors of reasoning; if so, whether they are

---

[6] The Nobel Prize in economics began in 1969, when it was awarded jointly to Ragnar Frisch, of Oslo University, and to Jan Tinbergen, of The Netherlands School of Economics. The co-author of the last eight editions of the textbook (1985-2010), William Nordhaus, a former student of Samuelson's, was one of the two recipients of the Nobel Prize in economics in 2018.

[7] Admittedly, there exists a textbook that may rival Samuelson's in popularity; first published in 1960 (McConnell and Bingham 1960), it is now (2018) in its 21th edition (McConnell et al. 2018). However, there is no comparison in terms of novelty of original publication, translation into foreign languages, and scientific accomplishments of the authors.

[8] See Finocchiaro 2013a, 2015a, 2015b, 2016a, 2016b.

indeed fallacies of composition; if not, what kind of arguments and errors they exemplify; and so on.

More generally, this paper also aims to further illustrate and pursue the empirical or naturalistic approach to the study of reasoning, argumentation, and fallacies, and especially the historical-textual version of this approach.[9] Also generally and methodologically speaking, this investigation is an illustration of the meta-argumentation approach to logic and argumentation theory; that is, an orientation that focuses on the meta-arguments advanced by various writers about the substantive or ground-level arguments attributed to others (see Finocchiaro 2013b). Furthermore, obviously, I aim to shed light on the nature of fallacies, which is a central and widely discussed topic in logic and argumentation theory, and on the nature of economic reasoning, which may be regarded as a special topic.

Next, at the practical level, this investigation also aims to better understand at least two globally relevant economic issues which are usually connected to the fallacy of composition. The first is the problem of government deficits and debts, which has played a key role in the Great Recession that afflicted the world economy following 2008; according to some economists, the root of this problem is the policy of austerity, which embodies the fallacy of composition.[10] The second is the problem of import tariffs and quotas that has recently gained the spotlight, ever since in 2018 the American government announced such tariffs and quotas in an attempt to bring its international trade under control. Some economists immediately cried "fallacy of composition": one (Epstein 2018) opined that "Trump's view is the pure embodiment of the fallacy of composition—insisting that a proposition that holds for the part is necessarily true for the larger whole"; another (Boudreaux 2018) found it "deeply disturbing that the Commerce secretary ... commits the sophomoric fallacy of composition—namely here, inferring that what is true for one can of soup is therefore true for the entire economy of which that one can is but a minuscule part."

Last but not least, especially in the present context, this investigation is a follow-up to some previous discussions between myself and John Woods. This should already be apparent from what I said above, in describing this investigation as an empirical or naturalistic approach to the fallacy of composition in economic reasoning, with the proviso that empirical does not mean empiricist or value-free, but rather should be combined with theoretical interpretation and critical evaluation. In fact, even a superficial acquaintance with Woods's works would easily reveal his focus on the naturalistic approach, the nature of fallacies, the fallacy of composition, and economic

---

[9] Cf. Barth 1985, Woods 2013, and Finocchiaro (2005, 1-20; 2014).
[10] Krugman (2013a; 2013b); for some details, cf. Finocchiaro 2015a, 25.

135

reasoning.[11] However, the connection between Woods's work and the present investigation is deeper, more concrete, and more direct than such an initial impression might suggest. Let me explain.

Woods and I have already had the opportunity to exchange views about the problem of the susceptibility of economic reasoning to the fallacy of composition.[12] Now, although our views are by no means identical, several important points of agreement have emerged from these discussions. However, here I want to call attention to several explicit claims by Woods that provide a basis for the present investigation, in the sense that this investigation could be regarded as an attempt to further test these claims; and as we shall see, the result is by and large a confirmation, an elaboration, and a refinement of these Woodsian claims.

The first claim is that, as Woods (2016a, 42) puts it, professional "economists are simply not paying attention"; that is, in their penchant to find and attribute fallacies of composition, economists themselves may be in error. Second, there is Woods's (2016a, 39, 41) point about the "elusiveness of compositionality"; that is, given that fallacies of composition are fallacious arguments embodying the compositional form, the compositional argument-form is conceptually difficult to understand and empirically hard to find. Third, combining the first two claims just made, Woods formulates the conjecture that perhaps one of the ways in which economists are not paying attention is that they are themselves committing a fallacy *about* composition: "it can't simply be ruled out that the significance of Finocchiaro's economic examples lies not in their compositionality but rather in the fact that they lack the structure that economists claim for them. If that were so, … It would show that their claim is true with such little frequency as to make it an error in the general case and, moreover, one that economists are much drawn to and at ease with. That would be a kind of fallacy about compositionality, but of course it wouldn't be the fallacy of composition" (Woods 2016a, 43).

Fourth, and more specifically, Woods advances a plausible criticism of one of the economists' most common examples of the fallacy of composition. This example is the argument from private to public debts, which is instead a faulty argument from analogy. In Woods's (2016a, 41) own words: "when the householder reasons that if high consumer debt loads are bad household economics how could it not also be bad government economics, his failure (if there is one) arises from his not knowing how differently structured national economies are from the way in which household economies work. The mistake lies in the faulty assumption that national economies are

---

[11] See, for example, Woods (2004a; 2004b; 2013; 2016a; 2016b); Woods and Walton (1977; 1982; 1989); Woods, Irvine, and Walton (2000; 2004). Cf. Finocchiaro (2014; 2016a).

[12] Finocchiaro (2016a; 2016b); Woods (2016a; 2016b).

analogues of household ones, only much bigger."

Fifth, and finally, Woods gives a subtle criticism of another one of the economists' examples; this is an illustration that involves noneconomic matters, but also serves almost as their ostensive definition of what they mean by fallacy of composition:

> the prominent example of standing up in a football game to get a better view of things—also found in one variation or another in Silk, Samuelson and Krugman—lies markedly askew from compositionality's canonical structure. If a few of the people in the stadium who aren't seeing very well get to their feet, they'll have a better view of things. But if everyone with an impoverished view gets to his feet, none of them will attain a better one. Schematize this (crudely) as "If some x who has P stands up, x will have not-P". This is not an inaccurate example of the type of case in question, but it is an unexpectedly instructive one all the same. The syntactic structure of this conditional shows it as reasoning from particulars to particulars in a way that replaces properties in antecedent-position with their complements in consequent-position. It is an interesting structure, but in and of itself tells us nothing about compositionality. [Woods 2016a, 42]

2. The Concept

Samuelson's textbook discusses the fallacy of composition partly in the introductory chapter, where he defines the concept in general, and partly in several subsequent chapters, whenever some particular example becomes relevant to the substantive topic being treated.[13] Let us begin with the former.

The introductory chapter discusses such topics as the basic concepts of economics (e.g., scarcity, supply and demand), the status of economics as a social science, the difference between macroeconomics and microeconomics, and the distinctions of description vs. policy vs. analysis. Another one of these introductory topics is what Samuelson variously calls (i.e., in different editions of his textbook) sometimes "pitfalls of economic reasoning," sometimes "methodology of economics," and sometimes "logic of economics." The most common subtopics of the last-mentioned introductory section are the importance of the qualification "other things being equal"; the fact that economic truths are statistical, probabilistic, generic, or tendential rather than exact or universal; the fallacy of *post hoc, ergo propter hoc*; and the relationship between parts and whole, or the fallacy of composition. Let us focus on the latter.

The discussion of this fallacy usually starts with a list of several

---

[13] For complete details, see the "Table of Samuelson's References to the Fallacy of Composition," found below, after the concluding section (no. 9).

situations, each described by a cryptic statement which Samuelson claims to be apparently paradoxical but actually true. Most of these cryptic examples are elaborated and explained in later chapters, and I too will discuss them later in due course. For now, let us look at the general concept.

The first edition does not explicitly give a definition, but does so implicitly, when Samuelson states: "many of the above paradoxes hinge around one single confusion or fallacy, called by logicians the 'fallacy of composition'. What is true for each is not necessarily true for all; and conversely, what is true for all may be quite false for each individual" (Samuelson 1948, 9). It is obvious that here Samuelson is saying that the fallacy of composition is committed when one does not understand that what is true for each is not necessarily true for all; eliminating the double negative, we get that the fallacy of composition is committed when one thinks that what is true for each is true for all.

It is also obvious that here the essential meaning is that this fallacy is committed when one thinks that what is true for each *separately* or *individually* is also true for all *together* or *collectively*. Without this qualification, that is, according to one literal meaning of the words 'each' and 'all', it would be analytically true that what is true for each is also true for all, and so the definition would be referring to an absurd or impossible situation.

Samuelson's implicit definition does contain one questionable item. That is, the inclusion of the "converse" condition in the second sentence may involve a possible confusion of the fallacy of composition with the fallacy of division. In fact, "fallacy of division" is the label usually reserved for the error of reasoning when one assumes that what is true for all together is also true for each individually. The two are of course related, and to some extent they raise similar issues; but they also involve some differences, and so they should be kept distinct.

Samuelson's essential meaning becomes clearer in the textbook's later editions. For example, already in the third edition he gives an explicit definition: "many of the above paradoxes hinge around one single confusion or fallacy, called by logicians the 'fallacy of composition'. In books on logic, this is defined as follows: *a fallacy in which what is true of a part is, on that account alone, alleged to be also true of the whole*. Very definitely, in the field of economics, it turns out that what seems to be true for each individual is not always true for society as a whole; and conversely, what seems to be true for all may be quite false for any one individual" (Samuelson 1955, 10).

Although this conception continues to be afflicted by a possible confusion with the fallacy of division, this is less problematic now because the converse condition is not mentioned in the official definition, but merely in the explanatory remark (second clause of the third sentence). More importantly, this formal definition further clarifies the essential meaning by using the terminology of "parts" and "whole." Moreover, the explanation provided in the first clause of the third sentence makes clear that Samuelson is talking about reasoning from what is true of *each* part to the same being true of the whole; in other words, the explanation makes clear that when the definition speaks of "what is true of *a* part," it means "what is true of *any one* part," and not "what is true of *some* part."

Unfortunately, this definition also adds a new questionable item. The problem stems from the phrase "on that account alone," which is an arbitrary restriction. There is no good general reason for including such a restrictive clause in the definition of the fallacy of composition. Nor is such a restrictivist formulation to be found in logic books, including those that were available at that time.[14]

The basics of the conception of the third edition are retained in the next several editions. However, in the eighth edition, a new problematic condition is added in the definiens: "in books on logic, this is defined as follows: ***Fallacy of composition*: a fallacy in which what is true of a part is, on that account alone, alleged to be also necessarily true of the whole**" (Samuelson 1970, 12). The problem stems from the word "necessarily." When so formulated, the definition is conceiving the fallacious argument as a deductive, rather than inductive, argument. That is, the argument committing the fallacy is being interpreted as claiming that, based on what is true of each part, it follows necessarily that the same is true of the whole. The inductive alternative would be to say that the fallacious argument is claiming that, based on what is true of each part, it is probable that the same is true of the whole; namely, there is some support for concluding that the same is true of the whole.

This is an important problem because the deductivist interpretation attributes a stronger claim to the argument, and so makes it more susceptible to criticism; thus, the existence of a fallacy is easier to prove. In other words, the deductivist formulation runs the risk of being uncharitable, or committing the straw-man fallacy; and so it is generally avoided by logicians.[15]

The discussion of the concept of fallacy of composition continues in the same vein for the next several editions, even when (starting with the 10th edition of 1976) the textbook acquires a co-author. Thus, as late as 1985, when Nordhaus became Samuelson's permanent collaborator and co-author, the discussion combined both of the elements reported above: a relatively clear account of the essential meaning of the fallacy, as consisting of erroneous reasoning from what holds for all parts or individuals of a system to the same holding for the whole or aggregate; and a relatively problematic

---

[14] Cf. Cohen and Nagel 1934, 377; Black 1946, 211-12.
[15] Cohen and Nagel 1934, 377; Black 1946, 211-12. Cf. Finocchiaro 2015a, 38.

triad of conditions, involving a possible confusion with the fallacy of division, an exclusivist stress on the inference being based only on what holds for all parts, and a deductivist exaggeration of the strength of the inference.

However, in the 14th edition of 1992, the three problematic conditions are completely dropped. In fact, the explicit definition now reads simply: "the fallacy of composition is the misconception that what is true for a part is therefore true for the whole" (Samuelson and Nordhaus 1992, 6). I believe this must be considered an improvement in the conception.

On the other hand, it's unclear whether such a potential improvement is consciously and reflectively motivated, or the result of a decision to avoid serious involvement with and discussion of the fallacy of composition. In fact, beginning with the 1992 edition, the introductory discussion of the concept is significantly shortened. Moreover, as we shall see later, the discussion of examples of this fallacy in subsequent chapters is drastically reduced and tends to disappear. More importantly, the new formulation embodies a serious and perhaps fatal misconception.

The problem stems from the talk of "a part" in this definition.[16] We saw earlier that, although abstractly speaking this phrase can mean either "*any one* part" or "*some* part," the accompanying explanations made it clear that the meaning was the former, so that the reasoning in question was from what is true for all parts to the same being true for the whole. However, in the 1992 edition the accompanying explanation conveys a very different meaning: "Have you ever seen people jump up at a football game to gain a better view? They usually find that, once everybody is standing up, the view has not improved at all. This example, in which what is true for an individual is not necessarily true for everyone, illustrates the 'fallacy of composition', which is defined as follows: … " (Samuelson and Nordhaus 1992, 6). Unfortunately, the reasoning here is an inference from one to all, which is usually problematic, but which is very different as compared to a compositional inference from all individually to all together. Such a problematic inference[17] is closer (although not identical) to what is usually called the fallacy of hasty generalization, rather than to the fallacy of composition.

This conceptual misconception is reinforced by the formulation found in the latest editions of the textbook, which seem to speak explicitly and unambiguously of reasoning from part of a system to the whole system: "Sometimes we assume that what holds true for part of a system also hold true for the whole. In economics, however, we often find that the whole is different from the sum of the parts. *When you assume that what is true for*

---

[16] Woods (2016a, 41-42) points out that Archer (1973, 45-46) too seems to share this confusion.

[17] Cf. Woods's (2016a, 42) criticism of this example, quoted in the Introduction above.

the part is also true for the whole, you are committing the fallacy of composition."[18] In order to be talking about the fallacy of composition, this passage should instead read something like the following, where the crucial changes are printed in italics: Sometimes we assume that what holds true for *each* part of a system also hold true for the whole ... When you assume that what is true for *all* the parts is also true for the whole, you are committing the fallacy of composition.

These last editions also contain a lengthy and useful glossary of terms, which duly includes the fallacy of composition, now defined as follows: "the fallacy of assuming that what holds for individuals also holds for the group or the entire system."[19] This seems almost completely right, since it suggests that we are talking about reasoning in accordance with the principle that what holds for all individuals or parts also holds for the whole group or system. However, one could now cavil that the authors seem unaware that their definition in the introductory chapter is not equivalent to their definition in the glossary.

Let us end this account of Samuelson's concept of the fallacy of composition on a more positive note. His discussion of the concept in the introductory chapter usually includes a methodological reflection which is extremely important, deeply revealing, and essentially accurate. For ease of reference, I shall call it Samuelson's manifesto on critical thinking. As I have already mentioned, that section of the introduction begins with a list of several examples described by cryptic statements that are claimed to be apparently paradoxical but actually true. After such a list, and before mentioning the fallacy of composition, we find the following reflection: "In the course of this book, each of the above seeming paradoxes will be resolved. Once explained, each is so obvious that you will wonder how anyone could ever have failed to notice it. This again is typical of economics. There are no magic formulas or hidden tricks. Anything that is really correct will seem perfectly reasonable once the argument is carefully developed."[20]

That is, Samuelson seems to want to make the truths of economics as being based on careful argumentation, understandable through explanation, and susceptible of being made reasonable. I believe that, by and large, he succeeds in this aim, and that these qualities may account for the success, popularity, and longevity of his textbook. Thus, my criticism of his concept and examples of the fallacy of composition should not be misinterpreted as being general, but should be limited to this particular issue. However, it must be reported that in later editions, the critical-thinking manifesto is basically

---

[18] Samuelson and Nordhaus 2001, 6; 2010, 6.
[19] Samuelson and Nordhaus 2001, 764; 2010, 662.
[20] Samuelson 1948, 8-9. Cf. Samuelson (1955, 10; 1961, 13; 1964, 11; 1970, 12); Samuelson and Temin 1976, 14.

or totally missing.[21]

3. The Paradox of Thrift

The so-called "paradox of thrift" is the example most commonly given and discussed for the fallacy of composition. The best explanation is perhaps the one found in the 10th edition of 1976:

> An increased desire to consume—which is another way of looking at a decreased desire to save—is likely to boost business sales and increase investment. On the other hand, a decreased desire to consume — i.e., an increase in thriftiness — is likely to reduce inflationary pressure in times of booming incomes; but in time of depression, it could make the depression worse and reduce the amount of actual net capital formation in the community. *High consumption and high investment are then hand in hand rather than opposed to each other.*
>
> This surprising result is sometimes called the "paradox of thrift." It is a paradox because most of us used to be taught that thrift is *always* a good thing. Ben Franklin's *Poor Richard's Almanac* never tired of preaching the doctrine of saving ... Let us for the moment leave our cherished beliefs aside and try to disentangle the paradox in a dispassionate, scientific manner. Two considerations will help to clarify the whole matter.
>
> The first is this. In economics, remember, we must always be on guard against the logical fallacy of composition. That is to say, what is good for each person separately need *not* thereby always be good for all; under some circumstances, private prudence may be social folly. Specifically, this means that the *attempt* of each and every person to increase his saving may — under the conditions to be described — result in a reduction in *actual* saving by all the people. Note the italicized words "attempt" and "actual"; between them, in our imperfect mixed economy, there may be a world of difference when people find themselves thrown out of jobs and with lowered incomes.
>
> The second clue to the paradox of thrift lies in the question of whether or not national income is at a depressed level. If we were at full employment and always remained there, then obviously the more of our national product we devoted to current consumption, the less would be available for capital formation. If output could be assumed to be always at its maximum, then the old-fashioned doctrine of thrift would be absolutely correct — correct, be it noted, from both the individual and the social standpoints. In primitive agricultural economics, such as the American colonies of Franklin's day, there was some truth in Franklin's prescription. The same was true during World Wars I and II, and during periods of boom and inflation: if people then become more thrifty, less consumption means more investment.

---

[21] Cf. Samuelson and Nordhaus 1985, 8-9; 1992, 6; 1995, 5; 2001, 6; 2010, 6.

But, according to statistical records, full employment and inflationary demand conditions have occurred only at intervals in our nation's history. Most of the time under laissez faire there were some wasting of resources, some unemployment, and some insufficiency of demand, investment, and purchasing power. When such is the case, everything can go into reverse. What was once a social virtue may then become a social vice. What is true for the individual — that extra thriftiness means increased saving and wealth — may then become completely untrue for the community as a whole.

Under conditions of unemployment, the *attempt* to save may result in *less*, not more, saving. The individual who saves cuts down on his consumption. He passes on less purchasing power than before; therefore, someone else's income is reduced, for one man's outgo is another man's income. If one man succeeds in saving more, maybe it is because someone else is forced to dissave. If one man succeeds in hoarding more money, someone else must do without. [Samuelson and Temin 1976, 237-38]

This passage seems to be advancing the following argument. To begin with, thriftiness may be defined as an individual's habit of spending and consuming less than he could afford, so as to save some money for future contingencies and for the accumulation of wealth. Now, it is a mistake to think that thriftiness is always a good thing, that is, under all economic conditions. On the contrary, thrift is sometimes harmful, specifically when there is unemployment or the economy is otherwise depressed. The reason for this is that, in a depressed economy, saving leads to less consumption; this results in less sales; this in turn causes cuts in production; less production implies a decrease in jobs or wages; and so poverty increases and the economy becomes even more depressed. On the other hand, when the economy is not depressed, that means that consumption, sales, production, and wages are at some maximum level, and so the only thing that saving can and does produce is investment, which grows the economy and increases general wealth; assuming, of course, that the economy is sufficiently developed as to have a mechanism, such as interest-rate adjustment, to stimulate investment when greater savings produce lower interest rates.

What, or where, exactly is the error of the traditional doctrine of thrift? It is to extrapolate what is true only under some economic condition, such as the American economy in Franklin's time, or during World War I, or during World War II. In such conditions, what is true is that thriftiness is *both an individual and a social virtue*. The extrapolation is to over-generalize this claim and think that thriftiness is both individually and socially virtuous always, under all economic conditions, even in a depressed economy. However, the error here is one of over-generalization or hasty generalization.

Here I am treating these two labels as inter-changeable, and there is no need to distinguish them, or make other finer distinctions within the concept

143

of generalization.[22] For the main point I want to make is that the traditional doctrine of thrift involves an error of generalization, insofar as its main conclusion is claiming more than warranted by the evidence, but would be correct if formulated in a more guarded manner. Moreover, I am saying that this is what *Samuelson's own criticism amounts to*; that is, here I am merely reconstructing his criticism, and not advancing my own additional criticism of the traditional doctrine.

Is there a fallacy of composition being committed? There would be if the error was to think that thrift was not only an individual virtue but also a social virtue. However, this is not the error because, according to Samuelson himself, there are times (during full employment) when thrift is thus doubly virtuous. The error is rather to think that, because thrift is doubly virtuous in a non-depressed economy, it is also doubly virtuous in a depressed economy. This is reasoning from what hold true only sometimes to what always holds true, not reasoning from what holds true of the parts or the individuals to the same holding true of the whole or the aggregate. Again, the mistake is standard and classic over-generalizing.

I believe that Samuelson's mis-characterization of a case of hasty generalization as an example of fallacy of composition is clear. Less clear is the import of his second criticism of the traditional doctrine of thrift. There, we seem to have a problem of unintended consequences. In a depressed economy, not all attempts or plans to save can be fulfilled. As Samuelson points out, most such attempts will be frustrated sooner or later by the worsening conditions caused by whatever saving has been accomplished. This is perhaps another instance of a generalization problem, since the main point of this criticism seems to be that in a depressed economy, not all attempts to save can be fulfilled, only some can come to fruition. Moreover, although Samuelson does not pretend to connect this second problem with the fallacy of composition, there may be a roundabout connection.

That is, recall that composition involves reasoning for all parts or individuals to the whole or aggregate. A fallacy here would supposedly have to involve the mistake of concluding that, given that all individuals were actually saving (actually being thrifty), then the whole economy would also be saving (i.e., growing or further investing). However, this would *not* be an error; for if the premise were true, the conclusion would indeed follow. The real problem is that the premise can be true only in a non-depressed economy; whereas when the economy is depressed the premise comes out false. In other words, if we are talking about a non-depressed economy, a non-erroneous argument of composition could be advanced; whereas if we are talking about

---

[22] For discussions of such issues, see Walton 1999; Woods (2004b; 2013, 209-16). Cf. Finocchiaro (2005, 109-47; 2014).

a depressed economy, no argument of composition could be advanced (the premise being unavailable), and hence no fallacy of composition could be committed.

In sum, the traditional doctrine of thrift does seem to embody some mistakes, chiefly an over-generalization or hasty generalization, but not a compositional error. The "paradox of thrift" does not really provide an example of the fallacy of composition.

4. Public vs. Private Deficits and Debts

Earlier (in the Introduction), I hinted at a popular misconception about private and public deficits and debts, and at professional economists' preoccupation to expose it. In fact, as Samuelson states in several editions, "the man in the street, if asked to make a list of important economic problems, will usually put the size of the public debt near the top of his list. A panel of economic experts, in this country or anywhere in the free world, will usually put the debt toward the bottom of any such list, and indeed some will actually include it on the credit side as a positive blessing.[23]

Of course, even among economic experts, this was not always so. Indeed, Samuelson himself tells us on more than one occasion that as late as "sixty years ago, economic textbooks dealing with public finance read much as they had in Adam Smith's time. From 1776 to 1929 there was little discernible progress. The Democratic President Grover Cleveland differed not a bit in his ideology of public finance from Republican William McKinley — or for that matter from Calvin Coolidge and Herbert Hoover. What were the clichés of oldfangled shirt-sleeve economics, the doctrines our grandparent were taught and preached to us in turn?"[24] One of the most persistent of these old-fashioned doctrines is formulated thus: "Public finance is simply an application of family finances. If a husband and wife spend more than their monthly income, they go bankrupt and misery follows. The same is true for Uncle Sam."[25]

Moreover, Samuelson labels this doctrine a myth, and explicitly charges it with the fallacy of composition: "Before we turn to the genuine burdens of the debt, it will be useful first to dispose of some ancient but hardy myths. 'How can the government go on running up debt? If my wife and I lived beyond our means and ran a debt, we'd soon learn what trouble is'. The person speaking thus has overlooked the fallacy of composition: what is true

---

[23] Samuelson 1964, 355. Cf. Samuelson 1970, 341; Samuelson and Temin 1976, 366.
[24] Samuelson and Nordhaus 1985, 347; cf. Samuelson and Nordhaus 1992, 624.
[25] Samuelson and Nordhaus 1985, 347; cf. Samuelson and Nordhaus 1992, 624.

for each unit may be false for the whole of society. ... What is true for individuals is not necessarily true for nations. We cannot simply assume that private vices are public vices" (Samuelson and Nordhaus 1985, 359-60).

This example has been a constant feature of the textbook since its first (1948) edition, where we find that this argument is explicitly charged not only with the fallacy of composition, but also with being unscientific: "In appraising the burdens involved in a public debt, we must carefully avoid the unscientific practice of making up our minds in advance that whatever is true of one small merchant's debt is also necessarily true of the government's debt. Prejudging the problem in this way might come perilously close to the logical fallacy of composition; and, instead of permitting us to isolate the true — all too real — burdens of the public debt, might only confuse the issue."[26]

Let us now see how Samuelson justifies his criticism that this argument commits the fallacy of composition. His justification apparently consists of two main parts. One part seems to amount to a direct destructive refutation of the reasoning in this argument, and will be discussed later. The other part may be viewed as an indirect criticism elaborating a positive constructive account of the burdens and benefits of public deficits and debts; this account, in turn, amounts to a denial of the argument's conclusion. That is, the argument's conclusion is that a public debt is bad (or, a "vice," or harmful, or irresponsible, etc.); whereas Samuelson's own claim is that a public debt is partly bad (or burdensome) but partly good (or beneficial). Let us see how and why.

As a preliminary terminological clarification, Samuelson points out that the deficit is a specific (e.g., annual) imbalance between expenditures and income, and the debt is simply the accumulation of previous deficits. This enables us to focus our discussion on the debt.

With that in mind, we must begin by making a crucial distinction between an external (or foreign) and an internal (or domestic) public debt. The former is indeed mostly bad. Or to be more precise: "Any public debt that is externally held does involve a current burden on the citizens at home, since in the end they have to send goods abroad corresponding to the interest payments and debt service. (Of course, if the original borrowing from abroad resulted in equivalent fruitful capital goods here, their fruits will cover the external-service debt; so the net effect of such borrowing, taken as a package, would be favorable to us.)"[27]

Next, let us understand one of the main effects of the growth of an internal public debt: "The principal way one generation puts a burden on

---

[26] Samuelson 1948, 426. Cf. Samuelson (1955, 350; 1961, 393; 1964, 354; 1970, 341); and Samuelson and Temin 1976, 365.

[27] Samuelson and Temin 1976, 377. In earlier editions, Samuelson literally begins his discussion with this distinction (1948, 426-27; 1955, 351; 1961, 394-95).

itself later or on a later generation is by bequeathing it less real capital than would otherwise have been the case" (Samuelson and Temin 1976, 377). For example, such a burden results not only when government borrowing is used to finance a war, but also when a war is financed through taxation.

Moreover, the later payments stemming from an internal public debt will usually involve "various internal transfer effects as one group in the community receives a larger share of the goods then produced at the expense of another group ... transfer effects between people of different ages then alive and certain effects within each generation's lifetime on how much they will receive of such consumption and at what ages. And the process of taxing Peter to pay Paul, or taxing Peter to pay Peter, can have definite costs: these can involve various distortions of production and efficiency" (Samuelson 1964, 364).

On the other hand, there are also beneficial effects of a growing public debt. One is that the greater amount of bonds owned by an individual "makes the average man feel wealthier. For good or evil, it raises his propensity-to-consume schedule: this may, in a poorly functioning system, be a great thing to reduce unemployment and increase both consumption and investment" (Samuelson and Temin 1976, 377).

Furthermore, there is a beneficial effect involving debt management and monetary policy: "the existence of a broad market in government securities makes possible extensive open-market operations of a stabilizing type and tends to enhance the effectiveness of monetary policy. Debt management by the Treasury and the Fed through a proper policy of open-market operations in bonds of all maturities that was properly carried out could enhance the stability of a modern system" (Samuelson and Temin 1976, 377-78).

Finally, there is a crucial quantitative consideration to keep in mind. As we saw from our initial letter to a newspaper editor, the numbers involved are often astronomically large. However, "it is important, also, to keep in perspective the size of the ... federal debt in relation to gross national product and interest charges" (Samuelson and Temin 1976, 375).

Samuelson's conclusion from such considerations is a model of judiciousness: "it would be a tragedy if people, in giving up their irrational fears of deficit spending, were thereby led to call the sky the limit. Unlimited spending can produce inflation, chaos, and waste. It is to be hoped that the discipline of rationality can replace the discipline of superstition and misunderstanding. After the shibboleth of a balanced budget has lost its power to limit public spending, the good society will have to replace it by a calculus of cost-and benefit" (Samuelson and Temin 1976, 378).

All these considerations are informative and enlightening about the truth of the matter, namely about what is true of public deficits and debt. In other words, they tell us that it is *not* true that a public debt is bad in every respect.

However, it is unclear that they tell us much about what is wrong with the argument that a public debt is bad because private debts (by families, merchants, and firms) are bad. On the other hand, Samuelson's account does include discussions that criticize explicitly and directly the reasoning in this argument. To these I now turn.

In many editions of his textbook, Samuelson adapts a criticism originally advanced by the nineteenth-century English historian Lord Thomas B. Macaulay, who was commenting on the public debt in England:

> At every stage in the growth of that debt the nation has set up the same cry of anguish and despair. At every stage in the growth of that debt it has been seriously asserted by wise men that bankruptcy and ruin were at hand. Yet still the debt went on growing, and still bankruptcy and ruin were as remote as ever. … The prophets of evil were under a double delusion. They erroneously imagined that there was an exact analogy between the case of an individual who is in debt to another individual and the case of a society which is in debt to a part of itself. … They made no allowance for the effect produced by the incessant progress of every experimental science, and by the incessant efforts of every man to get on in life. They saw that the debt grew; and they forgot that other things grew as well …[28]

The second "delusion" alleged by Macaulay corresponds to the final point of Samuelson's constructive account summarized above. The first alleged delusion corresponds in part to Samuelson's distinction between an external and an internal public debt. However, more importantly, Macaulay's first objection is a clear and incisive critical interpretation of the argument from private to public debt. Macaulay is interpreting it as an argument from analogy, and criticizing it as a weak analogy. I believe this captures the essence of what laypersons have in mind when they advance that argument: they are making a comparison between private debts and the public debt; they are asserting that (constant) private debts are a "vice"; and they are inferring that the public debt is also a vice. And the critique provides an effective way to refute this argument by undermining the analogy, pointing out various crucial differences: private debts are normally external, whereas the public debt is mostly internal; and private debts lack the benefits which the public debt enjoys deriving from its effect on private wealth and consumption and on monetary policy and debt management.

In short, the argument from private to public debt is a weak, erroneous, or flawed argument from analogy.[29] This criticism explicitly and clearly

---

[28] Quoted in Samuelson (1948, 439; 1955, 362; 1961, 406-7; 1964, 264; 1970, 345); Samuelson and Temin 1976, 370; Samuelson and Nordhaus (1985, 363; 1989, 404; 1992, 636). Cf. Macaulay 1875, 261-64.

[29] Cf. Woods's (2016a, 41) similar criticism, mentioned in the Introduction above.

advanced by Macaulay is shared by Samuelson (however implicitly and unwittingly). If so, however, it follows that Samuelson's attribution of a fallacy of composition to this example is misconceived lip service.[30]

This conclusion of mine is reinforced by the fact that in some of the later editions Samuelson added a discussion of an analogy between private and public debts. This discussion is essentially an analogical argument *supporting* the conclusion that the public debt is *not* harmful, and based on two claims: that there are cases of private debt that are not harmful, and that these instances of private debt are analogous to the case of public debt.

The case of a private debt elaborated by Samuelson is that of a large corporation, namely the American Telephone and Telegraph Company (AT&T). This is an American firm which originated in the 19th century, and which in the second part of the 20th century enjoyed a monopoly and became the world's largest corporation. Eventually, in the 1990's, the firm was split up and lost its monopoly. It is still a large firm, but since then other firms in the high-tech industry are much larger. Samuelson's elaboration of this analogical argument is found only in the textbook editions of the 1960's and 1970's.

> AT&T has grown all this century. It has floated new debt throughout this century, with never an end to it. If our economy remains healthy, AT&T will undoubtedly have a rising bond debt for the rest of this century. This is prudent finance. It is prudent to buy that bond debt, but not for the reason that the company has plants and equipment bought from that debt financing and which it could liquidate in a pinch. There is no one to whom AT&T could sell such specialized items in an emergency, since they are good only for the telephone business in which AT&T has complete local monopoly.
>
> Why is never-ending growth in AT&T debt prudent? It is prudent because *the dollar receipts the company can earn from its telephone services are sure to grow along with the population and GNP.* The interest on the debt, and the occasional refunding of the debt, can be paid for out of the revenues from the telephone company's customers. If they all become impoverished, say, by atomic war, AT&T would have to go bankrupt and not repay its debt. But in a growing economy, no going concern proceeds on the assumption that all the people will go bankrupt.
>
> What does the federal government use to pay its debt interest and refundings? Obviously, *it is the taxing capacity of the country's national product that any government can rely on.*
>
> So long as the money GNP grows at 5 or 6 per cent from now until kingdom come, the public debt of the federal government can grow at those rates,

---

[30] Many other economists have a tendency to pay lip service to the fallacy of composition, while implicitly or explicitly criticizing various arguments as flawed analogies: see Cline 1982, and Wray 2006; and cf. Finocchiaro 2016b, 52-53.

ultimately passing one, two, or any number of trillion dollars. No inflation need result if the process takes place in balance. And no bankruptcy or increase in relative tax burden. And no embarrassment to the Secretary of the Treasury. Like life itself, there is no end to the process.[31]

Samuelson is well aware that this reasoning is not, and is not meant to be, conclusive. The argument is only meant to be suggestive and to have some degree of strength. The analogy used and elaborated in the argument is meant to be positive, "reassuring … and … an antidote to misleading pessimistic analogies" (Samuelson and Temin 1976, 372). Here is, then, a strong analogical argument that a public debt is prudent because the private debt of a firm like AT&T is prudent, to be contrasted to the weak analogical argument on the other side, that a public debt is bad because the private debt of families or small merchants is bad.

However, the main point I want to stress is that here too we are dealing primarily with analogical reasoning, just as we were in the case of the traditional argument criticized by Macaulay. The fallacy of composition is nowhere in sight. Thus, the problem of private vs. public debt does not provide an example of the fallacy of composition, any more than earlier the paradox of thrift did, although for a different reason. Earlier, the reason why the paradox of thrift does not embody a fallacy of composition was that it actually embodies a hasty generalization; now, the reason why the argument from private to public debt is not a fallacy of composition is that it actually embodies a bad analogy. However, one final clarification is worth making here.

An important aspect of the problem of the public debt is that, although government deficits are likely to be beneficial when the economy is in recession, they are likely to be harmful in conditions of full employment and economic growth.[32] Thus, the claim that the public debt is harmful could be regarded as a generalization which is not always true, but must be qualified by specifying the conditions under which it is correct. This might suggest that the logical problem with the example of the public debt is one of generalization, and that one must avoid formulating it in a manner that is too sweeping. If so, then the error here would be similar to that in the paradox of thrift, for in both cases the pitfall to be avoided would be hasty generalization.

However, I believe that the important difference between the two cases remains, for the following reason. First of all, let us stress that we are talking

---

[31] Samuelson and Temin 1976, 372. Cf. Samuelson 1964, 368; 1970, 347.

[32] Samuelson would not deny this, although he does not stress it; see, for example, Samuelson and Nordhaus 2010, 632-33. Economists who are stricter followers of John Maynard Keynes stress and exploit this point to a much greater extent; see, for example, Krugman (2012a; 2012b).

150

about reasoning or argumentation, since in order to have a fallacy we must have an error of reasoning or an incorrect argument. Now, recall that for the case of the paradox of thrift the error was *not* to argue from thrift being an individual virtue to its being a social virtue, but rather to argue from thrift being both an individual and a social virtue under some conditions (full employment) to thrift being also doubly virtuous under all conditions (including during a recession). But for the case of the public debt, the error is to argue from private debt being (always) bad to public debt being (always) bad; and because of the disanalogy between public and private debts, such reasoning is incorrect, even during full employment, when both private and public debts are bad. The point is that, if and when public debt is bad, this is not *because* private debt is bad, but for other reasons.

5. Bank Creation of Money

A third common example of the fallacy of composition involves the topic of how banks create money. In the first edition (1948), Samuelson introduces the problem as follows:

> We now turn to one of the most interesting aspects of money and credit, the process called "multiple expansion of bank deposits." This is little understood. Most people have heard that in some mysterious manner banks are able to create money out of thin air, but too few really understand how the process works.
>
> Actually, there is nothing magical or incomprehensible about the creation of bank deposits. At every step of the way, any intelligent person can follow what is happening to the banks' accounts. The true explanation of deposit creation is simple. What is difficult to grasp are the false explanations still in wide circulation.
>
> According to these false explanations, the managers of an ordinary bank are able, by some use of their fountain pens, to lend several dollars for each dollar left on deposit with them. No wonder practical bankers see red when such behavior is attributed to them. They only wish they could do so. As every banker well knows, he cannot invest money that he does not have; and any money that he does invest in buying a security or making a loan will soon leave his bank.
>
> Bankers, therefore, often go to the opposite extreme. Because each small bank is limited in the way it can "create money," they sometimes argue that the whole banking system cannot create money. "After all," they say, "we can invest only what is left with us. We don't create anything. We only put the communities' savings to work." Bankers who argue in this way are quite wrong. They have become enmeshed in our old friend, the fallacy of composition: what is true for each is not true for all. The banking system as a whole can do what each small bank cannot do! [Samuelson 1948, 323-24]

151

This introductory account is repeated essentially unchanged in subsequent editions for the next four decades.[33] Let us note, to begin with, Samuelson's appealing and informal style of exposition that is typical of his textbook, as well as what I have previously called his reflective stress on critical-thinking and his judicious attempt to balance opposite extremes. On the substance of the issue, let us first focus on the thinking which Samuelson attributes to some bankers and which allegedly commits the fallacy of composition.

The bankers' thinking seems to amount to the following argument: banks (namely, the whole banking system) cannot create money because no individual bank can; in other words, each individual bank by itself is unable to create money, and so all banks collectively are unable to create money. Samuelson objects that "the banking system as a whole can do what each small bank cannot do: it can expand its loans, and thereby bank money, many times the new reserves created for it, even though each small bank is always lending out a fraction of its deposits."[34] This objection amounts to the criticism that while the premise of the bankers' argument is true, its conclusion is false. To justify this criticism, Samuelson primarily shows how and why their conclusion is false; namely, why it is false that the banking system cannot create money; or in positive terms, why it is true that the banking system does create money.

As Samuelson explains, the key to the process of banks' creation of money lies in the fact that they keep only a fraction of the money deposited with them, and lend or invest the rest. This was not always so. Banks evolved from goldsmith establishments, which originally were merely places for the safekeeping of valuables and charged a fee for the service. Eventually, goldsmiths realized that they did not have to keep 100% of all deposits in storage, since not all depositors would withdraw their valuables simultaneously. The goldsmith establishments would have to keep enough to accommodate the likely number of withdrawals. Thus came into being the system of fractional-reserve banking, which was nothing less than "revolutionary."[35]

With fractional reserves, what happens is the following. The amount of needed reserves is nowadays usually regulated by law and administered by the central bank. At the time of the earlier editions of Samuelson's textbook the required reserves in the United States were about 20% of deposits; at the

---

[33] Samuelson (1955, 272-73; 1961, 331; 1964, 296; 1970, 280-81); Samuelson and Temin 1976, 300-301; and Samuelson and Nordhaus 1985, 275-76.

[34] Samuelson and Nordhaus 1985, 276. Cf. Samuelson (1955, 273; 1961, 331; 1964, 296; 1970, 2810; Samuelson and Temin 1976, 301.

[35] Samuelson and Nordhaus 1992, 508; Samuelson, Nordhaus, and Mandel 1995, 490; Samuelson and Nordhaus 2001, 523.

time of the later editions, the reserves were required to be about 10%. I shall use the latter figure in my illustrations.

When a given amount of money M is deposited, the bank keeps 0.1M in reserve, and lends or invests the remaining 0.9M. The recipient of this loan usually deposits it in some bank, which keeps (0.1x0.9)M in reserve, and lends (0.9x0.9)M. Next, the recipient of this second loan also deposits it, and his bank keeps (0.1x0.9x0.9)M in reserve, and lends (0.9x0.9x0.9)M. This process continues indefinitely, so that the total amount of money in circulation becomes:[36]

M+0.9M+(0.9x0.9)M+(0.9x0.9x0.9)M+ ... =
$$= M(1+0.9+0.9^2+0.9^3+ ...) = M(1/1-0.9) = M(1/0.1) = 10M.$$

In general, given that the required amount of reserves is p percent of deposits D, the total amount of money circulating in the banking system is $D/(p/100)$. That is, in the original goldsmith system of 100% reserves, there is no change in deposits D; with 20% reserves, from a deposit of D the total generated is 5D; and with 10% reserves, the deposit D generates 10D.

This argument strikes me as being clear, plausible, and convincing, and does demonstrate how and why banks collectively create money. However, our focus is on whether, how, or why the bankers' argument from individual banks to the banking system is wrong and commits the fallacy of composition. And on this issue, I am not sure that Samuelson's criticism hits the mark. My main criticism would be to point out that Samuelson's own argument about the creation of money by the banking system also shows how an individual bank *can* create money.

Here, let me begin with his discussion of a "monopoly bank."[37] Samuelson himself points out that in some countries the banking system consists of a single bank with many branches, or perhaps a few such large banks. Although this is not true in the United States, such a situation is approximated in some particular states (chiefly California), and also within some large cities (such as New York); in such places, most of the banking is handled by a few large banks. It is easy to see that a monopoly bank can perform the same process which Samuelson's main argument attributes to the whole banking system, even though the various branches of the monopoly bank might be limited in the same way as individual banks are claimed to be. Thus, Samuelson himself shows how a monopoly bank can create money in the same way as a banking system does. To be less precise, but without loss of generality, instead of speaking of monopoly banks, let us speak of "large" banks, as Samuelson himself occasionally does. The point is that a large bank can and does create money, although not as much as the whole banking

---

[36] Cf. Samuelson 1948, 328; Samuelson and Nordhaus 2010, 465.
[37] Samuelson 1948, 330; 1955, 279; 1961, 338; 1964, 303; and 1970, 287.

system, or a monopoly bank, or even a "larger" bank.

This in turn raises the issue of "small" banks. In fact, when Samuelson agrees with the bankers' premise that no individual bank can create money, he is referring to small banks; and often he explicitly says so, as in the above quotations. Thus, presumably, it is only small banks that cannot create money. But is even this qualified claim true? I don't think so.

As Samuelson's main argument indicates, let us focus on the first step of the indefinitely long process of money creation in the whole system that generates a total amount that is a function of the required fractional reserve. Even the first-generation bank, where a deposit D has been made, generates the extra amount of 0.9D; when this is added to the original deposit D, we get a total of 1.9D. That is, the individual bank has almost doubled the amount of money in circulation. Admittedly, a small bank cannot do much more than this, although it can easily take the second step, when it receives a second deposit of 0.9D, for which it keeps only (0.1x0.9)D, and re-lends (0.9x0.9)D, or about 0.8D. Thus, the situation is not that an individual small bank is unable to create any money, but rather that it is unable to create the fully multiplied amount which the whole banking system can; it can create some money, although not as much as the whole banking system, or even as much as a "large" bank.

Actually, one other qualification or refinement is needed. Not even the whole banking system can really or literally create a total of D/(p/100), from a deposit of D, when the required reserve is p%. The reason lies in what Samuelson calls leakages, of which there are three main types. People do not leave into banks all the money which they have deposited, but withdraw some cash for pocket money. Second, banks themselves keep some cash on hand, without re-loaning or re-investing all that they could. And thirdly, for various reasons, banks sometimes keep excess reserves above the required percentage of deposits.

The upshot of these considerations is that it's not just the conclusion of the bankers' argument that is false, but also its premise. Thus, their argument cannot be invalidated by claiming that although its premise is true, its conclusion is false, which is the way Samuelson's criticism pretends. Actually, what his criticism really shows is that the fault of the bankers' argument is that it starts with a false premise and then arrives at a false conclusion. Let us now ask whether this fault makes it into a fallacy of composition.

To resolve this question, a crucial point to note is that the bankers' argument is indeed an argument of composition, or compositional argument. That is, the argument starts from a premise claiming that something is true of the individual parts of a system, and arrives at the conclusion that the same thing is true of the whole system; thus, the bankers are indeed assuming that what holds for the parts also holds for the whole. This interpretation seems accurate as applied to the argument which Samuelson attributes to the bankers. He gives no references, and I must report that this argument does not seem to be very common in the historical record and in empirical reality; at least this is so as compared with the argument from private to public debt, which is ubiquitous, but which turns out to be an argument from analogy rather than a compositional argument. However, here I shall not pursue this issue of who, when, and where advanced the bankers' argument; rather I shall focus on the argument as presented by Samuelson.

A second crucial point is that, generally speaking, not all arguments of composition are fallacious; some are inferentially correct, meaning that if the premises are true then the conclusion would also be true. Samuelson seems to uncritically assume that arguments of composition are always fallacious, so that all one needs to do to show or suggest that they are fallacious is to show or suggest that they have this form. However, this assumption is incorrect, and is refuted by the following argument, which has a compositional form but is valid: all the parts of this automobile have weight (mass); therefore, the whole automobile has weight (mass).[38] Thus, more would need to be said to show that bankers are committing the fallacy of composition when they advance the argument from individual banks to the whole banking system. Actually, Samuelson does say more, but as we have seen, his criticism shows something different.

That criticism shows not only that the conclusion of the bankers' argument is false, but also that its premise is false. However, this is not equivalent to showing that that there is an error of reasoning in arguing from their premise to the conclusion. The error of reasoning would depend on whether or not the conclusion *would be* true if the premise *were* true. Is this the case? Is it wrong to reason from how individual banks create or do not create money to how the banking system does or does not do so? I think that Samuelson's own account shows that such reasoning is *not* erroneous.

For, as already elaborated above, Samuelson's own account shows that the key to this phenomenon is the institution of fractional reserves. Given this practice, a particular bank can immediately expand the money supply by keeping 10% of a deposit in reserve and circulating the remaining 90%; this amount roughly to doubling the money supply. A larger bank with more branches can expand it more than that. The whole banking system can expand a given deposit ten-fold. However, none of this means that the whole system is doing something that particular banks cannot do. Rather, particular banks and the whole system are doing the same thing, namely expanding the money

---

[38] For details, see Bar-Hillel 1964; Walton 1989, 130; Finocchiaro (2015a, 27; 2016b, 53).

supply through the mechanism of fractional reserves. Moreover, if individual banks were unable to create money at all, so would the whole banking system. The whole banking system can create money as a function of the required reserve, because each particular bank contributes to that creation to some extent.

On the other hand, suppose a critic were to focus on a quantitative measure, and claim that individual banks cannot expand the money supply ten-fold (but only double it), whereas the whole banking system can do so. Then one could invent the argument that the whole banking system cannot expand the money supply ten-fold because no individual bank can do so. This would be a compositional argument with a true premise but false conclusion. And so one could criticize such an argument as a fallacy of composition.

However, such criticism would itself commit a fallacy, the straw-man fallacy and/or the violation of the principle of charity. For no sane person would modify the original bankers' argument by inserting the word "ten-fold" as this invented argument does, for when so modified the incorrectness of the reasoning is strikingly obvious; and in order to be a fallacy, an incorrect argument must also be common (namely, commonly occurring) and apparently correct. In any case, there is no reason to re-interpret the original bankers' argument in this manner. That would be like reformulating the above mentioned valid argument about the weight of an automobile as follows: all parts of this automobile weigh less than 1000 pounds, therefore, the whole automobile weighs less than 1000 pounds; this reasoning is clearly incorrect, but does not invalidate the other argument that speaks of weight in general, and does not quantify it as "less than 1000 pounds."

In short, Samuelson's example of the bankers' argument about the creation of money by banks is indeed an argument of composition, and it has a false premise and a false conclusion. Such a critical interpretation of the argument is implicitly demonstrated by Samuelson's own account. However, this is not to say that the example is a fallacy of composition, namely an argument of composition that is fallacious because it has a true premise and a false conclusion. This is the analysis to which Samuelson pays lip service; but once again, as in earlier examples, such lip service betrays logical misconceptions.

6. The Paradox of the Bumper Harvest

Another one of Samuelson's examples of the fallacy of composition is the so-called "paradox of the bumper harvest." He does not adopt this label until the very latest editions of his textbook,[39] and its explicit analysis in terms of the fallacy of composition is found in only a few editions.[40] However, this example happens to be one of the two or three whose introductory and cryptic description is found in almost every edition.[41] Moreover, this paradox raises interesting and novel issues. Thus, it is worth discussing here.

The paradox may be introduced as follows: "We have learned that an increase in supply, because of an abundant harvest or for whatever reason, is likely to depress price. So it is not surprising that Gregory King, the previously mentioned English writer of the seventeenth century, should have remarked on this fact. But King also observed a fact perhaps less obvious. His statistical studies convinced him that farmers as a whole receive *less* total revenue when the harvest is good than when it is bad. Paradoxically, then, good weather is bad for farmers as a whole" (Samuelson and Nordhaus 1985, 379).

The theoretical explanation of the paradox is in terms of the concept of elasticity, as applied to supply and demand: "The demands for basic food products such as wheat and corn tend to be inelastic; [that is,] for these necessities, consumption changes very little in response to price. But this means farmers as a whole receive less total revenue when the harvest is good than when it is bad. [The reason is that] the increase in supply arising from an abundant harvest tends to lower the price. But the lower price doesn't increase quantity demanded very much. The implication is that a low price elasticity of food means that large harvests ... tend to be associated with low revenue" (Samuelson and Nordhaus 2010, 71).

The analysis in terms of the fallacy of composition is this:

> The following examples are true statements that might surprise people who have fallen into the fallacy of composition ... If all farmers produce a big crop, total farm income will probably fall. To see how the fallacy of composition works, take the last example. A corn farmer works from dawn to dusk to increase yields, apply the right amount of fertilizer, and so forth. If she is successful in increasing output, then her income will rise handsomely. But if *all* farmers succeed in raising their output, the price of corn may fall so sharply that the total sales of corn (price times quantity) actually fall. This shows how what holds for an individual does not necessarily hold for the group. [Samuelson and Nordhaus 1992, 6]

Let us to clarify what is going on. Let us try to find the thing (namely, the condition) that holds for each farmer individually but not for all farmers

---

[39] Samuelson and Nordhaus 2001, 73-74; 2010, 71.

[40] Samuelson (1948, 452-53; 1955, 373-74); Samuelson and Nordhaus 1992, 6.

[41] Samuelson (1948, 8; 1955, 9; 1961, 12; 1964, 11; 1970, 11); Samuelson and Temin 1976, 14; Samuelson and Nordhaus (1985, 8; 1992, 6; 2001, 6; 2010, 6).

as a whole. It is *not* the amount or size of the harvest, for if each farmer produces a big ("bumper") crop, then the total production of all farmers will also be a big or bumper crop; indeed, this consideration would embody a valid compositional argument. Nor is the condition in question monetary income; for if total farm income falls, then the income of all or most farmers will fall on the average.

However, such considerations may be an oversimplification. Perhaps they reflect what is really the oversimplified statement of the example which Samuelson gives in the book's earlier editions, and which I myself have been calling "cryptic"; that is, "if all farmers work hard and nature cooperates in producing a bumper crop, total farm income *falls*."[42] Let us instead focus on the formulation which he adopts in the book's later editions. That is, "here are some true statements that might surprise you if you ignored the fallacy of composition: (1) If one farmer has a bumper crop, she has a higher income; if all farmers produce a record crop, farm incomes will fall. (2) ..."[43]

In terms of this latter formulation, what is it that holds for each individual farmer but not for the whole group of farmers?

What holds for each farmer looks like this: if a farmer is successful in increasing output, then her income will rise. However, this is not really or exactly true; this situation does not hold without qualification. What does hold instead is: if a farmer is successful in increasing output, *and not too many other farmers are similarly successful*, then her income will rise. And this is also true of each farmer; that is, if any one farmer is successful in increasing output, and not too many others are similarly successful, then her income will rise.[44]

On the other hand, what does *not* hold for the whole group? What does *not* hold is that if all farmers are successful in increasing output, then their total income will rise. This is not true. In other words, what is true is that if all farmers are successful in increasing output, then their total income will *decrease*. However, this is also true of each farmer; that is, if an individual farmer is successful in increasing output (when all other farmers are similarly successful), then the income of each will *decrease*.

In short, I don't think we have found something which holds (or is true) of each farmer, but does not hold (or is not true) of all farmers as a whole. Thus, it is not at all clear that we can properly formulate a claim that what holds for each farmer's income also holds for total farm income, such that the assumption of this claim would be an error, namely a fallacy of

---

[42] Samuelson 1948, 8. Cf. Samuelson (1955, 9; 1961, 12; 1964, 11; 1970, 11); Samuelson and Temin 1976, 14; Samuelson and Nordhaus (1985, 8; 1992, 6).
[43] Samuelson and Nordhaus 2001, 6; 2010, 6.
[44] On this type of criticism, cf. Woods's (2016a, 42) fifth point mentioned in the Introduction above.

composition. The idea of increasing income by increasing the harvest does not hold for farmers as a whole, but neither does it hold for individual farmers, unless the individuals involved are few in number. To commit a fallacy of composition one would have to believe that this idea holds for each individual farmer and so it holds for all farmers as a whole.

Finally, one more possibility is worth examining. This corresponds to how Samuelson describes the situation on some occasions. That is, "in the first chapter we learned that it is a fallacy to think that what is true for each is also true for all together. Here we have an instance as applied to farmers. Although the demand for each competitive farmer's wheat is very elastic, we already know that the demand for all wheat is very inelastic."[45] Thus, perhaps the concept of elasticity can help us define something that holds for each individual farmer but not for all farmers as a whole. One would then be committing the fallacy of composition, if one were to argue that, because the demand for each farmer's wheat is elastic, therefore the total demand for all farmers' wheat is also elastic. Here we would have an argument with the proper compositional form; we would be assuming that what holds for each individual farmer also holds for all farmers as a whole; and in the process we would be reasoning by starting with a true premise and arriving at a false conclusion. What better way to illustrate the fallacy of composition? Isn't the argument so interpreted a good example of the fallacy of composition?

The trouble with such criticism is similar to the one discussed earlier with regard to the topic of banks' creation of money, when the critic would invent the quantitatively specified argument that because no individual small bank can create money ten-fold, the whole banking system cannot do so either. As in that earlier situation, such criticism would be committing the straw-man fallacy and/or a violation of the principle of charity with regard to the argument that, because the demand for the wheat produced by each farmer is elastic, so is the demand for the total amount of wheat produced by all farmers as a whole. Indeed, the fallaciousness of the criticism would be more obvious in the present case because of the presence of the (relatively) technical terminology of elasticity. The point is that anyone who understands the concept of elasticity would be extremely unlikely to advance the just-invented argument from individual to total demand. Let us see why.

As Samuelson explains, "elasticity of demand measures the degree to which sales expand as price is reduced. Demand is elastic, inelastic, or unitary, depending upon whether a reduction in price increases, decreases, or does not change total revenue. This follows from the definition of elasticity of demand as the percentage change in quantity divided by the percentage change in price" (Samuelson 1948, 466). Thus, anyone wishing to determine

---

[45] Samuelson 1948, 452; 1955, 374.

whether the demand for an individual farmer's wheat harvest is elastic would have to examine whether the individual farmer's reduction in price increases his revenue; an individual "bumper" harvest would have this effect, and then one could conclude that the individual demand was elastic. However, anyone wanting to determine whether the total demand for all farmers' harvest was elastic would have to examine whether a price reduction by all farmers increased the total revenue of all farmers; a bumper harvest by all farmers would have the opposite effect, that is, decrease total revenue, because the price would have decreased but the total demand would have remained essentially unchanged; the conclusion would be that the total demand for all farmers' harvest was inelastic. To reach this latter conclusion one would not examine what was happening to the harvest, price, and revenue of an individual farmer; no one who understood the meaning of the concept of elasticity of demand would do it that way.

In other words, if one understood the concept of elasticity, one would know that you do not determine the elasticity of one variable on the basis of the elasticity of another variable. Rather, elasticity is a concept "used in economics to denote the responsiveness of one variable to changes in another variable. Thus the elasticity of X [individual quantity demand] with respect to Y [price] means the percentage change in X for every 1 percent change in Y" (Samuelson 2010, 660); it cannot be based on the percentage change in Z (total quantity demanded) for every 1 percent change in Y (price).

Going back to the substance of the issue, let us see what would be the error of believing that the fact discovered by Gregory King was really paradoxical. What would be wrong with thinking that when all farmers produce a bumper harvest, their total revenue (and the individual average revenue) should increase? One would be overlooking the fact that the demand for some goods like wheat is relatively fixed and constant, and the fact that a higher supply of a product decreases its price (other things being equal). The problem would be the ignorance, misunderstanding, or misapplication of the facts and laws of supply and demand. It's unclear that we are dealing with a logical error, or a pitfall in economic reasoning, at all, let alone with a fallacy of composition. If there is a logical error around, it is that of claiming that this fallacy is exemplified by the paradox of the bumper harvest.[46]

7. The General Demand for Labor

There is another example which Samuelson sometimes discusses in terms of

---

[46] On this specific point, cf. the third one of Woods's (2016a, 43) points anticipated in the Introduction above.

elasticity, and which thus appears at first as a paradigm illustration of the fallacy of composition. It concerns the topic of the economics of labor, and in particular the demand for various kinds of labor, and the resulting wages earned by workers. The textbook's very first edition explains this example as follows:

> One last example. Let us consider the demand schedule for labor; i.e., the number of workers who will be hired at each different wage. If a union can keep outsiders out, if its members have a special skill that cannot be done without, if machinery cannot be substituted for labor, and if the consumers need the employer's product badly, then the demand for union labor will be *inelastic*. The wage can be raised without throwing many people out of work. If the demand for labor is *elastic* because of the absence of one or more of the above conditions, then if the union insists on raising wages, the result will be unemployment for many of its members.
>
> In the construction industry, workers are organized into many different craft unions such as carpenters, plasterers, and plumbers. Because a builder's outlay for any one of these skills represents only a *small fraction* of the total cost of building a house, any one union can raise its wage without having its employment react vary elastically. This principle is sometimes called "the importance of being unimportant." The result tends to be high wages set by each craft because there is no incentive for them to moderate their demands.
>
> But when all crafts raise their wage rates, the cost of housing goes up markedly and people stop building. Thus the demand for all construction labor tends to be *elastic*. Taken together with the technical backwardness and chaos of the construction industries, the result may be much less construction than we need and often unemployment both in the construction industry and elsewhere.
>
> … Again, this is an illustration of the fallacy of composition: what's valid for the part may be false for the whole. [Samuelson 1948, 453-55]

Here we have apparently a clear example of the fallacy of composition, although in the reverse direction as compared with the previously alleged example of the paradox of the bumper harvest. That is, now one would be arguing from inelastic individual demand to inelastic total demand. The error would be committed by anyone who thought that, because the demand for the labor of any one particular construction craft is inelastic, the demand for the labor of all construction crafts as a whole is also inelastic. Such reasoning would be starting with a true premise but arriving at a false conclusion.

Now, in a sense, such reasoning suffers from the same abstractness as the earlier example about bumper crops. However, in the present case such an argument may actually reflect the thinking of labor unions when engaged in the struggle for higher wages. Underlying the abstract talk of elastic or inelastic demand, we now face concrete issues, such as the benefits and harm of higher wages, and the distinction between nominal or money wages and

161

real or absolute wages. As Samuelson explains:

> It is legitimate to draw up a demand curve of the usual general shape for one *small* labor market: as long as *all other* prices and wages are more or less unaffected, it is indeed true that a higher money wage in one sector is the same as a higher real wage there; it is true also that employment there can be expected to fall off somewhat at the higher wage.
>
> But remember the fallacy of composition. What is true for any *small* sector of the economy need not be true for *the whole aggregate*. If all wage rates rise, it is dangerous to suppose that commodity prices will remain constant. Thus, doubling all money wages *might* well result in a doubling of all prices. Were that the case, the real wage would not be changed at all. ...
>
> Remember that wages are not simply costs: they also represent *incomes* of most of the population. Therefore the sales revenue of business enterprises is vastly affected by a substantial change in wage levels. Since the demand for labor is a demand derived from the demand for business products, it is clear that any change in general wages must shift the general demand curve for labor.
>
> To illustrate this pitfall, ask the following question: In 1932 or 1975 when there was widespread unemployment, would an all-round cut in money wages have *increased* employment? Or, as claimed by trade-unionists, would such a decrease in general money wages have decreased "purchasing power" and *decreased* employment?
>
> To the extent that a halving of wages would result is a halving of *all* prices, and of *all* money incomes, and of *all* money spending, the answer must be obvious. Such a completely balanced deflation would neither help nor harm the unemployment situation. This serves as a warning against accepting the superficial claims of those critics of labor who argue in terms of simple *dd* [demand] curves, and of those friends of labor who argue in terms of crude "purchasing power." [Samuelson and Temin 1976, 592]

It should be noted that, as indicated at the end of this passage, Samuelson sees himself, with some plausibility, as advancing a judicious analysis that avoids the one-sidedness and exaggerations of both advocates and critics of labor-union activities and interests. However, I am not sure this applies to the question of the fallacy of composition, which is our concern here.

Samuelson is pointing out that we must be careful in advancing or opposing union and workers' demands for higher wages. The workers in any one sector of the economy or of an industry can benefit from asking for and obtaining higher (money) wages, insofar as such higher wages will correspond to higher real wages. But this holds at best only as long as not too many other sectors ask for and obtain higher wages. If and when all sectors do, then what goes up is not only wages, but also prices, and so wages relative to prices do not change; that is, only nominal or money wages have risen, not real wages.

Certainly, we can agree with Samuelson that the failure to understand the clarification just made is an error, even an error of reasoning. But is it a fallacy of composition? In other words, is it an error describable as involving the assumption that what holds for each individual sector of the economy also holds for the whole economy? I don't think so. I believe that the error is to think that what holds for some parts also holds for the whole, whether the parts are particular crafts of the construction industry and the aggregate is the whole construction industry, or whether the individual parts are particular industries and the aggregate is the economic system as a whole. However, the latter is a generalization error. To have a compositional fallacy, we would have to have a compositional argument to begin with; and to have a compositional argument, our reasoning would have to start from the claim that it was beneficial and effective to raise the real wages of all particular sectors. However, Samuelson's criticism points out that this is an inherently impossible or self-defeating goal, and so a compositional argument cannot even get started, and hence there is no fallacy of composition.

As in previous examples, I am using the substance of Samuelson's own account to show that there is an error to be avoided, but that the error does not involve the logical fallacy of composition. In the present case, perhaps Samuelson himself is groping toward the generalization criticism, rather than the compositional criticism. This is reflected in the fact that in many editions of his textbook (from the second to the tenth) he discusses this problem under the label of "pitfalls in the concept of a general demand for labor."[47] This phrase could be interpreted to mean something like "errors in the process of generalizing about labor issues."

Let us now examine, however briefly, what type of generalization error we have here. Recall that earlier I argued that (according to Samuelson's own criticism) the paradox of thrift also embodies a generalization error, a kind of hasty generalization, rather than a fallacy of composition: the traditional doctrine of thrift (à la Franklin) claimed that thrift is prudent under all conditions, including a depressed economy, whereas it is actually harmful when there is unemployment, and so it is prudent only in conditions of full employment and economic growth. The generalization that is correct is one which is less sweeping than what the traditional doctrine advocated.

Now, for the present case of labor wages, we also have an incorrect generalization when stated universally as claiming that all laborers can benefit from a raise in their money wages. The truth is that only some can benefit this way; benefits (i.e., increases in real wages and purchasing power) can result only as long as not too many sectors get raises in labor wages. This is a situation similar to that of farmers producing a bumper harvest: farmers'

---

[47] Samuelson (1955, 550-51; 1961, 638-39; 1964, 570-71; 1970, 566-67); Samuelson and Temin 1976, 592.

income can increase only as long as not too many farmers produce a bumper crop; as we have seen, when all do, their income actually decreases. One difference between these two situations is that, when *all* are involved, the real wages of labor-union workers do not change (despite the increase in nominal wages), whereas the income of farmers actually decreases with a bumper harvest. In both of these cases, the correct claims must be formulated in a guarded or qualified manner: some individuals can increase their incomes (from higher wages or bigger crop sales) only as long as their number is not too large relative to the whole group of which they are part; only a part of the whole can increase their income, not the whole.

Perhaps such claims could be labeled generalizations, as long as we understand that they are not universal generalizations, nor generic generalizations, nor statistical generalizations. They are somewhat akin to existential generalizations, at least in the logicians' sense, i.e., statements of the form "Some A's are B," which in turn are taken to mean "at least one A is B"; but I would avoid this terminology, because such statements are usually contrasted to those of the form "All A's are B," and so it might be misleading to label them "generalizations." Moreover, the claims in question acquire importance and significance insofar as they refer to more than just a single individual member of a group. Perhaps the label "partial generalizations" might avoid all such difficulties, and yet convey the right idea.

Our conclusion is that the problem of individual vs. general demand for labor does not provide us with an example of the fallacy of composition, any more than Samuelson's other examples examined earlier do. The problem does embody an error of reasoning that may be plausibly attributed to some labor unions and workers asking for higher wages, and to those advocating reduced wages to cure depressions. And the error is the failure to be clear about the nature of partial generalizations ("Some, but not too many, A's are B"), and to distinguish them from universal generalizations ("All A are B"), generic generalizations ("A's are, typically, B"), existential generalizations ("Some A, at least, is B"), and collective generalizations ("The A's, as a whole, are B").[48] Such a generalization error is not exactly equivalent to hasty generalization, but is also present in some of Samuelson's other examples. In any case, the fallacy of composition is still nowhere in sight.

8. Beggar-thy-neighbor Policies

The phrase "beggar-thy-neighbor policies" refers to tactics and strategies

---

[48] These considerations could be compared and contrasted with the one contained in Woods's (2016a, 42) fifth point anticipated in the Introduction above.

which countries sometimes adopt and follow with regard to international trade. Here are some instances: tariffs on imported goods; quotas on the amount of goods that can be imported; bilateral exchange controls; and depreciation of the currency. The phrase obviously carries a negative connotation, so that such policies are meant to be intrinsically or usually wrong or harmful from an economic or political point of view.

Moreover, Samuelson sometimes discusses such policies as providing an example of the fallacy of composition. To be sure, this is not his most frequent, explicit, or extensive example, as compared to the ones already discussed. However, he does present it explicitly on at least three occasions, in the textbook editions of the 1960's and 1970's;[49] also, on at least two occasions, in earlier editions of the 1940's and 1950's,[50] he introduces it by analogy with the case of the paradox of thrift, which, as I mentioned earlier, is his most frequent example of the fallacy of composition; and in the cryptic descriptions found in the textbook introductory chapter, he gives some kind of tariff example in almost every edition.

What is the problem? In Samuelson's own words:

Great Depression and beggar-my-neighbor policies After the 1929 stock-market crash, foreign loans became worthless, new foreign lending ceased, and in every country there was much unemployment and unrest. With jobs scarce at home, the political forces of protectionism became rampant. Tariffs were raised, quotas imposed, and in many countries exchange controls were also imposed. Against the advice of almost 100% of the economics profession (who signed a petition to Congress), the Smoot-Hawley (1930) high tariff was passed. Cynics were delighted at the spectacle of a country *trying to collect debts from abroad and at the same time shutting out the import goods that could alone have provided the payment for those debts*; and at the swindle perpetrated on farmers—who were net exporters and not importers, and who were being given import tariffs on the export(!) products in exchange for their voting for tariffs on manufactures.

The fallacy of composition was at work. Each country believed that if *it* could develop a favorable balance of trade, *its* employment would increase at the expense of its neighbors; in effect, it would be succeeding in exporting some of its joblessness. But for everybody to run a favorable trade balance simultaneously is a self-contradiction—as impossible as for everybody to be taller than anybody else. [Samuelson and Temin 1976, 706]

Before we examine this fallacy-of-composition claim, let us look at the substance of Samuelson's criticism of beggar-thy-neighbor policies. The

---

[49] Samuelson (1964, 698-700; 1970, 682-83); Samuelson and Temin 1976, 706-707.
[50] Samuelson 1948, 373; 1955, 664.

harm of such policies stems from the fact that other countries are likely to adopt them as well; this will then reduce or nullify the comparative advantages which make international trade beneficial to all; and the end result will be drastically reduced international trade and highly inefficient production of goods in wrong places. As Samuelson puts is:

> One does not need much intelligence to see that foreign nations will not stand idly by while we attempt these policies. They too have economics textbooks, and legislators. They too, during a great depression, will be following beggar-my-neighbor tactics; they too will be raising tariffs and introducing import quotas and exchange control; they will be trying to depreciate the pound (or the franc as the case may be) so that the dollar will appreciate in value. In fact, they will be trying to up their exports and cut imports.
>
> What is the result when all countries try to beggar their neighbors in this way—when all try to climb on each other's shoulders to see the parade? Obviously, we cannot succeed in exporting to England more than she is exporting to us, while *at the same time* England is succeeding in exporting to us more than she is importing. Our mutual attempts to develop favorable balances of trade are worse than canceling. International trade drops to the lowest level of exports and imports. Both nations are worse off. [Samuelson 1955, 666]

None of this is or should be surprising. Underlying this whole process is the fact that "the attempt ... to generate a favorable surplus of exports over imports ... could be predicted to cut down on the fruitful division of labor" (Samuelson and Temin 1976, 706).

This criticism of beggar-thy-neighbor policies is plausible and acceptable as a first approximation. To be sure, there are qualifications and provisos which would have to be considered for a fuller and finer analysis, and which Samuelson himself elaborates in various places. For example, "if our neighbor abroad has overfull employment and inflation while at the same time we have unemployment, the above beggar-my-neighbor policies may then paradoxically be pleasing to both of us" (Samuelson 1955, 666, n. 1). Furthermore, "historical studies show that retaliatory tariffs usually lead other nations to raise their tariffs still higher and are rarely an effective bargaining chip for multilateral tariff reduction" (Samuelson and Nordhaus 2010, 357). And it cannot be denied that there are "noneconomic arguments that suggest it is desirable to sacrifice economic welfare to subsidize other national objectives ... there is more to life than economic welfare. A nation surely should not sacrifice its liberty, culture, and human rights for a few dollars of extra income" (Samuelson and Nordhaus 2010, 355). National security should, of course, be included in such a list of noneconomic aims. However, our main question is whether, how, and why beggar-thy-neighbor policies embody a fallacy of composition.

It should be boringly obvious by now that to find a fallacy of composition

166

we have to find someone thinking that what holds for each individual part also holds for the whole aggregate or system. Were the proponents and supporters of the Smoot-Hawley law of 1930 thinking along these lines? They were certainly thinking that, as Samuelson says in a passage above, if the United States "could develop a favorable balance of trade, *its* employment would increase" (Samuelson and Temin 1976, 706). But were they also thinking that if all countries could develop a favorable balance of trade, total employment in the whole world would increase? Now, Samuelson points out, correctly, that it is self-contradictory that all countries would develop a favorable balance of trade; this impossibility is as obvious as the impossibility of everyone being taller than everyone else. This obviousness leads me to say that the Smoot-Hawley supporters knew that it is impossible for all countries to develop a favorable balance of trade; thus, they did not think that if all countries developed a favorable balance of trade then world employment would increase. This, then, was *not* their error. Nor was their error to believe that if the United States could develop a favorable balance of trade then its employment would increase; for this belief was in fact correct.

Their error may have been to overlook the retaliatory policies of other countries. That is, their mistake was perhaps to think that if the USA instituted tariffs, quotas, etc., then it would develop a favorable balance of trade. This belief was incorrect; for it could be predicted that if the USA instituted such policies, then other countries would also adopt them; but if other countries also adopted beggar-thy-neighbor policies, then international trade would collapse.

On the other hand, it is unlikely that the Smoot-Hawley supporters completely overlooked the possibility of retaliatory policies. As Samuelson (1955, 666) himself says, "one does not need much intelligence to see that foreign nations will not stand idly by while we attempt these policies." Of course, one could be attributing them a lack of intelligence, but to do so would be a step toward oneself committing the straw-man fallacy or a violation of the principle of charity, a problem which we have encountered before. If we want to steer clear of this problem, we could say that the Smoot-Hawley supporters misjudged the predicted retaliation of other countries. That is, perhaps they over-estimated the intelligence of other countries, and attributed to them Samuelson's own argument that retaliatory policies usually do not work, reported above as one of the needed qualifications to his main argument. Or perhaps they predicted the retaliation, but were confident that they would win the resulting trade war.

The upshot of my considerations is that "beggar-thy-neighbor policies" may involve or exemplify errors of judgment regarding the law of comparative advantages, the retaliatory behavior of other countries, and the effects that would result. Certainly one should be on the lookout for avoiding

167

such errors. However, the fallacy of composition, again, does not seem to be one of these errors. Obsessing about it may even distract us from the main problems.

9. Conclusion

This investigation has been a case study in the empirical or naturalistic approach to logic and argumentation theory, and more specifically the historical-textual approach. This approach is an orientation that studies reasoning, argumentation, and critical thinking as found in actual texts produced in various concrete contexts in the course of history; moreover, the approach does not limit itself to observing such phenomena with a *tabula rasa*, but includes theoretical interpretation and critical evaluation. The concrete actual reasoning under investigation has been Paul Samuelson's textbook *Economics*, in all its 19 editions from 1948 to 2010.

Another methodological aspect of this investigation has been a sensitivity to meta-argumentation, that is, to arguments about arguments as found in the texts being studied. In other words, the arguments by Samuelson which we have examined are those that deal with a particular topic, namely the fallacy of composition. Now, this fallacy is an erroneous argument from premises about what holds for all the individuals of a group or parts of a system to a conclusion that the same hold for the whole group or system. Thus, Samuelson's own arguments are meta-arguments, and my own emphasis on them reflects my meta-argumentational approach.

We have seen that Samuelson's definition of the concept of fallacy of composition and his interpretation of the examples he gives are problematic or questionable (to say the least). Obviously, this corresponds to Wood's (2016a, 42) talk of economists not paying attention, mentioned in the Introduction above.

With regard to the concept, Samuelson's various definitions do contain a kernel that is self-consistent and adequate, namely that the fallacy of composition is the error of assuming that what holds for all individuals or parts also holds for the whole group or system. However, this core is often confused with the error of assuming that what holds for *some* individuals or parts also holds for the whole group or system; but the latter is actually an error of generalization rather than of composition. Moreover, to this kernel there are sometimes added other extraneous elements, such as: a possible confusion with the fallacy of division, which is actually the *converse* of the fallacy of composition; an exclusivist emphasis on the conclusion about the whole being based *only* on what holds for the parts; and a deductivist *exaggeration* of the strength claimed for the inference.

168

With regard to Samuelson's examples, they illustrate many things, but not the fallacy of composition. Sometimes the situation involves a hasty generalization, as is the case with the paradox of thrift. Other times the example is really a faulty argument from analogy, as it happens with the argument from private to public debt; and as we saw earlier in the Introduction, this criticism was anticipated by Woods (2016a, 41). Sometimes we do have an argument of composition that is *not* fallacious but essentially correct, unless it is misinterpreted in a straw-man or uncharitable manner; such is the case for the example of banks' creation of money. In the paradox of the bumper harvest, we do have an argument of composition (explicitly using the concept of elasticity) which is indeed erroneous, but which is artificial, abstract, and essentially irrelevant to the problem; the actual argument that is relevant does not commit a logical error, but a substantive one, such as the misunderstanding of the concept of elasticity and of the law of supply and demand. In the example of the general demand for labor, there is again an artificial and irrelevant argument of composition (involving elasticity) that is incorrect; but the real difficulty is primarily a generalization error different from a hasty generalization, and involving the failure to be clear about the nature of partial generalizations ("Some, but not too many, A's are B"). And for the example of beggar-thy-neighbor policies, there is no argument of composition, and the errors are not primarily errors of reasoning but rather errors of judgment; they pertain to the economic law of comparative advantages and to the historical vicissitudes of trade wars.

It would have been interesting, gratifying, and exciting if Samuelson's misconceptions and misinterpretations fit into a simple, nice, or elegant pattern of error. In that case, one would have been tempted to define a new fallacy consisting of erroneously claiming that a fallacy of composition has been committed, when in fact no such fallacy has occurred, because the argument is either non-compositional or non-fallacious. This abstract possibility is conjectured by Woods,[51] as we saw in the Introduction above.

However, there does not seem to be any such easily discernible pattern. Although that possibility might become the subject of some future deeper analysis, for the time being we must rest content with a more modest conclusion: Samuelson's (and other economists') concern with the "logical" fallacy of composition seems misguided and misplaced; the fallacy of composition does not seem to have the important role which Samuelson and other professional economists (often) attach to it.[52]

On the other hand, it may be possible to end the present investigation on

---

[51] For some additional reflections on this issue, see Woods 2016a, 43; cf. also Finocchiaro 2016b, 54.
[52] For some further evidence, see Woods 2016b, 59-60.

a more positive note, of sorts. That is, there is some evidence, from Samuelson's own textbook, that strengthens the modest negative conclusion reached here. Two distinct pieces of evidence are involved.

First, I have already mentioned in Section 2 above that the later editions of the textbook *de facto* drop the talk of and the concern with the fallacy of composition. Let me elaborate briefly.

The Preface to the 12th edition of 1985 begins by saying that "this twelfth edition is the most sweeping revision since the landmark 1948 first edition" (Samuelson and Nordhaus 1985, p. vii). Then it goes on to describe the various revisions in detail. These are also summarized as follows: "We have completely reorganized the order of presentation; the chapters on macroeconomics now use the comprehensive aggregate supply and demand approach; the microeconomics chapters have been streamlined; the application chapters have been refocused on problems of the 1980's; and, of course, the examples and factual material have been brought right up-to-date" (Samuelson and Nordhaus 1985, p. vii). Not to be missed is also the fact that "a major addition to the twelfth edition is the Glossary. This dictionary of economics has been especially designed for the introductory student — providing a capsule summary of all the major terms encountered in this text" (Samuelson and Nordhaus 1985, p. x). It is also worth mentioning that for this 12th edition Samuelson had a new collaborator, William D. Nordhaus, his former student and then professor of economics at Yale University; and Nordhaus was to remain Samuelson's constant co-author for all subsequent seven editions, up to the posthumous 19th edition of 2010.

The 1985 Preface says nothing about the fallacy of composition or revisions concerning it. However, the following changes may be noted. In the introductory chapter, there is, as before, a general discussion of the fallacy of composition in a section on the "methodology of economics." However, the list of examples, briefly described in a manner that I have been labeling "cryptic," is reduced from seven to five. Later, the 1992 edition lists only four such examples, and the editions of 2001 and of 2010 list only three.

More importantly, the 1985 edition begins a trend that reduces the number of subsequent explicit discussions of examples of the fallacy of composition. It has only four such explicit discussions, whereas the 1976 edition had had six. The editions of 1992, of 1995, and of 2001 each have only one such explicit discussion. The last edition, the 19th of 2010, has *none*. To be sure, this last edition still duly lists the term in the Glossary, and retains a shortened general discussion in the introductory chapter.

These changes in the textbook seem to be an indication that slowly and gradually Samuelson himself (perhaps stimulated by Nordhaus) realized that the fallacy of composition is not an important part of learning the science of economics; is not a crucial part of the "methodology of economics"; is not one of the main "pitfalls of economic reasoning"; is not a key part of the "logic of economics." It is none of these things, at least not to the extent that for more than four decades Samuelson himself thought. This is the same conclusion which I have justified in meticulous detail in the course of this essay. Thus, the negative and critical tenor of this investigation should not itself be judged negatively or critically, for it may now be balanced by the constructive and positive result showing that eventually Samuelson agreed with this thesis. It is, of course, unclear whether other economists have learned this lesson — another issue worthy of future exploration.[53]

The second piece of evidence is this. It is obvious that the motivation underlying Samuelson's concern with the fallacy of composition is the attempt to deal with the problematic relationship between microeconomics and macroeconomics. Certainly we must be careful when reasoning in both directions of this logical and methodological divide: from microeconomic premises to macroeconomic conclusions, and vice versa from macroeconomic premises to microeconomic conclusions. However, attempts to inject the fallacy of composition (and the converse fallacy of division) are misleading, confusing, and distracting over-simplifications or misconceptions.

Although this topic too deserves further investigation, the following example from Samuelson illustrates my point beautifully. It deals with the relationship between land rent and commodity prices, and explains the difference in the microeconomic and the macroeconomic points of view. The explanation is clear, insightful, and eloquent, provided that we drop talk of the fallacy of composition and forget about it. In the following passage, this can be easily accomplished merely by deleting the first sentence of the fourth paragraph, which is the only one that mentions the fallacy of composition.

> A factor of production like cornland is said to earn a pure economic rent (1) when its total supply is fixed or perfectly inelastic; and (2) when the factor has no other uses, such as land being used in the production of cotton. Adam Smith's great follower in England, David Ricardo, noted in 1815 that the case of such an inelastically supplied factor could be described in the following way: "It is not really true that the price of corn is high because the price of cornland is high. Actually the reverse is more nearly the truth. The price of cornland is high because the price of corn is high. Because the supply of land is inelastic, land will always work for whatever competition gives it. Thus the value of the land derives entirely from the value of the product, and not vice versa."
>
> **Rent and Costs**. Economists sometimes go further and say, "Rent does not enter into the cost of production." There is a grain of truth in this, but still it is very dangerous reasoning. If you were a corn farmer, you would certainly have to pay your landlord just like anybody else. You would certainly include rent in

---

[53] Again, on this point, cf. Woods 2016b, 59-60.

your costs of production, and if you failed to pay your rent, you would end up in court.

Relativity of Viewpoint. What then are economists saying when they claim that rent does not enter into society's cost of production? They are reminding us that rent is the return to a factor that is completely inelastic in supply, so that the same quantity would be supplied whatever the price. Therefore, the prices of goods really determine land rent — rather than land rent determining the prices of goods.

In fact, the paradox of land costs involves our old enemy, the fallacy of composition. What appears as a cost of production to an individual firm using a particular kind of land may be only a price-determined rent to the whole community.

This point is most easily seen when the land is specialized and can be used for production by only one industry. If a piece of land is inelastically supplied to one industry and has no place to go, it will always work for whatever it can earn there; its return will thus appear to every small firm as a cost like any other. But as observers of the whole industry, we must still recognize that the land return is a price-determined rent and not a price-determining cost.

In conclusion:

Whether rent is or is not a price-determining cost depends upon the viewpoint. What looks like a price-determining cost to a single firm or industry may for the entire economy be a pure economic rent paid to an inelastically supplied factor.[54]

Table of Samuelson's References to the Fallacy of Composition

The following table gives the page numbers where explicit discussions of the fallacy of composition may be found in the various editions of Paul Samuelson's textbook *Economics*. The first column lists in each row the edition number for which information is provided in a particular row. The second column lists the dates of each edition, and starting in 1976 the co-author(s). The third column gives the pages listed in the Index under the entry "fallacy of composition." The fourth column contains two items of information: the page numbers where there is a general discussion of the fallacy in the introductory chapter; and the number of briefly described examples given; not shown in the table, but worthy of note, is the fact that these introductory discussions are parts of chapter sections whose titles change in the following sequence: the whole and the part; methodology of economics; pitfalls in economic reasoning; and logic of economics. From the 5th to the 13th column we have page numbers on which various explicit

---

[54] Samuelson and Nordhaus 1992, 265-66. Cf. Samuelson (1955, 504-9; 1961, 596-97; 1964, 540; 1970, 538-40); Samuelson and Temin 1976, 561-64; Samuelson and Nordhaus (1985, 602-10; 1989, 666-67).

discussions of this fallacy may be found or not found. When a particular example of the fallacy of composition is *not explicitly* discussed, the word "NO" appears in the corresponding box. In some cases where the word "NO" indicates such an absence, some page numbers are given within brackets to indicate the pages where there is a relevant discussion, but without any explicit mention of the label "fallacy of composition." The first row, from column 5 to column 13, gives respectively identifying descriptions of the various examples: the paradox of thrift; banks' creation of money; public vs. private debt; general demand for labor; the paradox of the bumper harvest; land rent vs. commodity prices; beggar-thy-neighbor policies; general price rise fallacy; and microeconomics vs. macroeconomics. Finally, note also that some boxes are empty, which indicates that the corresponding editions (1951, 1958, 1967, 1973, 1980) have not been examined.

Table of Samuelson's References to the Fallacy of Composition

ed	Date co-author	Index refs	intro section pp / # e.g.	paradox of thrift	banks' creation of money	public vs private debt	general demand for labor	paradox bumper harvest	land rent vs comm prices	tariffs / beggar-my-neighbor	general price rise	micro vs macro
1	1948	8-9, 270, 324, 426, 452	pp. 8-9 7 e.g.	269-72	323-24	426-31	453-55	452-53	NO	NO[370-75, 539, 567]	NO	NO
2	1951											
3	1955	9-10, 237, 273, 350, 374, 505, 550, 693	pp. 9-10 7 e.g.	235-38	272-73	350-55	550-51 554#7	373-74	504-9	NO[664-66]	692-94	NO[360]
4	1958											
5	1961	12-14	pp. 12-14 7 e.g.	270-74	331	392-406	638-39 642#7	NO	596-97	NO[754-57]	403	NO
6	1964	11	pp. 11-12 7 e.g.	236-39	296	354-63	570-71 575#7	NO	540	698-700	361	NO
7	1967											
8	1970	11-12, 539, 566	pp. 11-12 7 e.g.	224-26 232#2	280-87 291-92	341-53	566-67 570#15	NO	538-40	682-83	NO	NO
9	1973											
10	1976 Temin	14, 238, 370, 563, 592, 596, 706	p. 14 7 e.g.	237-39, 247#2	300-302	365-78	592 596#15	NO [381-88]	561-64	706-7	NO	NO
11	1980 W. Samuelson											
12	1985 Nordhaus	8-9, 172, 276, 360, 604	pp. 8-9 5 e.g.	171-74	275-83	357-64	NO	NO [379]	602-10	NO [686]	NO	NO
13	1989 Nordhaus	?	pp. 7-10 4 e.g.	183-84		399-404	NO	NO	666-67	NO	NO	NO
14	1992 Nordhaus	6, 736	p. 6 4 e.g.	NO [480-85]	NO [506-13]	NO [624, 627-36]	NO [88-91, 222-24]	NO [69-71]	265-66	NO	NO	NO
15	1995 Nordhaus Mandel	456-57	NO	455-57	NO [488-96]	NO	NO [79-82]	NO [62-63]	NO	NO	NO	NO
16	1998 Nordhaus	6-7	pp. 6-7 4 e.g.	NO	NO [475-82]	NO [644-53]	NO [86-88]	NO [68-70]	NO [248-50, 264#1c]	NO [702-07]	NO	NO
17	2001 Nordhaus	6	p. 6 3 e.g.	510	NO [521-29]	NO	NO [91-93]	NO [73-74]	NO	NO	NO	NO
18	2005 Nordhaus	6	p. 6 3 e.g.	NO [454-58, 501]	NO [515-21]	NO [709-17]	NO [90-93, 232-34]	NO [71-72]	NO [264-66, 281#1c]	NO [311-12]	NO	NO
19	2010 Nordhaus	6	p. 6 3 e.g.	NO [416-20]	NO [463-65]	NO [630-38]	NO [91-93, 236-38]	NO [71]	NO[269-71, 81#3c]	NO [357-58]	NO	NO

References

Anderson, William L. 2010. Fallacy of composition, or a non sequitur? At http://krugman-in-wonderland.blogspot.com/2010/09/fallacy-of-composition-or-non-sequitur.html; consulted on December 14, 2015.

Archer, Maurice. 1973. *Introductory Macroeconomics: A Canadian Analysis*. Toronto: Macmillan.

Bar-Hillel, Yehoshua. 1964. More on the fallacy of composition. *Mind* 73: 125-26.

Barth, Else M. 1985. A new field: Empirical logic. *Synthese* 63: 375-88.

Black, Max. 1946. *Critical Thinking: An Introduction to Logic and scientific Method*. New York: Prentice-Hall.

Boudreaux, Donald J. 2018. Wilbur Ross flunks arithmetic — and basic logic. At http://cafehayek.com/2018/03/wilbur-ross-flunks-arithmetic-basic-logic.html; consulted on April 19, 2018.

Caballero, Ricardo J. 1992. A fallacy of composition. *American Economic Review* 82: 1279-92.

Cline, William R. 1982. "Can the East Asian model of development be Generalized?" *World Development* 10: 81-90.

Cohen, Morris R., and Ernest Nagel. 1934. *An Introduction to Logic and Scientific Method*. New York: Harcourt, Brace and Company.

Epstein, Richard A. 2018. Trumped-up economics. At https://www.hoover.org/research/trumped-economics; consulted on April 19, 2018.

Finocchiaro, Maurice A. 2005. *Arguments about Arguments: Systematic, Critical, and Historical Essays in Logical Theory*. New York: Cambridge University Press.

Finocchiaro, Maurice A. 2013a. Debts, oligarchies, and holisms: Deconstructing the fallacy of composition. *Informal Logic* 33: 143-74.

Finocchiaro, Maurice A. 2013b. *Meta-argumentation: An Approach to Logic and Argumentation Theory*. London: College Publications.

Finocchiaro, Maurice A. 2014. Essay-review of J. Woods's *Errors of Reasoning: Naturalizing the Logic of Inference. Argumentation* 28: 231-39.

Finocchiaro, Maurice A. 2015a. The fallacy of composition: Guiding concepts, historical cases, and research problems." *Journal of Applied Logic*, vol. 13, issue 2, part B, June 2015, pp. 24–43.

Finocchiaro, Maurice A. 2015b. Ubiquity, ambiguity, and metarationality: Searching for the fallacy of composition. In *Reflections on Theoretical Issues in Argumentation Theory*, ed. Frans H. van Eemeren and B.

Garssen, 131-41. Dordrecht: Springer.

Finocchiaro, Maurice A. 2016a. Economic reasoning and fallacy of composition, part I: The problem. *Eris: Rivista internazionale di argomentazione e dibattito*, vol. 1, no. 2, pp. 17-38. ISSN 2421-6747; at http://eris.fisppa.unipd.it/Eris.

Finocchiaro, Maurice A. 2016b. Economic reasoning and fallacy of composition, part III: Response to John Woods's comments." *Eris: Rivista internazionale di argomentazione e dibattito*, vol. 1, no. 2, pp. 46-56. ISSN 2421-6747; at http://eris.fisppa.unipd.it/Eris.

Kelly, Jr., William A., and Elizabeth S. Kelly. 2015. Obama and the 'fallacy of composition'. *The Wall Street Journal*, February 4. At http://www.wsj.com/articles/bill-kelly-and-elizabeth-sawyer-kelly-obama-and-the-fallacy-of-composition-1423095533; consulted on March 18, 2015.

Krugman, Paul. 2010. Paradoxes of deleveraging and releveraging. At http://krugman.blogs.nytimes.com/2010/09/03/paradoxes-of-deleveraging-and-releveraging/; consulted on December 17, 2015.

Krugman, Paul. 2012a. *End This Depression Now!* New York: Norton.

Krugman, Paul. 2012b. Nobody understands debt. *New York Times*, January 2, p. A21. At http://www.nytimes.com/2012/01/02/opinion/krugman-nobody-understands-debt.html?_r=0; consulted on December 15, 2015.

Krugman, Paul. 2013a. Austerity wrought pain, no gain. *Las Vegas Sun*, January 8, p. 3. At http://lasvegassun.com/news/2013/jan/08/austerity-wrought-pain-no-gain/#.VHPVyW1c75E.gmail.

Krugman, Paul. 2013b. The punishment cure. *The New York Times*, December 9. At http://www.nytimes.com/2013/12/09/opinion/krugman-the-punishment-cure.html?_r=0; consulted on December 15, 2013.

Macaulay, Thomas B. 1875. *The History of England from the Accession of James II*, vol. 4. Philadelphia: J. B. Lippincott & Co.

Mayer, Jörg. 2002. The fallacy of composition: A review of the literature. *The World Economy* 25: 875-94.

McConnell, Campbell R., and Robert C Bingham. 1960. *Elementary Economics: Principles, Problems, and Policies*. New York, McGraw-Hill.

McConnell, Campbell R., Stanley L Brue, and Sean Masaki Flynn. 2018. *Economics: Principles, Problems, and Policies*, 21st edn. Dubuque (Iowa): McGraw-Hill Education.

Samuelson, Paul A. 1948. *Economics, an Introductory Analysis*, 1st edn. New York: McGraw-Hill.

Samuelson, Paul A. 1951. *Economics, an Introductory Analysis*, 2nd edn. New York: McGraw-Hill.

Samuelson, Paul A. 1955. *Economics, an Introductory Analysis*, 3rd edn.

New York: McGraw-Hill.

Samuelson, Paul A. 1958. *Economics, an Introductory Analysis*, 4th edn. New York: McGraw-Hill.

Samuelson, Paul A. 1961. *Economics, an Introductory Analysis*, 5th edn. New York: McGraw-Hill.

Samuelson, Paul A. 1964. *Economics, an Introductory Analysis*, 6th edn. New York: McGraw-Hill.

Samuelson, Paul A. 1967. *Economics, an Introductory Analysis*, 7th edn. New York: McGraw-Hill.

Samuelson, Paul A. 1970. *Economics, an Introductory Analysis*, 8th edn. New York: McGraw-Hill.

Samuelson, Paul A. 1973. *Economics, an Introductory Analysis*, 9th edn. New York: McGraw-Hill.

Samuelson, Paul A, and Peter Temin. 1976. *Economics*, 10th edn. New York: McGraw-Hill.

Samuelson, Paul A., and William Samuelson. 1980. *Economics*, 11th edn. New York: McGraw-Hill.

Samuelson, Paul A., and William D. Nordhaus. 1985. *Economics*, 12th edn. New York: McGraw-Hill.

Samuelson, Paul A., and William D. Nordhaus. 1989. *Economics*, 13th edn. New York: McGraw-Hill.

Samuelson, Paul A., and William D. Nordhaus. 1992. *Economics*, 14th edn. New York: McGraw-Hill.

Samuelson, Paul A., William D. Nordhaus, and Michael J. Mandel. 1995. *Economics*, 15th edn. New York: McGraw-Hill.

Samuelson, Paul A., and William D. Nordhaus. 1998. *Economics*, 16th edn. Boston: McGraw-Hill.

Samuelson, Paul A., and William D. Nordhaus. 2001. *Economics*, 17th edn. Boston: McGraw-Hill.

Samuelson, Paul A., and William D. Nordhaus. 2005. *Economics*, 18th edn. Boston: McGraw-Hill.

Samuelson, Paul A., and William D. Nordhaus. 2010. *Economics*, 19th edn. Boston: McGraw-Hill.

Silk, Leonard. 1978. *Economics in Plain English*. New York: Simon and Schuster.

Sumner, Scott. 2011. Small is irrelevant (in macro). Posted February 25, 2011. At http://www.themoneyillusion.com/?p=9056; consulted on December 15, 2015.

Walton, Douglas N. 1989. *Informal Logic*. Cambridge: Cambridge University Press.

Walton, Douglas N. 1999. Rethinking the fallacy of hasty generalization. *Argumentation* 13: 161-82.

Woods, John. 2004a. *The Death of Argument: Fallacies in Agent-Based Reasoning*. Dordrecht: Kluwer.

Woods, John. 2004b. Hasty generalization. In Woods 2004a, 311-34 (Chapter 19).

Woods, John. 2013. *Errors of Reasoning: Naturalizing the Logic of Inference*. London: College Publications.

Woods, John. 2016a. Economic reasoning and fallacy of composition, part II: Comments on Maurice Finocchiaro's paper. *Eris: Rivista internazionale di argomentazione e dibattito*, vol. 1, no. 2, pp. 39-45. ISSN 2421-6747; at http://eris.fisppa.unipd.it/Eris.

Woods, John. 2016b. Economic reasoning and fallacy of composition, part IV: Some parting words. *Eris: Rivista internazionale di argomentazione e dibattito*, vol. 1, no. 2, pp. 57-61. ISSN 2421-6747; at http://eris.fisppa.unipd.it/Eris.

Woods, John, A. Irvine, and D. Walton. 2000. *Argument: Critical Thinking, Logic and the Fallacies*. Toronto: Prentice-Hall.

Woods, John, A. Irvine, and D. Walton. 2004. *Argument: Critical Thinking, Logic and the Fallacies*, 2nd edn. Toronto: Prentice-Hall.

Woods, John, and D. N. Walton. 1977. Composition and division. *Studia Logica* 36: 381-406. Reprinted in Woods and Walton 1989, 93-119, 279-81.

Woods, John, and D.N. Walton. 1982. *Argument: The Logic of Fallacies*. Toronto: McGraw-Hill Ryerson Limited.

Woods, John, and D.N. Walton. 1989. *Fallacies: Selected Papers 1972-1982*. Dordrecht: Foris Publications.

Wray, L. Randall. 2006. Teaching the fallacy of composition: The federal budget deficit. At https://edi.bard.edu/research/cfeps-archive/; first consulted on October 19, 2012; later on May 25, 2023.

Chapter 8
Argumentation Schemes for Composition and Division Arguments: A Critique of Walton's Account

1. My Acquaintance with Walton's Work

My acquaintance and involvement with Douglas Walton's scholarly work goes back a long time. In the 1970's, one of my main lines of research was the nature of fallacies, and so I read several of the articles on the topic that were being co-authored by him and John Woods; thus, one of my own major articles stemming from that period included a critical appreciation of their essay on the *post hoc ergo propter hoc*.[1] In 1985, Walton published an important book on *ad hominem* arguments entitled *Arguer's Position: A Pragmatic Study of Ad Hominem Attack, Criticism, Refutation, and Fallacy*; and upon the invitation of Henry Johnstone Jr, editor of the journal *Philosophy and Rhetoric*, I wrote a review of it that was extremely favorable, although not uncritical.[2] Next, in the 1990's, one strand of my work was a critique of the dialogical and dialectical approaches to the study of argumentation, and at one point I criticized Walton's own approach, as he had elaborated it in the first two chapters of his then-recent *Argument Structure: A Pragmatic Theory*.[3] More recently, in the context of my work on the fallacy of composition, I found myself studying a theoretical article on the topic co-authored by Woods and Walton, and a practical application of the concept to economic reasoning, as elaborated in their textbook *Argument: Critical Thinking, Logic and the Fallacies*; I found their work on the fallacy of composition in economics inspiring, fruitful, and important, but criticized them for not having continued to pursue such a project, and committed myself to doing so.[4]

Besides the occasions just mentioned, which left a published record, I had other encounters with Walton's work which did not, but were also important. I certainly read his *Informal Logic: A Handbook for Critical Argumentation* (Walton 1989), and I could see that the book had some value for students and outsiders to the field. However, from the point of view of a specialist who had contributed to the development of the field, my overall impression was that (to use a cliché) what was new was not true and what

---

[1] Woods and Walton 1977b; cf. Finocchiaro 1981, 18-20.
[2] Walton 1985; cf. Finocchiaro 1987.
[3] Walton 1996b; cf. Finocchiaro 1999, 270-71.
[4] Woods and Walton 1977a; Woods, Irvine, and Walton 2004, 250-67. Cf. Finocchiaro 2015; 2016a; 2016b.

was true was not new.

Analogous but appropriately different was my reaction to *A Pragmatic Theory of Fallacy* (Walton 1995); again I avidly read it when it first appeared, but I was disappointed to have to conclude that this book was (to paraphrase Voltaire) neither pragmatic, nor a theory, nor a work on fallacies. Let me elaborate. First, the work did not strike as being pragmatic because the material and examples used to illustrate concepts were not sufficiently realistic and down-to-earth; to be sure, they were more realistic than the typical examples used in most textbooks, but not enough. Second, I did not find the book to be advancing a theory because it seemed to lack any ideas or principles that had the requisite simplicity, systematicity, unity, or explanatory power; that is, the book was too unfocused to be a theory, and too many topics came under discussion which had little connection with one another. Third, the reason why the subject matter of the work did not seem to be fallacy is the following: the book focused on various types of argument (e.g., *ad hominem*, analogy, and affirming the consequent) which, although deductively invalid, are not always logically incorrect; in fact, Walton himself tried to find the conditions under which such arguments are correct, and so such arguments are not always fallacies; thus, what we really had here was a study of certain argumentation techniques that are of special interest in informal logic, and a book that was not essentially different from the author's previous *Informal Logic*.

The next book by Walton that attracted my attention was *Abductive Reasoning* (Walton 2004). This topic was obviously much more focused than that of Walton's two previously mentioned works. Moreover, the subject matter happened to be much closer to my own interests, in light of my own long-standing work in the theory of explanation and the history and philosophy of science (cf., e.g., Finocchiaro 1973). Unfortunately, this ensured that my disappointment would be greater as a result of reading the book. In fact, the examples used continued to be insufficiently realistic (as previously encountered), but also insufficiently scientific; and by the latter I mean that for the most part they were not taken from science, but from the law and from everyday reasoning. Moreover, at the conceptual level the book advanced a muddled account of the meaning of the notions of abductive, deductive, inductive, probable, plausible, and presumptive arguments; and as far as I could tell, a root cause of this confusion was the failure to be clear and critical about the distinction between interpretation aimed to understand arguments and evaluation aimed to determine their strengths or weaknesses.

Finally, there was a fourth book with which I became acquainted, *Argumentation Schemes*.[5] Its contents included discussions of almost all types of arguments, and so it seemed relevant to several of my own research

---

[5] Walton, Reed, and Macagno 2008; cf. Walton and Macagno 2016.

projects. Moreover, because of the amount of scholarly attention and citations it received, this work was hard to miss. I concluded that this book would be worth consulting as needed in the future.

Now, despite the fact (just recounted) that my acquaintance with Walton's scholarship is long-standing and two-fold, I could readily admit that it was also meager and incomplete, for I was also aware of the obvious fact that his scholarly output was massive. Thus, for the purpose of the present contribution, I decided to become better acquainted with it. However, again, because of the magnitude of Walton's work, my plan was not to study or read all of it, which would have necessitated the unrealistic abandonment of all my other scholarly interests and involvements; rather, my plan was to learn more of, and about, his work in the hope of finding a manageable topic amenable to discussion in a brief essay appropriate to the present context.

Accordingly, I read various reviews of Walton's books. To begin with, regarding Walton's *Pragmatic Theory of Fallacy* (1995), Ralph Johnson's (1998) review was mostly critical, and thus reinforced my own unpublished opinion of this book. On the other hand, I also read Woods's (2001) review of Walton's (1998) *Ad Hominem Arguments*; I was pleased to discover that the review was highly positive, thus confirming my own judgment about Walton's earlier book on this particular topic. I also read Tony Blair's (1999a; 1999b) review of *Argumentation Schemes for Presumptive Reasoning* (Walton 1996a), which is mostly critical despite some deferential lip service. For the *Fundamentals of Critical Argumentation* (Walton 2006), I found Marcin Lewinski's (2009) review very valuable. Regarding *Argumentation Schemes* (Walton, Macagno, and Reed 2008), I found the critical analysis by Christoph Lumer (2011; 2016) very informative, insightful, and incisive. For *Methods of Argumentation* (Walton 2013), the review by Corina Andone (2014) was very useful.

As a result of this increased acquaintance with Walton's work, and of the evolution of my own scholarly involvements, it became increasingly clear to me that I should try to write something on the connection between the notion of argumentation scheme and the fallacy of composition. To this end, one more piece of research I undertook was to see whether this topic had been discussed by Walton in places other than those I was already acquainted with, such as the 1977 article co-authored with Woods, the co-authored textbook *Argument*, the book *Informal Logic*, and the book *Argumentation Schemes*. Although I found no additional sustained discussions, a few other minor ones emerged. For example, there is a discussion of "composition and division" in a very brief section of Chapter 8 of *Informal Fallacies: Towards a Theory of Argument Criticisms* (Walton 1987, 214-15); there is a one-paragraph mention in *Fallacies Arising from Ambiguity* (Walton 1996c, 99-100, 274-75); and there is a repetition of the four-page discussion from the first edition of *Informal Logic* in the second edition of this book.[6]

2. Walton on Argumentation Schemes for Arguments from Composition and Division

Let us now try to reconstruct Walton's account of argumentation schemes as they apply to the fallacy of composition, including the related concepts of argument from composition, argument from division, and fallacy of division.

To begin with, Walton is clear that we must make a distinction between the traditional concept of the fallacy of composition stemming from Aristotle and the current conception. The Aristotelian notion is based on the distinction between the distributive and the collective meaning of words. To say that a term is used distributively means that it refers to each entity described by the term; whereas to say that a term is used collectively means that it refers to the whole set of entities it describes. Thus, one possible error (a "fallacy") is to argue from premises that use a term distributively to a conclusion that uses it collectively. One common example of this, repeated by Walton (1989, 129) is the following argument: "A bus uses more gas than a car. Therefore, all buses use more gas than all cars." Here, the premise uses the words 'bus' and 'car' distributively: it is talking about each and every bus and car, and saying that if you take any one bus and any one car, and compare their gasoline consumption for the same distance, the bus will be using more gasoline than the car; in this sense the premise is true. However, the conclusion is using the same two words in a collective sense, since it is claiming that the entire class of buses consumes more gasoline than the entire class of cars; this is not true for the simple reason that there happen to be many fewer buses than cars.

Instead, the concept Walton has in mind (and discusses in more detail) is that of a fallacy of composition as an argument which erroneously reasons from parts to the whole, in the sense that the premises assert that something is true of the parts and the conclusion infers that the same thing is true of the whole. A common example, also mentioned by Walton (1989, 129), is this: "All the parts of this machine are light. Therefore, this machine is light." Obviously, there are many machines which are heavy (not light) even though all their many parts are light; being light-weight is not a property that can be transferred from parts to whole; weight adds up, so to speak.

A second important point which Walton hastens to add is that not all arguments having this form from parts to whole are fallacious; some are deductively valid. He gives the following example: "All the parts of this machine are iron. Therefore, this machine is made of iron" (Walton 1989,

---

[6] Walton 1989, 128-31; 2008, 156-58.

130); indeed, the property of chemical composition does transfer from parts to whole. In this connection, Walton wisely introduces the term "argument from composition" (Walton et. al. 2008, 113) to refer to an argument having this form from what is true of the parts to the same thing being true of the whole; thus, arguments from composition are sometimes correct and sometimes incorrect. It is only when such an argument is incorrect that one may speak of a fallacy of composition. Thus, the present point may be formulated by saying that Walton makes a second important distinction— between fallacy of composition and argument from composition.

Next, a third distinction is also worth emphasizing, namely that between composition and division. Walton is clear that there is a type of reasoning which is the reverse of composition: "an argument from division" is one that reasons from what is true of the whole to the same thing being true of the parts (Walton et al. 2008, 113). It too is sometimes correct and sometimes incorrect. In the latter case it may be called a fallacy of division, for example: "This machine is heavy. Therefore, all the parts of this machine are heavy" (Walton 1989, 130).

Using the notion of an argumentation scheme, the three points elaborated above may be formulated as follows. An argument from composition is one whose form fits the following scheme:

Premise: All the parts of X have property Y.
Conclusion: Therefore, X has property Y.
[Walton 1989, 130; Walton et al. 2008, 113, 316]

An argument from division is one whose form fits the following scheme:

Premise: X has property Y.
Conclusion: Therefore, all the parts of X have property Y.
[Walton et al. 2008, 114, 317]

In my opinion, these definitions in terms of these schemes are essentially correct. However, they are over-simplifications,[7] as we shall begin to see below when we discuss other versions of these arguments which Walton mentions, and also when I undertake a constructive and empirically based account. For the time being, I want to focus on a number of other issues.

The most immediately relevant issue pertains to the conditions under which such arguments are fallacious, or at least incorrect. Whether or not such arguments are incorrect, depends, according to Walton, on the answer

---

[7] Without intending to make invidious comparisons or to sow discord among friends, I should mention that such criticism seems to me to corresponds to John Woods's charge of "over-abstraction" against such a scheme (Woods 2016b; cf. Woods 2016a, Finocchiaro 2016a, and Finocchiaro 2016b).

to some corresponding "critical questions." For arguments from composition, the critical question is:

> Is property Y compositionally hereditary with regard to aggregate X? That is, when every part that composes X has property Y, does X (the whole) have property Y? [Walton et al. 2008, 113]

For arguments from division, the critical question is:

> Is property Y divisionally hereditary with regard to aggregate X? That is, when X (the whole) has property Y, does every part that composes X have property Y? [Walton et al. 2008, 114]

By way of criticism, I would like to point that these critical questions are unsatisfactory. The most striking flaw, which applies equally to both, is that they are completely useless and unhelpful. Each is merely a restatement of what it means to advance the corresponding argument; to infer a conclusion C from a premise P is to claim that when P is true, so is C.

Moreover, I would point out that both critical questions contain implicit definitions of technical terms, respectively, 'compositionally hereditary' and 'divisionally hereditary'. This is worse than unnecessary; it is distracting. They should be restated more simply. The first should read: "when every part that composes X has property Y, does X (the whole) have property Y?" The second should read: "when X (the whole) has property Y, does every part that composes X have property Y?".

A third criticism I would make involves the formulation of these critical questions in the so-called "User's Compendium of Schemes" of the book *Argumentation Schemes*. There, the critical question for the argument from composition reads: "Is property Y compositionally hereditary with regard to aggregate X (when X [the whole] has property Y, then every part that composes X has property Y)?" (Walton et al. 2008, 316). And the critical question for the argument from division reads: "Is property Y divisionally hereditary with regard to aggregate Y (when every part that composes X has property Y, then X [the whole] has property Y)?" (Walton et al. 2008, 317). Obviously, these formulations are incorrectly reversing the definitions of 'compositionally hereditary' and 'divisionally hereditary'. This reversal could be merely a trivial slip of the pen or typographical error, rather than a conceptual confusion. However, even so, I believe the reversal is significant evidence that Walton himself is not taking seriously these critical questions — that he too really regards them as useless.

Later, I shall try to be more constructive with regard to such critical questions, just as I shall also be regarding the form of the schemes. Before that, however, some more criticism is in order, which involves some of what Walton allegedly derives from, and attributes to, Chaim Perelman's *New*

Rhetoric (Perelman and Olbrechts-Tyteca 1969).

3. Walton on Perelman on Composition and Division

The above-mentioned "User's Compendium of Schemes" in the book *Argumentation Schemes* contains 60 sections each of which summarizes the definition and critical questions of a major type of argument. However, most such sections also include subsections that summarize subtypes of major arguments, to yield a grand total of more than 100 argument schemes. Thus, the section dealing with the argument from composition (Walton et al. 2008, 316) includes partly the scheme discussed above, which is labeled "generic," and for which the only reference given is to Walton's (1989, 130) *Informal Logic*; but that same section also discusses another scheme labeled "inclusion of the part in the whole," for which the only reference is a 10-page section of Perelman and Olbrechts-Tyteca's *New Rhetoric* (1969, 231-41). Similarly, the section dealing with the argument from division (Walton et al. 2008, 317) includes partly the scheme discussed above, which is also labeled "generic," and for which the only reference given is to Woods and Walton's (1982, 206-208) textbook *Argument: The Logic of Fallacies*; but this same section also discusses another scheme labeled "division of the whole into its parts," for which the only reference is once again the same 10-page section of Perelman and Olbrechts-Tyteca's *New Rhetoric* (1969, 231-41). In short, under the general labels of composition and division, besides the two types of argument on which I commented earlier, Walton discusses two other (sub)types, labeled respectively "inclusion of the part in the whole" and "division of the whole into its parts," and attributed basically to Perelman's *New Rhetoric*. Obviously, these two other types also need some discussion here.

Walton defines these two schemes as follows:

Inclusion of the Part in the Whole
Premise 1: y is a species (part) of X.
Premise 2: X is A.
Conclusion: y is A (is less A than X, because it is part of it; it is less A than X because it is a smaller part of it). [Walton et al. 2008, 316]

Division of the Whole into its Parts
Premise 1: X is the whole of $x_1, x_2, \ldots x_n$ ($x_1, x_2, \ldots x_n$ are the parts of the whole X).
Premise 2: Only if x_1, or x_2, or $\ldots x_n$ is A, X is A.
Premise 3: x_1 is A (no x is A).
Conclusion: X is A (X is not A). [Walton et al. 2008, 317]

No critical questions are listed for either one of these schemes. For this reason, and also because of various difficulties with these definitions, it is only natural to want to consult Perelman's *New Rhetoric*, to which Walton refers. But before we do that, let me add some comments.

First of all, it is undeniable that these schemes are a step in the right direction of correcting the over-simplification of Walton's "generic" versions of the arguments. The main improvement is the addition (in both schemes) of premise 1, which specifies which entities are parts of which whole.

On the other hand, from the point of view of simplicity vs. complexity, these schemes are unnecessarily complicated by the inclusion of additional possibilities added in parenthesis; this happens in the conclusion of the "inclusion of the part in the whole" scheme and in premise 3 and conclusion of the "division of the whole into its parts" scheme. Moreover, in Walton's definition of "division of the whole into its parts," it's unclear whether the 'only if' of the second premise is meant literally, or whether it is to be understood as 'if and only if'; if meant literally, then the third premise corresponds to the consequent of the conditional second premise, and so this scheme becomes a version of affirming the consequent, and the definition becomes whimsical and arbitrary.

Finally, there is what is perhaps a more serious difficulty. That is, Walton regards the "inclusion of the part in the whole" as a special case of the argument from composition. This is certainly a misconception because, according to his own definition, such "inclusion" is an argument from what is true of the whole to the same thing being true of the parts, namely an argument from division. Similarly, but in reverse, Walton's "division of the whole into its parts" is reasoning from what is true of parts to the same thing being true of the whole; thus, it is a version of the argument from composition, and not of the argument from division. It is now time to look at Perelman's account to see whether it is to blame for Walton's difficulties.

Let us begin with what Perelman labels "division of the whole into its parts" (Perelman and Olbrechts-Tyteca 1969, 234-41):

> The concept of the whole as the sum of its parts provides the basis for a series of arguments that can be called arguments of *division* … [p. 234]. We shall consider that in the argument by *division* the parts must be exhaustively enumerable, but that they can be chosen at will in a variety of ways on condition that by adding them up the given whole may be reconstituted. [P. 235] … the argument by division presupposes that the sum of the parts equals the whole and that the situation being considered exhaust the possibilities … [p. 238]. All the arguments by division obviously imply relations between the parts such that their sum can reconstitute the whole. [P. 239]

In other words, by "division of the whole into its parts," or more specifically by "argument of division," Perelman means what is commonly called argument from composition!!!

This point is reinforced by the clearest example he gives of such an argument: "one might prove to someone who doubts it that a city has been completely destroyed by enumerating exhaustively the districts that have been destroyed" (Perelman and Olbrechts-Tyteca 1969, 236). Here, I would add that this is a good example of a non-fallacious argument from composition.

Obviously, Perelman's terminology is linguistically deviant[8] and conceptually confusing (as it seems to have confused Walton and/or his co-authors). However, Perelman is at least consistent and does not seem to be himself confused, since the other type of argument which he labels "inclusion of the part in the whole" corresponds to what is normally called argument from division. In fact, his basic definition of "inclusion of the part in the whole" makes it clear that he is talking about "arguments … which are based on the principle 'what is true of the whole is true of the part'" (Perelman and Olbrechts-Tyteca 1969, 231). And as an illustration, he quotes "this assertion of Locke: For whatsoever is not lawful to the whole Church cannot by any ecclesiastical right become lawful to any of its members" (Perelman and Olbrechts-Tyteca 1969, 231). As it stands, this assertion is certainly cryptic,[9] but fortunately it can be clearly deciphered by consulting the original passage in Locke.

Perelman tells us in a note that this quotation comes from John Locke's "Letter Concerning Toleration," published in 1689. The context of this assertion is the following argument (Locke 1952, 4-7). Locke first argues that a Church is a free and voluntary society whose aim is to worship God and to acquire eternal life; it follows that a Church cannot use force to deprive its members of civil rights like liberty and private property; rather the only thing which a Church can do against persons who do not follow its rules is to expel them from membership in the Church; from this Locke thinks it also follows that clergymen, "whether they be bishops, priests, presbyters, ministers, or however else dignified or distinguished" (Locke 1952, 7) also cannot deprive Church members of liberty or property; "for whatsoever is not lawful for the whole Church cannot by any ecclesiastical right become lawful to any of its members" (Locke 1952, 7). In this sequence, the second, fourth, and fifth

---

[8] I am aware, of course, that Perelman and Olbrechts-Tyteca's *New Rhetoric* (1969) is a translation from the French (Perelman and Olbrechts-Tyteca 1958), and that perhaps the original French is not beset by this oddity. It would be interesting to check, but that is beyond the scope of the present investigation.

[9] Perelman's *New Rhetoric* has the merit of frequently giving illustrations consisting of texts quoted from classical sources, but also the demerit that such quotations are usually so cryptic as to require further analysis for an adequate understanding. Another example of such a double-edged presentation by Perelman involves the concept of begging the question and a quotation from Antiphon's speech on the murder of Herodes; this is criticized by Finocchiaro (1980, 273-77).

assertions make up a subargument with the form commonly termed "argument from division" and here labeled by Perelman "inclusion of the part in the whole." And, I would add, this is an interesting, plausible, and nonfallacious argument, although also not deductively valid.

4. Some Constructive Suggestions

Let us now try to move in a more constructive direction. Let us begin with the over-simplified and overly abstract (though essentially correct) scheme for the argument from composition: (P1) All parts of W have property Y; (C) Therefore, W has property Y. The first improvement to make here might be to split the premise into two parts: (P11) all a's have property Y; and (P12) all parts of W are a's. One reason for this is that in such argumentation one seldom asserts explicitly a claim such as (P1). Instead, one is more likely to explicitly assert (P11) and leave (P12) implicit. Similarly, regarding the connection between the parts and the whole, one needs to assume, and perhaps leave implicit, a third claim: (P13) if all parts of W are Y, then W is Y. Thus, we get the following scheme:

Scheme 4.1:
(P11) All a's are Y.
(P12) All parts of W are a's.
(P13) If all parts of W are Y, then W is Y.
Therefore, (C) W is Y.

This may also regarded as a cleaned-up or simplified version of what Walton, allegedly following Perelman, labels "division of the whole into its parts" (Walton et al. 2008, 317). The (P11) here corresponds to "Premise 3" there; (P12) here to "Premise 1" there; and (P13) here to "Premise 2" there.

Actually, various nuances may be added to this scheme. One is that sometimes there are two main subsets of W that have the property Y; besides the already mentioned a's, we have what we shall call b's. The above scheme would then become:

Scheme 4.2:
(P11') All a's and b's are Y.
(P12') All parts of W are a's or b's.
(P13) If all parts of W are Y, then W is Y.
Therefore, (C) W is Y.

More importantly, with regard to the first mentioned claim (P12), one is more likely to think of it as, or to formulate it as: W is a whole whose *relevant* parts are the a's. A similar qualification should be made for (P11), so that it

188

does not sound like a universal generalization, but rather like a generic or normic generalization, namely: *a*'s, normally, or typically, have property Y. (P11) might also have to be replaced by a statistical generalization, to the effect that: most *a*'s are Y. And (P13) might have to be formulated as a probabilistic claim. Then we would get a scheme such as the following:

Scheme 4.3:
(P11'') *a*'s are, normally, Y.
(P12'') The relevant parts of W are *a*'s.
(P13'') If all relevant parts of W are Y, then W is probably Y.
Therefore, probably, (C) W is Y.

Let me give some examples, which are not merely illustrations of the schematic concepts just presented, but rather actual argumentative situations from which I have derived these concepts.

Consider the problem of public vs. private deficits and debts in economics.[10] One of the most popular arguments on this topic is the following. It would obviously be wrong (irresponsible, unsustainable, and unacceptable) for a family to constantly live beyond its means by always spending more that it earns, borrowing money, and accumulating a growing debt. Therefore, it is wrong (irresponsible, unsustainable, and unacceptable) for the national government to constantly have unbalanced budgets, run deficits, and maintain a growing national debt. Without worrying for the moment about evaluating this argument, the focus now is on understanding that this is an argument from composition: the property Y is the irresponsibility of the practice of operating constantly with a deficit and accumulating a growing debt; the W is the national government; and the parts are families. Furthermore, one does not bother saying explicitly that families are parts of a national economy. But note also that one is assuming that families are the crucial or relevant parts of a national economy.

However, in this case, families ("the *a*'s") are not the only relevant parts of a national economy. Business firms ("*b*'s") are equally important and relevant. Now, it so happens that the same thing ("Y") is true of them as it is of families: it is wrong (and unsustainable, etc.) for a business firm to operate with constant deficits and a growing debt. Thus, the attribution of the same requirement to a national government can also be based on these parts, and the conclusion of the compositional argument is thereby strengthened.

Another example involves a topic widely discussed in political science and political sociology, the so-called "iron law of oligarchy."[11] This is the claim that a democratic society has an irresistible tendency to become

---

[10] Cf. Samuelson 1948, 426-31; Samuelson and Nordhaus 1985, 357-64; Krugman 2013a; Krugman 2013b; Finocchiaro 2019, 138-44.
[11] Cf. Michels 1915; Michels 1962; Finocchiaro 2015, 34-36.

oligarchical or anti-democratic. The evidence for this claim is the fact that, if one studies some crucial institutions advocating democratic values (e.g., political parties and labor unions), one finds that they inevitably become oligarchical in their own internal operations. Now, in such a context, political parties and labor unions may be regarded as the relevant parts of the whole society. Then assuming that whatever holds for the parts also holds for the whole, the argument infers the conclusion attributing the same property to the whole society.

Next, it may be of some interest to sketch the sub-argument supporting the above mentioned crucial factual premise about the oligarchic tendency of political parties and labor unions. That is: it is technically impossible for the majority of members to directly administer such institutions; they have to elect leaders; leaders get constantly re-elected, partly because at first they have an advantage over newcomers; moreover, they control party machinery, such as the press; and they change psychologically in their attitude due to the salary they receive, the power they exercise, their interaction with the ruling class, their age, and their attachment to their own accomplishments.

In this overall argument, the a's and b's of the scheme are political parties and labor unions. The W is the whole society. There is no pretension that they make up all parts of the whole society, but only the relevant parts. The property Y is the development of unavoidable anti-democratic tendencies.

Let us now try to formulate some principles for the evaluation of such arguments from composition. This corresponds to what Walton and his followers call "critical questions," but I shall call them "evaluative principles" or "principles of evaluation." Recall that the only such principle formulated by Walton was completely useless, being merely a definition of the term 'compositionally hereditary'.

The first principle I would formulate is one that makes clear that we are concerned primarily, not with the question of the deductive validity of the argument, but with the question of whether the inference is reasonable, plausible, probable, cogent, or strong; and if it is, how much. These terms are not given a precise or explicit definition, but are taken in their ordinary meaning. The point is primarily to provide an alternative to deductive evaluation. This is my formulation of a principle that has also been suggested by Juho Ritola (2009b), in the context of a commentary to a paper by James Gough and Mano Daniel (2009). Thus, we have:

Evaluative Principle 1:
Independently of the deductive validity of an argument from composition, the primary aim is to determine whether the inference from the premises to the conclusion is reasonable, plausible, probable, cogent, or strong, and, if so, how much.

A second principle may be gathered from some suggestions by Frans van

190

Eemeren and Rob Grootendorst.[12] It is based on two distinctions. One is between absolute and relative properties, for example, square vs. heavy. The second distinction is between structured or heterogeneous and unstructured or homogeneous wholes, for example a basketball team and a pile of sand. The principle asserts that properties can be transferred from parts to the whole if only if the properties are absolute and the whole is unstructured. This means that a property cannot be transferred from parts to whole when the properties are relative or the whole is structured; in all such cases, the corresponding argument from composition would be incorrect. Thus, for example, it would be correct to argue that this pile of sand is white because all its grains of sand are white; for in this case the property of being white is absolute and the whole pile is unstructured. On the other hand, in the other three possible cases the arguments would be incorrect: this figure, a rectangle consisting of two squares side by side, is square because all its parts are square (absolute property and structured whole); this pile of sand, from several truck loads, is light because all its grains of sand are light (relative property and unstructured whole); and this football team is good because its players are good (case of relative property and structured whole).

This principle is of some use, at least as long as one does not interpret it in too precise a manner. However, as van Eemeren and Grootendorst themselves recognize, aside from simple cases, it is difficult to determine whether a given property is absolute or relative, and whether a given whole is homogeneous or heterogeneous; frequently, this cannot be determined prior to, or independently of, knowing the correctness of the corresponding compositional arguments. In any case, we have:

Evaluative Principle 2:
In an argument from composition, determine whether the property ("Y") to be transferred is absolute or relative, and whether the whole ("W") is structured (heterogeneous) or unstructured (homogeneous). The argument is basically correct if and only if the property is absolute and the whole is unstructured (homogeneous).

There is a third evaluative principle, which I derive from the evaluative practice of the social scientists who have criticized the two arguments from composition presented above, dealing with private and public deficits and debts and with the iron law of oligarchy. Let us begin with the latter.

Recall that the argument for the iron law of oligarchy derives a claim about the unavoidable anti-democratic tendencies of a democratic society from the inevitable anti-democratic tendencies of political parties and labor unions, despite the democratic aims of the latter. Critics have objected that this inference from these parts to the societal whole is illegitimate because

---

[12] van Eemeren and Grootendorst (1992, 177; 1999).

there are some crucial differences or dissimilarities between parties and unions on the one hand and the society as a whole. Political theorist Robert Dahl[13] has focused on the phenomenon of competition: he has argued that a democratic political system usually allows competition among different political parties and labor unions, and such competition enables it to counteract the oligarchical tendencies at the societal level; however, political parties and labor unions are usually founded and run in a one-sided or partisan manner, which seeks to defend and foster the particular interests and aims of the members. And political sociologist Seymour Martin Lipset[14] has objected that there exists a crucial condition in democratic societies which is absent in undemocratic societies and in particular institutions of democratic ones: a constitutional stipulation or a traditional practice banning any one group from exercising tyrannical power over opposing groups.

Let us now look at the criticism of the argument from private to public debt. Economists[15] usually point out that there are significant dissimilarities between private and public debts, and that is the main reason why one cannot argue from what is true of the former to the same thing between true of the latter. To begin with, debts by families and firms are usually "external," whereas public debts are mostly "internal." That is, private debts usually involve money owed by families or firms to other entities, such as banks, or other families, or other firms. On the other hand, national debts mostly involve money which the citizens of a country owe to themselves. (Note the qualifications denoted by "mostly" here; for to some extent, many nations also borrow money from other countries; and insofar as such external debt grows, so does the analogy between public and private.) The next point to understand is that a public (internal) debt has many benefits which a private one does not: one of these benefits is that a public debt generates government bonds, and the private wealth and the consumption of the citizens who own such bonds increases; another is that the management of the public debt enables a government to manage such things as interest rates and the printing of money, and thus improve the economy.

Now, in the present context, the upshot of such criticism seems to be that an argument from composition is weakened insofar as there are important dissimilarities between the parts and the whole. However, by evaluating the argument in this manner, we seem to be interpreting it as an argument from analogy, rather than as an argument from composition. Now, even if this were true, perhaps the point to make would be to say that sometimes arguments that seem to be compositional are really analogical. And indeed, this point has already been suggested by Trudy Govier and partly endorsed by others.[16]

---

[13] Dahl 1989, 276; cf. Finocchiaro 2015, 34-36.
[14] Lipset 1962; cf. Finocchiaro 2015, 34-36.
[15] E.g., Samuelson and Temin 1976, 365-78; cf. Finocchiaro 2019, 138-44.
[16] Govier 2009; Finocchiaro 2013; Woods 2016a.

However, in the present context, I would like to explore whether such an argument can retain some aspect of compositionality while also having an aspect of analogy. The following scheme might do the trick:

Scheme 4.4:
(1) *a*'s and *b*'s are parts of W (perhaps the only parts, or the only relevant parts).
(2) *a*'s and *b*'s are Y.
(3) *a*'s and *b*'s are analogous to W (they have many properties in common).
(4) If two entities share many known similarities, they are likely to share additional ones.
(5) Therefore, probably, W is Y.

In such a scheme, one is still reasoning from what is true of parts to the same thing being true of the whole, which would amount to an argument from composition. But one is also claiming that there is an analogy between two entities, and that this analogy justifies attributing to one of them a property known to belong to the other. This scheme also seems to embody a connection between the two aspects; in fact, the analogy (claim no. 3) is being grounded mostly, and perhaps exclusively, on the part-whole relationship claim (no. 1). Moreover, just as in the usual argument from composition the part-whole claim is often not explicitly asserted, but implicitly assumed, the same thing happens here with the analogy claim. With these provisos and qualifications, we can assert that both the argument from private to public debts and the argument for the iron law of oligarchy fit this scheme.

This scheme also enables us to formulate the evaluative principle which the critics of these arguments were implicitly using. That is, we can interpret their criticism as an attempt to undermine claim no. 4 of this scheme. As stated this claim is not true: its truth depends on the absence of significant dissimilarities between the two alleged analogues. Thus, the claim should be stated as follows: if and only if, two entities share many known similarities, and they do not embody significant dissimilarities, are they likely to share additional similarities; in other words, two entities are likely to share additional similarities if and only if they share many known similarities, and they do not embody significant dissimilarities. Moreover, it should be noted that the other schemes (4.1, 4.2, and 4.3) discussed above also contain or assume a premise (the third one) that can be undermined by such dissimilarities. Thus, the evaluative principle we are searching for can also be applied to compositional arguments that do not explicitly have an analogical component. The principle might be stated as follows:

Evaluative Principle 3:
When evaluating an argument from composition, it is always relevant and important to check whether or not there exist significant dissimilarities between the parts and the whole. If so, the argument is thereby weakened; if not, the

argument is strengthened to some extent.

5. Epilogue

In this essay, I began by giving a general descriptive account of Douglas Walton's work in logic and argumentation theory. It is obvious that his work is impressive for its quantity and variety. Indeed, this point was further strengthened by the fact that, on the one hand, I have followed his work for about five decades, publishing several discussions of some parts of it, and privately studying other parts; on the other hand, I readily admitted that my acquaintance with it has been relatively meager. Thus, in the present context I undertook some further study of Walton's work. As a result, I decided to focus on the issue of argumentation schemes for the argument from composition and the argument from division. My reason for this choice was *not* that Walton had written a whole book on this type of argument; in fact, although (by one count) he wrote at least sixteen books on various special types of arguments (besides even more books on argumentation in general), and although he authored or co-authored several articles and chapters on arguments from composition and division, it so happens that his work did not include a whole book on such particular arguments. Rather my reason was partly that Walton wrote two books and many chapters and articles on argumentation schemes, and tried to apply the concept to every type of argument; partly that this aspect of his work has been very widely discussed in the scholarly literature; partly that in the last several years I have myself worked on the fallacy of composition; and partly that this fallacy continues to be widely regarded as extremely common and extremely important (Finocchiaro 2015, 25-26).

Thus, my next self-appointed task was to understand and reconstruct Walton's account of argumentation schemes as they applied to arguments from compositions and from division. This account is found primarily, although not exclusively, in his book *Informal Logic* and his co-authored work *Argumentation Schemes*. The account is relatively brief and involves one scheme and one critical question for each the argument from composition and the argument from division. Unfortunately, Walton's account is highly unsatisfactory. The main difficulties are over-simplification, uselessness, and muddled confusion.

Walton's account also includes some references to Chaim Perelman's account of "inclusion of the part in the whole" and "division of the whole into its parts," as he labels them in *The New Rhetoric*. These references motivated me to examine Perelman's account. This examination revealed that what Perelman calls "division of the whole into its parts" corresponds to what is usually called argument from composition, and what he calls "inclusion of

194

the part in the whole" corresponds to what is usually called argument from division; and Perelman also gives at least two interesting, clear, and plausible illustrations. Unfortunately, Walton's account misinterprets these correspondences as being the reverse of what they really are.

Finally, I attempted to sketch a constructive account of how the notion of argumentation scheme might be applied to arguments from composition and from division. My account elaborates four distinct (but interrelated) schemes for the argument from composition; such schemes are meant primarily to understand or interpret such arguments. Moreover, I also elaborate three principles of evaluation for such arguments, which are meant to correspond to Walton's "critical questions," whose terminology I wish to avoid; as my own terminology tries to make clear, such principles are meant primarily to evaluate or assess such arguments. Thirdly, my account is based on a presentation of some realistic examples, specifically the argument from private to public debts in economics, and the argument for the iron law of oligarchy in political science and political sociology. Fourthly, an interesting point that emerges in my account is that some arguments from composition are also simultaneously arguments from analogy.

Much more remains to be done, not only from the point of view of a general study of the fallacy of composition, as I have had the occasion of pointing out before (Finocchiaro 2015, 36-41). However, even from the point of view of the present focus (argumentation schemes for compositional arguments), further studies are needed. For example, perhaps more nuances need to be elaborated for the four schemes in my constructive account. Perhaps additional, although interrelated, schemes may have to be defined. Perhaps the same two points apply also to the three evaluative principles in my account; that is, more nuances for the principles already mentioned and additional principles to be formulated. And since such schemes and principles should be grounded on realistic examples, the search for the latter must continue.

References

Andone, Corina. 2014. Review of Douglas Walton's *Methods of Argumentation. History and Philosophy of Logic* 35: 304-306. DOI: 10.1080/01445340.2014.894711.

Blair, J. Anthony. 1999a. Review of D.N. Walton's *Argumentation Schemes for Presumptive Reasoning. Argumentation* 13: 338–43.

Blair, J. Anthony. 1999b. Walton's argumentation schemes for presumptive reasoning: A critique and development. In *Proceedings of the Fourth International Conference of the International Society for the Study of Argumentation*, ed. Frans H. van Eemeren, Rob Grootendorst, Anthony

Blair, and Charles A. Willard, 56-61. Amsterdam: SicSat.

Dahl, Robert A. 1989. *Democracy and Its Critics*. New Haven: Yale University Press.

Finocchiaro, Maurice A. 1973. *History of Science as Explanation*. Detroit: Wayne State University Press.

Finocchiaro, Maurice A. 1980. *Galileo and the Art of Reasoning: Rhetorical Foundations of Logic and Scientific Method*. (Boston Studies in the Philosophy of Science, vol. 61.) Boston: Reidel.

Finocchiaro, Maurice A. 1981. Fallacies and the evaluation of reasoning. *American Philosophical Quarterly* 18: 13-22. Reprinted in Finocchiaro 2005, Chapter 6, pp. 109-27.

Finocchiaro, Maurice A. 1987. Review of Douglas Walton's *Arguer's Position: A Pragmatic Study of Ad Hominem Attack, Criticism, Refutation, and Fallacy*. *Philosophy and Rhetoric* 20: 63-65.

Finocchiaro, Maurice A. 1999. A critique of the dialectical approach, part II. In *Proceedings of the Fourth International Conference of the International Society for the Study of Argumentation*, ed. Frans H. van Eemeren, Rob Grootendorst, Anthony Blair, and Charles A. Willard, 195-99. Amsterdam: SicSat. Reprinted in Finocchiaro 2005, Chapter 15, pp. 165-76.

Finocchiaro, Maurice A. 2005. *Arguments about Arguments: Systematic, Critical, and Historical essays in Logical Theory*. New York: Cambridge University Press.

Finocchiaro, Maurice A. 2013. Debts, oligarchies, and holisms: Deconstructing the fallacy of composition." *Informal Logic* 33: 143-74.

Finocchiaro, Maurice A. 2015. The fallacy of composition: Guiding concepts, historical cases, and research problems. *Journal of Applied Logic*, vol. 13, issue 2, part B, June 2015, pp. 24–43.

Finocchiaro, Maurice A. 2016a. Economic reasoning and fallacy of composition, part I: The problem. *Eris: Rivista internazionale di argomentazione e dibattito*, vol. 1, no. 2, pp. 17-38. ISSN 2421-6747; at http://eris.fisppa.unipd.it/Eris.

Finocchiaro, Maurice A. 2016b. Economic reasoning and fallacy of composition, part III: Response to John Woods's comments. *Eris: Rivista internazionale di argomentazione e dibattito*, vol. 1, no. 2, pp. 46-56. ISSN 2421-6747; at http://eris.fisppa.unipd.it/Eris.

Finocchiaro, Maurice A. 2019. Samuelson on the fallacy of composition in economics: A Woodsian critique." In *Natural Arguments: A Tribute to John Woods*, ed. Dov Gabbay, Lorenzo Magnani, Woosuk Park, and Ahti Veikko Pietarinen, 125-72. London: College Publications.

Gough, James E., and Mano Daniel. 2009. The fallacy of composition. In Ritola 2009a.

Govier, Trudy. 2009. Duets, cartoons, and tragedies: Struggles with the fallacy of composition. In *Pondering on Problems of Argumentation*, ed. Frans H. van Eemeren and B. Garssen, 91-104. Dordrecht: Springer.

Johnson, Ralph H. 1998. Review of Douglas Walton's *A Pragmatic Theory of Fallacy. Argumentation* 12: 115–23.

Krugman, Paul. 2013a. Austerity wrought pain, no gain. *Las Vegas Sun*, January 8, p. 3. At: http://lasvegassun.com/news/2013/jan/08/austerity-wrought-pain-no-gain/#.VHPVyW1c75E.gmail.

Krugman, Paul. 2013b. The punishment cure. *The New York Times*, December 8. At http://www.nytimes.com/2013/12/09/opinion/krugman-the-punishment-cure.html?_r=0.

Lewinski, Marcin. 2009. Review of Walton's *Fundamentals of Critical Argumentation. Argumentation* 23: 123–26. DOI 10.1007/s10503-008-9111-1.

Lipset, Seymour Martin. 1962. Introduction to Michels 1962, 15-39.

Locke, John. 1952. A letter concerning toleration. In *Great Books of the Western World*, vol. 35, *Locke, Berkeley, Hume*, pp. 1-22. Chicago: University of Chicago Press.

Lumer, Christoph. 2011. Argument schemes — An epistemological approach. In *Argumentation, Cognition and Community: Proceedings of the 9th International Conference of the Ontario Society for the Study of Argumentation (OSSA), 18-22 May 2011*, ed. Frank Zenker. Windsor, ON: University of Windsor. CD-rom; ISBN 978-0-920233-66-5; http://scholar.uwindsor.ca/cgi/viewcontent.cgi?article=1016&context=ossaarchive.

Lumer, Christoph. 2016. Walton's argumentation schemes. In *Argumentation, Objectivity, and Bias. Proceedings of the 11th International Conference of the Ontario Society for the Study of Argumentation (OSSA), 18-21 May 2016*, ed. P. Bondy and L. Benaquista. Windsor, Canada: University of Windsor. Online: https://scholar.uwindsor.ca/ossaarchive/OSSA11/papersandcommentaries/110.

Michels, Robert. 1915. *Political Parties: A Sociological Study of the Oligarchical Tendencies of Modern Democracy*. Trans. E. Paul and C. Paul. Glencoe: The Free Press.

Michels, Robert. 1962. *Political Parties: A Sociological Study of the Oligarchical Tendencies of Modern Democracy*. Trans. E. Paul and C. Paul. New York: Collier.

Perelman, Chaim, and L. Olbrechts-Tyteca. 1958. *La nouvelle rhétorique: Traité de l'argumentation*. Paris: Presses Universitaires de France.

Perelman, Chaim, and L. Olbrechts-Tyteca. 1969. *The New Rhetoric: A Treatise on Argumentation*. Trans. J. Wilkinson and P. Weaver. Notre Dame: University of Notre Dame.

Ritola, Juho, ed. 2009a. *Argument Cultures: Proceedings of the 8th Biennial*

Conference of the Ontario Society for the Study of Argumentation (OSSA, 2009). Windsor, ON: Ontario Society for the Study of Argumentation. CD-ROM, ISBN 978-0-920233-51-1.

Ritola, Juho. 2009b. Commentary on James E. Gough and Mano Daniel's 'The fallacy of composition'. In Ritola 2009a.

Samuelson, Paul A. 1948. *Economics, an Introductory Analysis*, 1st edn. New York: McGraw-Hill.

Samuelson, Paul A, and Peter Temin. 1976. *Economics*, 10th edn. New York: McGraw-Hill.

Samuelson, Paul A., and William D. Nordhaus. 1985. *Economics*, 12th edn. New York: McGraw-Hill.

van Eemeren, Frans H., and R. Grootendorst. 1992. *Argumentation, Communication, and Fallacies*. Hillsdale: Lawrence Erlbaum Associates.

van Eemeren, Frans H., and R. Grootendorst. 1999. The fallacies of composition and division. In *JFAK: Essays Dedicated to Johan van Benthem on the Occasion of His 50th Birthday*, ed. J. Gerbrandy, M. Marx, M. de Rijke, and Y. Venema. Amsterdam: University of Amsterdam, Institute for Logic, Language, and Computation. At www.illc.uva.nl/j50/; consulted on June 18, 2013.

Walton, Douglas N. 1985. *Arguer's Position: A Pragmatic Study of Ad Hominem Attack, Criticism, Refutation, and Fallacy*. Westport, CT: Greenwood Press.

Walton, Douglas N. 1987. *Informal Fallacies: Towards a Theory of Argument Criticisms*. Amsterdam and Philadelphia: John Benjamins.

Walton, Douglas N. 1989. *Informal Logic: A Handbook for Critical Argumentation*. New York: Cambridge University Press.

Walton, Douglas N. 1995. *A Pragmatic Theory of Fallacy*. Tuscaloosa, AL: University of Alabama Press.

Walton, Douglas N. 1996a. *Argumentation Schemes for Presumptive Reasoning*. Mahwah, NJ: Lawrence Erlbaum Associates.

Walton, Douglas N. 1996b. *Argument Structure: A Pragmatic Theory*. Toronto: University of Toronto Press.

Walton, Douglas N. 1996c. *Fallacies Arising from Ambiguity*. Dordrecht: Kluwer.

Walton, Douglas N. 1998. *Ad Hominem Arguments*. Tuscaloosa, AL: University of Alabama Press.

Walton, Douglas N. 2004. *Abductive Reasoning*. Tuscaloosa, AL: University of Alabama Press.

Walton, Douglas N. 2006. *Fundamentals of Critical Argumentation*. New York: Cambridge University Press.

Walton, Douglas N. 2008. *Informal Logic: A Pragmatic Approach*, 2nd ed. New York: Cambridge University Press.

Walton, Douglas N. 2013. *Methods of Argumentation*. New York: Cambridge University Press.

Walton, Douglas N., and F. Macagno. 2016. A classification system for argumentation schemes. *Argument and Computation* 6: 219-45.

Walton, Douglas N., Chris Reed, and Fabrizio Macagno. 2008. *Argumentation Schemes*. New York: Cambridge University Press.

Woods, John. 2001. Review of Douglas Walton's *Ad Hominem Arguments*. *Argumentation* 15: 503–507.

Woods, John. 2016a. Economic reasoning and fallacy of composition, part II: Comments on Maurice Finocchiaro's paper. *Eris: Rivista internazionale di argomentazione e dibattito*, vol. 1, no. 2, pp. 39-45. ISSN 2421-6747; at http://eris.fisppa.unipd.it/Eris.

Woods, John. 2016b. Economic reasoning and fallacy of composition, part IV: Some parting words. *Eris: Rivista internazionale di argomentazione e dibattito*, vol. 1, no. 2, pp. 57-61. ISSN 2421-6747; at http://eris.fisppa.unipd.it/Eris.

Woods, John, A. Irvine, and D. Walton. 2004. *Argument: Critical Thinking, Logic and the Fallacies*, 2nd edn. Toronto: Prentice-Hall.

Woods, John, and Douglas Walton. 1977a. Composition and division. *Studia Logica* 36: 381-406. Reprinted in Woods and Walton 1989, 93-119, 279-81.

Woods, John, and Douglas Walton. 1977b. *Post hoc, ergo propter hoc. The Review of Metaphysics* 30: 569-93.

Woods, John, and Douglas Walton. 1982. *Argument: The Logic of Fallacies*. Toronto: McGraw-Hill Ryerson Limited.

Woods, John, and Douglas Walton. 1989. *Fallacies: Selected Papers 1972-1982*. Dordrecht: Foris Publications.

Chapter 9
Do Arguments for Global Warming Commit a Fallacy of Composition?

1. Approach

This essay is a continuation of my previous work, at the level of methodology, of theoretical conceptualization, and of empirical research. Thus, it will be useful to briefly summarize some of that background material.

Methodologically, my approach is *historical-textual* in the sense that it focuses on the analysis of historically important texts containing reasoning, arguments, and critical thinking. It is a special case of an approach that is broadly empirical but also normative and theory-laden; it may be instructively contrasted not only to the apriorist orientation of formal deductive logic, but also to the experimental approach of cognitive psychology and the inductive-intuitive approach of analytical philosophy. Thus, my approach is similar (which is not to say identical) to what is called "informal logic" by Johnson and Blair, "empirical logic" by Barth, and "probative logic" by Scriven.[1]

Moreover, my approach is *dialectical,* in at least two senses of this controversial concept. One is that in the subject matter studied, I tend to stress counter-arguments, objections, criticism, evaluation, potential (and not necessarily actual) dialogue, and the clarification (rather than the resolution) of differences of opinion. The other sense of dialectical refers to my engagement in serious dialogue with other scholars. Thus, my fundamental definition is that "an argument is an attempt to justify a conclusion by giving reasons in support of it *or* defending it from objections [or both]."[2]

Within such a general approach, fallacies may be regarded as a special topic. My approach to the study of fallacies is aware that empirical observation is theory-laden. Thus, to begin with, I follow some of Woods's insights.[3] For example, I agree that fallacies are more like theoretical entities such as quarks in physics, rather than like concrete objects such as buttercups in everyday life. And I accept as a guiding idea the definition that a fallacy is

---

[1] See Johnson and Blair 1980, and cf. Finocchiaro 2005, 21-33; see Barth 1985, and cf. Finocchiaro 2005, 46-64; see Scriven (1987; 2009), and cf. Finocchiaro 2005, 5-7.

[2] Finocchiaro 2005, 319. Cf. Blair and Johnson 1987; Johnson 2000; Finocchiaro (2005, 292-326; 2013b, 65-74).

[3] Woods (1988; 2013). Cf. Hansen 2002; Finocchiaro (2014; 2015).

a (1) common (2) type of (3) argument that (4) appears to be correct but is (5) actually incorrect.[4]

Finally, in the study of fallacies, I have been practicing a meta-argumentational approach.[5] That is, one distinguishes a meta-argument from a ground-level argument, and defines the former as an argument about one or more arguments, or about argumentation in general. Then a ground-level argument can be defined as one about such things as natural phenomena, historical events, human actions, mathematical numbers, or metaphysical entities. A prototypical case of meta-argumentation is argument analysis, in which one advances and justifies interpretive or evaluative claims about ground-level arguments. Then we search for fallacies primarily in meta-argumentation rather than ground-level argumentation. However, this is not meant in the sense that we look for meta-arguments that commit various fallacies, but rather that we try to find meta-arguments advancing explicit conclusions that some fallacy has been committed, i.e., that some ground-level argument embodies or commits a fallacy.

2. The Fallacy of Composition

Now, there are both theoretical and practical reasons for wanting to focus on the fallacy of composition. In fact, many theorists have claimed this fallacy to be more frequent and important that any other. At the practical and empirical level, as I have elaborated elsewhere (Finocchiaro 2015; 2019), this fallacy happens to be committed in, and thus helps us to understand, some of the most consequential controversies in the history of thought and in contemporary culture. For example, during the Copernican revolution, there is Aristotle's geocentric argument from natural motion and Galileo's criticism of that argument; in argumentation for and against the existence of God, we have the argument from design and Hume's criticism of it; in political science and political sociology, the so-called iron law of oligarchy advanced by Robert Michels has been criticized by Robert A. Dahl and by Seymour Martin Lipset; and in the science of economics, the contributions of leading economists such as John M. Keynes and Paul Samuelson include exposing the fallacies of composition committed in popular thought about economic affairs.

---

[4] Here, the use of the term 'correct' is deliberatively vague or broad; thus correct argument is meant to correspond to what others call good argument, and incorrect argument to bad or erroneous argument; and so, using more precise terms, incorrect arguments may be deductively invalid, *or* inductively weak, *or* rhetorically inappropriate, *or* epistemologically unsound.
[5] Finocchiaro 2005, 130; 2013b; 2013c, 242-47; 2015; 2019. Cf. Strawson 1952, 15; Doury 2005.

However, this investigation cannot be conducted with a *tabula rasa*, for we need to be clear about what we mean by fallacy of composition, and also we need to examine real or realistic material which typically does not come with the label 'fallacy of composition' attached to it. In other words, we need to be mindful of the fact that observation is theory-laden, and that the examination of this material must be guided by some definition of what this fallacy is, and by some idea of what to do with the material under examination so as to test it for the occurrence of this fallacy. Let us begin with some very fundamental definitions (cf. Finocchiaro 2015).

By *fallacy of composition* I mean an argument of composition that commits a fallacy. An *argument of composition* is one which concludes that a whole has a certain property because the parts of the whole have that property. An argument of composition may also be called a *compositional argument*. And, as mentioned above, a *fallacy* is a common type of argument that appears to be correct but is actually incorrect.

It is important to distinguish between arguments of composition and fallacies of composition because not all compositional arguments are incorrect, let alone fallacious; some are correct, indeed deductively valid, although not formally valid. My favorite example is the following: all parts of this automobile have weight; therefore, the whole automobile has weight.

Note also that I am distinguishing between incorrect arguments and fallacious arguments. In order to be fallacious, namely to be a fallacy, an argument must meet (three) other conditions besides incorrectness: it must *seem* to be correct; it must be an instance of a *general type*; and it must occur *commonly* or *frequently*. Thus, although all fallacious arguments are incorrect, not all incorrect arguments are fallacious.

Furthermore, we should also distinguish clearly and explicitly arguments and fallacies of composition from arguments and fallacies of *division*. The latter are usually defined as being the reverse of the former. Then both composition and division are often discussed under the same heading, with the pretext that they both involve reasoning about parts and wholes: composition would be the special case when one reasons from parts to wholes, and division the special case when one reasons from wholes to parts.

Two other confusions are relatively widespread and should be avoided. The argument of composition as I have defined it above should not be equated with an argument that goes from using a term with a distributive meaning in the premises to using it with a collective meaning in the conclusion. An example of the latter is this: "because a bus uses more gasoline than an automobile, therefore all buses use more gasoline than all automobiles" (Copi 1968, 81). Nor should my definition be equated with reasoning from a property of some members of a group to the same property for the entire group. A memorable example of the latter is the following: "Have you ever seen people jump up at a football game to gain a better view? They usually

202

find that, once everybody is standing up, the view has not improved at all. Such behavior, where what is true for an individual is not necessarily true for everyone illustrates the 'fallacy of composition' " (Samuelson and Nordhaus 1989, 7-8). This second confusion should be easier to avoid once we realize that such arguments are really instances of inductive generalizations, and such fallacies instances of hasty generalizations.

Let us now add some nuances to my own fundamental definition stated above (cf. Finocchiaro 2021). Let us begin with the over-simplified and overly abstract (though essentially correct) scheme for the argument of composition:

Scheme 1:
(P1) All parts of W have property Y;
(C) Therefore, W has property Y.

The first improvement to make here might be to split the premise into two parts: (P1.1) all a's have property Y; and (P1.2) all parts of W are a's. The reason for this is that in such argumentation one seldom asserts explicitly a claim such as (P1); instead, one is more likely to explicitly assert (P1.1) and leave (P1.2) implicit. Similarly, regarding the connection between the parts and the whole, one needs to assume, and perhaps leave implicit, a third claim: (P1.3) if all parts of W are Y, then W is Y. Thus, we get:

Scheme 2:
(P1.1) All a's are Y.
(P1.2) All parts of W are a's.
(P1.3) If all parts of W are Y, then W is Y.
Therefore, (C) W is Y.

Next, let us note that sometimes there are two main subsets of W that have the property Y; besides the already mentioned a's, we have what we shall call b's.[6] The above scheme would then become:

Scheme 3:
(P1.1') All a's and b's are Y.
(P1.2') All parts of W are a's or b's.
(P1.3) If all parts of W are Y, then W is Y.
Therefore, (C) W is Y.

---

[6] For example, in economics, a common and controversial argument attempts to show that the government of a whole society should refrain from operating with constantly unbalanced budgets and increasingly accumulating debts; the alleged support of this conclusion is that families ("a's") should operate in this manner and that business firms ("b's") should also operate in this manner. For details, cf. Finocchiaro (2019, 138-44; 2021, 64-65).

More importantly, with regard to claim (P1.2), one is more likely to think of it as, or to formulate it as: W is a whole whose *relevant* parts are the *a*'s. A similar qualification should be made for (P1.1), so that it does not sound like a universal generalization, but rather like a generic or normic generalization,[7] namely: *a*'s, normally, or typically, have property Y. (P1.1) might also have to be replaced by a statistical generalization, to the effect that: most *a*'s are Y. And (P1.3) might have to be formulated as a probabilistic claim. Then we would get:

Scheme 4:
(P1.1'') *a*'s are, normally, Y.
(P1.2'') The relevant parts of W are *a*'s.
(P1.3'') If all relevant parts of W are Y, then W is probably Y.
Therefore, probably, (C) W is Y.

Next, it is important to sketch some principles for the evaluation of such arguments of composition. The first principle I would formulate[8] is one that makes clear that we are concerned primarily, not with the question of the deductive validity of the argument, but with the question of whether the inference is reasonable, plausible, probable, cogent, or strong; and if it is, how much. Here, these terms are not given a precise or explicit definition, but are taken in their ordinary meaning. The point is primarily to provide an alternative to deductive evaluation. Thus, we have:

Evaluative Principle 1:
Independently of the deductive validity of an argument of composition, the primary aim is to determine whether the inference from the premises to the conclusion is reasonable, plausible, probable, cogent, or strong, and, if so, how much.

A second principle may be gathered from some suggestions by van Eemeren and Grootendorst.[9] It is based on two distinctions. One is between absolute and relative properties, for example, square vs. heavy. The second distinction is between structured or heterogeneous and unstructured or homogeneous wholes, for example a basketball team vs. a pile of sand. This principle may be formulated thus:

---

[7] I adopt the term 'normic' from Scriven (1959; 1989; 2009); cf. Finocchiaro (2005, 5-7). And I have learned more about it from Woods (2009; 2013); cf. Finocchiaro 2014.
[8] Cf. Ritola 2009b; Gough and Daniel 2009; Finocchiaro (2015; 2021).
[9] van Eemeren and Grootendorst 1992, 177; 1999. Cf. Gough and Daniel 2009; Ritola 2009b; Finocchiaro 2021.

Evaluative Principle 2:
In an argument of composition, determine whether the property ("Y") to be transferred is absolute or relative, and whether the whole ("W") is structured (heterogeneous) or unstructured (homogeneous). The argument is basically correct if and only if the property is absolute and the whole is unstructured (homogeneous).

This principle is of some use, at least as long as one does not interpret it in too precise a manner. Moreover, as van Eemeren and Grootendorst (1999) themselves recognize, aside from simple cases, it is often difficult to determine whether a given property is absolute or relative, and whether a given whole is homogeneous or heterogeneous; frequently, this cannot be determined prior to, or independently of, knowing the correctness of the corresponding compositional arguments.

Finally, there is a third evaluative principle which is worth formulating in this context.[10] That is, sometimes an argument of composition is criticized by pointing out that there are important dissimilarities between the parts and the whole. By evaluating the argument in this manner, we seem to be interpreting it as being in a sense an argument from analogy. Here, my suggestion is that such an argument can retain some aspect of compositionality while also having an aspect of analogy. The following scheme might do the trick:

Scheme 5:
(1) a's and b's are parts of W (perhaps the only parts, or the only relevant parts).
(2) Therefore, a's and b's are analogous to W (they have many properties in common).
(3) But a's and b's are also known to have property Y.
(4) And, if two entities share many known similarities, they are likely to share additional ones.
(5) Therefore, probably, W has property Y.

This scheme has two subarguments: the first is from (1) to (2); the second is from (2), (3) and (4) to (5). The first exploits the (alleged) part-whole relationship; the second is basically an argument from analogy.

Besides its interpretive value and function, this scheme also enables us to formulate the evaluative principle which the critics of such arguments are implicitly using. That is, we can interpret their criticism as an attempt to undermine claim no. 4 of this scheme. As stated this claim is not true: its truth depends on the absence of significant dissimilarities between the two alleged analogues. Thus, the principle could be stated as follows:

---

[10] See Govier 2009, and cf. Finocchiaro 2013a; see Woods 2016, and cf. Finocchiaro 2016; see Finocchiaro 2021, especially p. 68..

Evaluative Principle 3:
When evaluating an argument of composition, it is always relevant and important to check whether or not there exist significant dissimilarities between the parts and the whole. If so, the argument is thereby weakened; if not, the argument is strengthened to some extent.

Moreover, it should be noted that the nuanced schemes (2, 3, and 4) discussed above also contain or assume a premise (the third one) that can be undermined by such dissimilarities. Thus, the evaluative principle just stated can also be applied to compositional arguments that do not explicitly have an analogical component.

3. Global Warming

There is obviously no need to stress the general cultural and practical importance and relevance of the current controversy about global warming and climate change. Nor should there be any difficulty in imagining how striking the following passage would be for someone engaged in scholarly research along the lines summarized above:

> Aggregation is a structural method that models use to simplify matters by grouping together several different quantities and assuming that they can all be lumped together and treated in the same way; for example, composite parameters are often used for things such as pollution, natural resources, and population. Global mean average temperatures are calculated instead of regional temperatures or day and night temperatures …
>
> However, … aggregation of all pollutants misses the fact that air pollution is localized mostly in cities and stems mostly from cars. Thus, this aggregation might lead to misleading conclusions about the limits of an entire system when, in actual fact, there might be only localized limits and regional problems.
>
> … Similarly, … aggregation also masks important features of global warming. Balling[11] holds that the predicted warming will most likely be manifested in a reduction in the diurnal temperature range (the difference between maximum and minimum daily temperatures), with the warming taking place mostly at night and mostly in winter. This important, and perhaps noncatastrophic nature of the warming is masked by aggregate reports of global temperature averages. …
>
> To group and average in this way is to commit the fallacy of composition. [Haller 2002, 48-50]

This passage comes from a book in which Haller argues for two main conclusions: first, that the evidence and arguments supporting global

---

[11] Here Haller refers to Balling 1992, pp. xxiv, 103.

warming and climate change are not completely conclusive; second, that the potential harm is so great and catastrophic that one can make a cogent probabilistic argument similar to Pascal's wager for the existence of God; and such an argument justifies many drastic actions which individuals, governments, societies, and international organizations should take to prevent the catastrophe.

Haller's book motivated me to read and study a number of other books by such authors as Gore (2000), Balling (1992), Nordhaus (2013), Pope Francis (2015), Gates (2021), Koonin (2021), and Lomborg (2021). I also read the latest (IPCC 2021) *Contribution of Working Group I to the Sixth Assessment Report of the Intergovernmental Panel on Climate Change*, dealing with the physical science basis of climate change. As a result, my analysis of the passage just quoted is as follows.

In this passage, Haller is talking about two situations and arguments, one involving pollution and the other global warming. The discussion of pollution is relatively clear and straightforward. In an earlier passage, Haller (2002, 47-48) refers to an essay by Ian Hacking (1986); so let us first examine Hacking's essay.

Hacking is discussing primarily the difference between side effects and interference effects. Side effects are effects resulting from something whose behavior is occurring in an isolated context. Interference effects are those resulting from two things whose behavior is occurring when they are placed together in a common context. For example, when a patient is taking only one prescription drug the results are side effects; but when a patient is taking two prescribed drugs simultaneously the results are interference effects.

Then Hacking gives the following example. Consider a power plant that burns coal to generate electricity. Such plants usually produce a lot of fly ash which is channeled through a long and tall chimney and then released into the atmosphere. The resulting pollution can be reduced by having the chimney layered with baffles that obstruct the motion of the ash and collect some of it, so that it can then be removed during periodical cleaning. The resulting pollution can also be reduced by having the walls of the chimney electrostatically charged so that they attract some of the fly ash and prevent it from escaping into the air. Now, suppose the chimney is built and operated in such a way so as to exploit both baffles and electrostatically charged walls. Hacking points out plausibly that without empirical evidence we cannot reliably predict in advance that a chimney with both features will be able to collect and prevent from escaping an amount of ash equal to the sum of that collected by the baffles alone and that collected by the electrostatically charged wall alone. Rather, the actual result is likely to be that there is some kind of interference between the two processes that lowers or raises that amount.

The context of Hacking's discussion is not an argument-theoretical one, but rather the legal and moral culpability of ignoring interference effects. On the other hand, Haller is more focused on argumentation, although he mostly uses the language of the epistemology and methodology of models vs. evidence. Haller seems to be suggesting that here we have the following argument: one premise states that the baffles alone can collect a certain amount of ash; another premise states that the electrostatically charged wall alone can collect some other amount of ash; and the conclusion claims that the chimney as a whole can collect the sum of these two amounts. And we can agree with Haller that such an argument is afflicted by the problem of aggregation, and so it can be evaluated as weak or incorrect. Moreover, although this argument as it stands is not exactly a compositional argument, it probably could be modified in that direction, and then it might be a candidate for a fallacy of composition.

However, let us now move on to the topic of global warming which is closer to the center of Haller's attention. Although he is not too explicit, he is certainly thinking of an argument whose conclusion claims that (in recent decades) the terrestrial globe has been undergoing a (significant) warming, in the sense of a significant increase of its (over-all or mean) temperature. And the evidence for this claim is that the various parts of the earth have been undergoing some warming. And here the argument is indeed a compositional one, because it starts from premises about the warming of the parts of the earth and infers the conclusion that the whole earth is warming.

In fact, if we examine works that discuss this issue in scientific detail,[12] we find the following. For several decades, there have been increasingly systematic efforts to measure and keep track of the temperature of numerous places on earth. Some of these observation stations are located on land; some in the atmosphere, at various heights; some on the surface of the oceans; and some at various depths in the oceans. Already three decades ago, at the time of the publication of the book to which Haller refers, there were about 20,000 of these stations (Balling 1992, 36). Nowadays, there are more than twice as many. From such data, one can then calculate their average to represent the global temperature. These calculations require computers to accomplish, but once we have such global mean temperatures, then we can detect their trend upwards.

Obviously, in such a process one is *not* inferring that the whole globe is warming by the same amount as any one part. Rather one is defining the temperature of the globe as the mathematical mean of the temperature of the parts; one is computing a temporal series of such mean temperatures; and then one is detecting that such mean temperatures are increasing. If the mathematics is correct, this will yield a deductively valid argument. Thus,

---

[12] Cf. Balling 1992, IPCC 2021, Koonin 2021, Lomborg 2021, Nordhaus 2013.

insofar as the argument is a compositional one, we have a correct argument of composition, and *not* a fallacy of composition.

However, Haller seems to support his evaluative claim with an argument, which certainly deserves examination. But before we do that, let us look at another work (Gough and Daniel 2009) which seems to agree with Haller's fallacy claim and to elaborate it, and which is more explicitly argument-oriented.

> *The Problem of Aggregation* is highlighted by Stephen Haller in his discussion of the climate change debate (Haller 2002, 48). Haller introduces his argument with a brief discussion of the attempt to arrive at a global averaging of pollution. He cautions us that there are different kinds of pollution such that, when combined, the result of these two forces is not simply an average or composite. This sort of argument, he avers, commits fallacious composition. The MP [missing premise] is unacceptable since there is an attempt to take pollution levels at the parts level that are not absolute (they are dependent on the context of the micro situations in which they emerge) and transferring them to the whole when the whole is neither undifferentiated nor homogenous. In these sorts of cases, where the parts being transferred are not undifferentiated and absolute, attempts to combine pollution that arise from two types of subsystems can often be surprising:
>
> … For example, increasing pollutants to the oceans which create more algae could have the positive effective of providing more food for some species of the aquatic population of the oceans, which has a positive effect on other species in danger of extinction for lack of food, and so on. That is, it is possible to aggregate some individual pollutants and not produce any overall catastrophic effect.
>
> … when scientists add the climate data from various regions of the world into one large grid, then (while ignoring regional differences) use this average (which is a relative number to the regional situation) to conclude that the global ecosystem is about to undergo an irreversible, catastrophic collapse, the composition mistake becomes more dangerous. The transfer from a set of parts in which "we are still unable to generate descriptions of the interactions among the components" to a heterogeneous whole or ecosystem is illegitimate. Hence Haller charges that: "To group and average in this way is to commit the fallacy of composition" (Haller 2002, 50).
>
> … For Haller, both arguments, the pollution and the global averaging argument, as well as the catastrophic collapse argument, commit the fallacy of composition. [Gough and Daniel 2009, 7-8]

Here, it is helpful that Gough and Daniel evaluate the pollution argument by using a version of the principle first elaborated by van Eemeren and Grootendorst (1999) and discussed above, involving the concepts of absolute vs. relative properties and heterogenous vs. homogeneous whole. This strengthens the evaluation of that argument as incorrect.

However, the situation is different for the evaluation of the global-warming argument. Gough and Daniel (2009, 8) are explicit that they are questioning the attempt "to conclude that the global ecosystem is about to undergo an irreversible, catastrophic collapse"; and their reason is that some effects of global warming are *not* catastrophic, but rather beneficial. This echoes Haller's (2002, 50) own meta-argument that, "with the warming taking place mostly at night and mostly in winter," the global warming may not be all catastrophic. Here a missing premise (and an acceptable one) is that warmer nights and warmer winters would be mostly beneficial.

Now, this meta-argument is basically cogent, but it is *not* about the compositional argument supporting the existence of global warming. It is rather about what I would interpret as an inductive generalization argument supporting the claim that all effects of global warming are harmful (not beneficial). And the criticism amounts to the claim that such an inductive argument is a hasty generalization. This issue about the nature of the effects of global warming is indeed an important and controversial issue, but a distinct one, in the controversy about climate change.

Going back to the issue of the *existence* of global warming, I have already stated that it strikes me as a deductively valid argument of composition. Let me now elaborate on this judgment by double-checking whether this argument could be criticized by extending or applying the criticism of these authors, which is actually directed at the pollution argument of composition and at the generalization argument for the harm of global warming.

For example, let us examine how to apply the distinction between absolute and relative properties and between homogeneous and heterogenous wholes to the compositional argument for the existence of global warming. One could say that the temperature, warming, and heat content of a body are not absolute properties, but relative ones. And the whole earth is not an unstructured and undifferentiated whole, but structured and heterogeneous; in fact, in these discussions, it is usually subdivided into: land surface, ocean surface, ocean depths, cryosphere (glaciers and ice), troposphere, and stratosphere. Then, by analogy with the case of the pollution argument, and by a literal application of van Eemeren and Grootendorst's (1999) principle, we get that the global-warming argument is incorrect, and perhaps fallacious.

However, this meta-argument will not work for the following reasons, stemming from the laws of physics pertaining to the nature of heat and thermodynamics. That is, from the point of view of heat, the structure and heterogeneity of the earth is irrelevant; what is relevant is the following. All parts of the earth consist of atoms and molecules that vibrate to some extent, and such vibration defines what heat is; and temperature measures the kinetic energy of such vibration. By the law of conservation of energy (first law of thermodynamics), such vibratory motion cannot disappear or be lost, but can only be transferred to other bodies; and by the second law of thermodynamics, such a transfer takes place in the direction from warmer to cooler bodies. Thus, the mean temperature of the whole earth is a consequence of the temperature of its parts. It follows further that the above mentioned principle of evaluation is not always valid or applicable.

At this point it is useful to add one complication, although it does not destroy the validity of the global-warming argument. There is now general agreement that, unlike all the other parts of the earth, the stratosphere (i.e., the upper part of the atmosphere) is undergoing a process of cooling.[13] The relevance of this in the present context is that it is not literally true that all parts of the earth have (recently) undergone some warming; and thus the main premise of the compositional argument for global warming is not exactly true. However, the amount of this cooling is relatively small, and the fact remains that all the other parts are indeed warming; thus, the calculation of the global mean temperature does yield a slightly lower figure than it would otherwise, but still characterized by an upward trend.

Nevertheless, from the point of view of argumentation theory a problem remains. That is, how shall we characterize or classify the global-warming argument when we add this complication? For, with this complication, the argument does not adhere to any of the nuanced schemes for compositional arguments discussed earlier (in Section 2 above), let alone the over-simplified and overly abstract scheme no. 1. The needed scheme would have to be something along the following lines:

Scheme 6:
(1) $a_1, a_2, a_3, ..., a_n$ and b are parts of W (perhaps, the only relevant parts).
(2) $a_1, a_2, a_3, ..., a_n$ are Y, but b is not.
(3) Taking into account the details of b as well as of the a_i's, the a_i's prevail over b.
(4) Therefore, W is Y.

Here, the concept of *prevail* is vague and would have to be clarified, but that will have to be postponed to some future investigation.

This analysis, I dare say, is pretty exhaustive with regard to the question whether the observational argument supporting the existence of global warming commits the fallacy of composition. My conclusion is that the main such argument does not commit such a fallacy. Moreover, the criticism of it advanced by Haller and by Gough and Daniel is untenable for several reasons. However, I would not deny that my present analysis merely scratches the surface of the controversy over climate change.

4. Epilogue

In fact, the just mentioned argument should not be confused with others

---

[13] Cf. Balling 1992, 75-76; IPCC 2021, Technical Summary, p. 65, and Chapter 1, Frequently Asked Questions 1.1.

supporting *future* global warming; or how long it will continue; or what the amount of the warming will be; or whether the temperature will increase more in the future than it has increased in the recent past. I have said nothing about these issues. Another distinct argument would be about the *effects* of global warming: what they would be and whether they would be beneficial or harmful; I have had the occasion to comment on Haller's and Gould and Daniel's suggestion that the warming of night-time and winter temperatures would probably be beneficial. However, this did not include anything about whether or not global warming results in more frequent and/or more intense floods, droughts, hurricanes, and wildfires; and these, of course, are extremely important issues. Nor have I addressed the question of the *cause(s)* of global warming; on this there is general agreement that one significant cause is the increase of carbon dioxide in the atmosphere, stemming from the burning of fossil fuels, and operating through the greenhouse effect; but there is less agreement on how significant this human cause is and on the role of natural causes. Nevertheless, my analysis above is a beginning, which is all I could do in the present context.

Finally, from the point of view of my meta-argumentational approach to fallacies in general, it so happens that my research for this paper revealed some possible candidates for future case studies. That is, these would be cases where some of the above mentioned authors criticize arguments by charging some kind of fallacy. For example, one of the works mentioned above, which I studied for the present paper, is a book entitled *The Climate Casino: Risk, Uncertainty, and Economics for a Warming World*, authored by William Nordhaus. Now, by and large, Nordhaus is a proponent of global warming and climate change, but he is critical of one particular argument. In his own words:

> … The group of 8 richest countries declared at the L'Aquila Summit in July 2009, "We recognize the scientific view that the increase in global average temperature above pre-industrial levels ought not to exceed 2 degrees C." … Where does this scientific view come from? … The surprising answer it that the scientific rationale for the 2° C target is not really very scientific. For example, in explaining the 2° C target, the most recent report [2010] of the U.S. National Academy of Sciences did little more than connect the circularity of the argument: "Subsequent scientific research has sought to better understand and quantify the links among GHG [green house gas] emissions, atmospheric GHC concentrations, changes in global climate, and the impacts of those changes on human and environmental systems. Based on this research, many policy makers in the international community recognize limiting the increase in global mean surface temperature to 2° C above pre-industrial levels as an important benchmark; this goal was embodied in the Copenhagen Accords, at a 2009 meeting of the G-8, and in other policy forums." So the politicians refer to the science, and the scientists refer to the politics. [Nordhaus 2013, 199-200]

Nordhaus seems to be criticizing the argument for limiting global warming to 2° centigrade as being circular or question-begging; that is, he is charging this argument with committing a common and important fallacy. Let us also note that Nordhaus was a 2018 recipient of the Nobel Prize in Economics, and that the motivation released by the Royal Swedish Academy of Sciences states that his merit has been "integrating climate change into long-run macroeconomic analysis."[14] Here, then, we have an interesting, important, and promising case-study for future investigation by anyone willing to pursue the study of fallacies by means of the approach advocated and illustrated in this paper, namely by means of a critical examination of meta-arguments claiming that some particular argument commits some particular fallacy.

References

Balling, Robert C., Jr. 1992. *The Heated Debate: Greenhouse Predictions versus Climate Reality*. San Francisco: Pacific Research Institute for Public Policy.

Barth, E.M. 1985. A new field: Empirical logic. *Synthese* 63: 375-88.

Blair, J. Anthony, and R.H. Johnson. 1987. Argumentation as dialectical. *Argumentation* 1: 41-56.

Copi, Irving M. 1968. *Introduction to logic,* 3rd edn. New York: MacMillan.

Doury, Marianne. 2005. The accusation of *Amalgame* as a meta-argumentative refutation. In *Argumentation in practice*, ed. Frans H. van Eemeren and P. Houtlosser, 145-61. Amsterdam: John Benjamins.

Finocchiaro, Maurice A. 2005. *Arguments about arguments*. New York: Cambridge University Press.

Finocchiaro, Maurice A. 2013a. Debts, oligarchies, and holisms. *Informal Logic* 33: 143-74.

Finocchiaro, Maurice A. 2013b. The fallacy of composition and meta-argumentation. In *Virtues of argumentation: Proceedings of the 10th International Conference of the Ontario Society for the Study of Argumentation (OSSA), 22-26 May 2013*, ed. D. Mohammed and M. Lewiński. Windsor: Ontario Society for the Study of Argumentation.

Finocchiaro, Maurice A. 2013c. *Meta-argumentation*. London: College Publications.

Finocchiaro, Maurice A. 2014. Essay-review of J. Woods's *Errors of Reasoning. Argumentation* 28: 231-39.

Finocchiaro, Maurice A. 2015. The fallacy of composition. *Journal of*

---

[14] See https://www.nobelprize.org/prizes/economic-sciences/2018/nordhaus/facts/; accessed June 2, 2022.

Applied Logic, vol. 13, issue 2, part B, June 2015, pp. 24–43.

Finocchiaro, Maurice A. 2016. Economic reasoning and fallacy of composition, part III: Response to John Woods's comments. *Eris: Rivista Internazionale di Argomentazione e Dibattito*, vol. 1, no. 2, pp. 46-56. http://eris.fisppa.unipd.it/Eris. Accessed March 15, 2017.

Finocchiaro, Maurice A. 2019. Samuelson on the fallacy of composition in economics. In *Natural Arguments*, ed. Dov Gabbay, Lorenzo Magnani, Woosuk Park, and Ahti Veikko Pietarinen, 125-72. London: College Publications.

Finocchiaro, Maurice A. 2021. Argumentation schemes for composition and division arguments. *Journal of Applied Logics* 8: 53-73.

Francis I, Pope. 2015. *Praise Be to You: Laudato Si'*. St. Francisco: Ignatius Press.

Gates, Bill. 2021. *How to Avoid a Climate Disaster: The Solutions We Have and the Breakthroughs We Need*. New York: Knopf.

Gore, Albert. 2000. *Earth in the Balance: Ecology and the Human Spirit*, 2nd edn. Boston: Houghton Mifflin.

Gough, James E., and M. Daniel. 2009. The fallacy of composition. In Ritola 2009a.

Govier, Trudy. 2009. Duets, cartoons, and tragedies. In *Pondering on Problems of Argumentation*, ed. Frans H. van Eemeren and Bart Garssen, 91-104. Dordrecht: Springer.

Hacking, Ian. 1986. Culpable ignorance of interference effects. In *Values at Risk*, ed. Douglas MacLean, 136-54. Totowa: Rowman & Allanheld.

Haller, Stephen F. 2002. *Apocalypse Soon?: Wagering on Warnings of Global Catastrophe*. Montréal: McGill-Queen's University Press.

Hansen, Hans V. 2002. The straw thing of fallacy theory. *Argumentation* 16: 133-55.

IPCC. 2021. *Climate change 2021: The physical science basis. Contribution of Working Group I to the Sixth Assessment Report of the Intergovernmental Panel on Climate Change* [Masson-Delmotte, V., P. Zhai, A. Pirani, S. L. Connors, C. Péan, S. Berger, N. Caud, Y. Chen, L. Goldfarb, M. I. Gomis, M. Huang, K. Leitzell, E. Lonnoy, J.B.R. Matthews, T. K. Maycock, T. Waterfield, O. Yelekçi, R. Yu and B. Zhou (eds.)]. Cambridge University Press. In Press.

Johnson, Ralph H. 2000. *Manifest Rationality*. Mahwah: Lawrence Erlbaum Associates.

Johnson, Ralph H., and J.A. Blair. 1980. The recent development of informal logic. In *Informal logic*, ed. J. Anthony Blair and R.H. Johnson, 3-28. Inverness: Edgepress.

Koonin, Steven E. 2021. *Unsettled: What Climate Science Tells Us, What It Doesn't, and Why It Matters*. Dallas: BenBella Books.

Lomborg, Bjorn. 2021. *False Alarm: How Climate Change Panic Costs Us Trillions, Hurts the Poor, and Fails to Fix the Planet*, reprint edn. New York: Basic Books.

Nordhaus, William. 2013. *The Climate Casino: Risk, Uncertainty, and Economics for a Warming World*. New Haven: Yale University Press.

Ritola, Juho, ed. 2009a. *Argument Cultures: Proceedings of the 8th OSSA Conference*, 2009. Windsor: Ontario Society for the Study of Argumentation.

Ritola, Juho. 2009b. Commentary on James E. Gough and Mano Daniel's 'The fallacy of composition'. In Ritola 2009a.

Samuelson, Paul A., and William D. Nordhaus. 1989. *Economics*, 13th edn. New York: McGraw-Hill.

Scriven, Michael. 1959. Truisms as the grounds for historical explanations. In *Theories of History*, ed. P. Gardiner, 443-75. Glencoe, IL: Free Press.

Scriven, Michael. 1987. Probative logic. In *Argumentation across the Lines of Discipline: Proceedings of the Conference on Argumentation* 1986, ed. Frans H. van Eemeren, R. Grootendorst, J.A. Blair, and C.A. Willard, 7-32. Dordrecht: Foris Publications.

Scriven, Michael. 2009. Probative inference. In Ritola 2009a.

Strawson, P .F. 1952. *Introduction to Logical Theory*. London: Methuen.

van Eemeren, Frans H., and R. Grootendorst. 1992. *Argumentation, Communication, and Fallacies*. Hillsdale: Lawrence Erlbaum Associates.

van Eemeren, Frans H., and R. Grootendorst. 1999. The fallacies of composition and division. In *JFAK: Essays Dedicated to Johan van Benthem on the Occasion of his 50th Birthday*, ed. J. Gerbrandy, M. Marx, M. de Rijke, and Y. Venema. Amsterdam: University of Amsterdam, Institute for Logic, Language, and Computation. At www.illc.uva.nl/j50/; consulted on June 18, 2013.

Woods, John. 1988. Buttercups, GNP's, and quarks. *Informal Logic* 10: 67-76.

Woods, John. 2009. Commentary on Michael Scriven's 'Probative inference'. In Ritola 2009a.

Woods, John. 2013. *Errors of Reasoning*. London: College Publications.

Woods, John. 2016. Economic reasoning and fallacy of composition, part II: Comments on Maurice Finocchiaro's paper. *Eris: Rivista Internazionale di Argomentazione e Dibattito*, vol. 1, no. 2, pp. 39-45. At http://eris.fisppa.unipd.it/Eris; accessed on March 15, 20

INDEX

abductive, 128, 180, 198

Aberdein, Andrew, 60, 79

ad hominem argument, 63, 88, 97,
179-181, 196-199

aggregation, 41, 53, 76-77, 114,
206-209

Allen, Derek, x

ambiguity, 2, 6, 41-43, 56, 80,
104, 175, 181, 198

analogy, 1, 16, 36-38, 46-50,
63, 67-75, 79, 87-88,
117-118, 121-124, 136,
148-151, 155, 165, 169,
180, 192-195, 205, 210

Anderson, William, 97, 103, 133,
175

Andone, Corina, 181, 195

Angell, Richard, 101-103

apocalypse, 51, 81, 214

Archer, Maurice, 87, 90-91, 103,
110, 120, 129, 133, 140,
175

argument analysis, 28, 34, 45, 62,
78, 201

argument from division, 60,
182-188, 194

argument of composition, 1, 5, 13,
16-17, 27, 36, 57-58, 66,
70, 75, 85, 99, 123, 131,
144-145, 154-156, 169,
202-206, 210

Aristotle, 1-2, 6, 47-48, 56, 64-65,
68, 73, 129-130, 182,
201

Arnauld, Antoine, 11, 27, 56, 65,
79

AT&T (American Telephone and
Telegraph Company),
149-150

austerity, 41, 51-53, 78, 82, 106,
135, 176, 197

balance of trade, 165-167

Balling, Robert, 77-79, 206-208,
211-213

Bar-Hillel, Yehoshua, 85,
102-103, 116, 125, 155,
175

Barth, Else, 10, 27, 135, 175, 200,

220

www.ingramcontent.com/pod-product-compliance
Lightning Source LLC
Chambersburg PA
CBHW062217270326
41930CB00009B/1763